THRESHOLD
EDITIONS

MERCURY
RADIO ARTS

ALSO BY GLENN BECK

The Original Argument: The Federalists' Case for the Constitution,
Adapted for the 21st Century

The 7: Seven Wonders That Will Change Your Life

Broke: The Plan to Restore Our Trust, Truth and Treasure

The Overton Window

Idiots Unplugged: Truth for Those Who Care to Listen (*audiobook*)

The Christmas Sweater: A Picture Book

Arguing with Idiots: How to Stop Small Minds and Big Government

Glenn Beck's Common Sense: The Case Against an Out-of-Control Government,
Inspired by Thomas Paine

America's March to Socialism: Why We're One Step Closer to
Giant Missile Parades (*audiobook*)

The Christmas Sweater

An Inconvenient Book: Real Solutions to the World's Biggest Problems

The Real America: Early Writings from the Heart and Heartland

LIARS

HOW PROGRESSIVES EXPLOIT OUR FEARS FOR POWER AND CONTROL

◆

GLENN BECK

THRESHOLD
EDITIONS

MERCURY
RADIO ARTS

THRESHOLD EDITIONS/MERCURY RADIO ARTS

NEW YORK LONDON TORONTO SYDNEY NEW DELHI

Threshold Editions/Mercury Radio Arts
An Imprint of Simon & Schuster, Inc.
1230 Avenue of the Americas
New York, NY 10020

Copyright © 2016 by Mercury Radio Arts, Inc.

First Threshold Editions/Mercury Radio Arts paperback edition August 2017

THRESHOLD EDITIONS and colophon are trademarks of Simon & Schuster, Inc.

GLENN BECK is a trademark of Mercury Radio Arts, Inc.

For information about special discounts for bulk purchases,
please contact Simon & Schuster Special Sales at
1-866-506-1949 or business@simonandschuster.com.

The Simon & Schuster Speakers Bureau can bring authors to your live event.
For more information, or to book an event, contact the Simon & Schuster Speakers
Bureau at 1-866-248-3049 or visit our website at www.simonspeakers.com.

Interior design by Renato Stanisic

Manufactured in the United States of America

1 3 5 7 9 10 8 6 4 2

Library of Congress Cataloging-in-Publication Data is available.

ISBN 978-1-4767-9885-1
ISBN 978-1-4767-9888-2 (pbk)
ISBN 978-1-4767-9891-2 (ebook)

FOR RAPHE, CHEYENNE, LORELAI, AND COEN,
AND ALL THOSE WHO WILL PLAY A ROLE IN THE REFOUNDING
OF OUR NATION. MAY THEY DO IT WITHOUT FEAR FROM LIARS.

CONT

PART I

THE ROAD WE'VE TRAVELED

INTRODUCTION

IN THE JUNGLE,
THE MIGHTY JUNGLE,
THE LION SLEEPS TONIGHT

I n 2001, an archeological team in the Djurab Desert discovered the
remains of what they described as mankind's oldest living ancestor,
an apelike mammal with prominent brows. They dubbed this new
species *Sahelanthropus tchadensis*. More chimpanzee than human, these
primates lived in groups in a lakeside forest that gave way seven million years ago to the Saharan desert sands of northern Africa.

During the excavation, the team also encountered the remains of
a large saber-toothed cat the size of a lion, which hunted these early
humans as prey. The cats' six-inch front sabers were perfectly suited
for carving through flesh and bone, and their low-slung frames were
adapted for stealthily stalking their next meals. Nothing could outrun
these powerful creatures, certainly not the primates of North Africa
that lived in constant fear of them.

"With our present data, we don't know what precisely the interactions were between a primate and a big carnivore," said Patrick

Vignaud, director of the University of Poitiers' Institute of Paleoprimatology and Human Paleontology. "But probably these interactions were not so friendly."

We can imagine that interaction seven million years ago: a pair of our ancestors foraging for food near a pool of water, their child playing cheerfully near the mother's feet. And then, without warning, a shadow in the brush becomes a living, breathing, snarling vision of death. The mother cries out and leaps to protect her baby. The father steps in between the beast and his family. The hairs on the back of both the hunter's and the hunted's necks stand up straight. Nostrils flare, eyes squint, jaws clench. Beads of sweat appear. Survival instincts kick in as the adrenaline flows.

They circle each other slowly. An instant later, the monster leaps forward. Nails and teeth dig into flesh. Dust swirls upward from the ground, lodging in the primate's throat, lungs, and eyes. The warm-iron taste of lifeblood fills the cat's mouth as saliva and blood spill out. Droplets of red-brown spatter the dry ground.

Then, with one swift and well-placed blow to the giant cat's head, the battle ends. The primate escapes this time—bruised, battered, and bloodied.

His mate brings over their frightened child, and they all embrace. Heart rates begin to slow, and adrenaline levels recede, but something has irrevocably changed for them. The fear has burrowed deep into their subconscious, and it will never really leave.

Whether we're aware of it or not, all of us are attracted to—and strangely beholden to—feelings of fear. Our bodies are simply wired that way. The ultimate fear, of course, is of the end. Of death itself. The fear of an encounter with a saber-toothed cat haunts *Sahelanthropus tchadensis* and his descendants—us—for eternity. Parents and children look carefully to every shadow for squinted yellow eyes hovering over sharp teeth.

Can you hear it? The low rumble that turns into a growl and eventually into a panting snarl? The beast is getting closer. The idea of death from the shadows, in all its forms, stalks us all.

What does any of this have to do with Woodrow Wilson or Hillary Clinton? It's a good question, and it's what we're going to explore in this book. Fear, as well as the hopeful (if not pointless) solutions offered to combat it, is ultimately what make progressivism so successful. It's what makes otherwise intelligent, rational, and good human beings succumb so easily to obviously absurd visions of the future painted by politicians. It's why our brothers and sisters and our children—and sometimes even you and I—are continually tempted by the progressive siren song.

Many experts have written about progressivism. I've talked about it on the air for more than a decade now, so I'm guessing you are already familiar with its frightening and demonstrable outcomes: the insatiable thirst for control and betterment of others; the determination to build a massive, all-controlling welfare state that holds the rest of us hostage to its preferences and whims; and the flirtation with totalitarianism masked by the guise of political correctness. Progressives regularly espouse ideas and support causes that openly involve the subjugation, murder, or mutilation of their fellow human beings, always in the name of a better world for all.

When their policies are actually implemented, they unfailingly achieve the opposite of their promised results. And yet, despite this, no amount of empirical data seems to dissuade progressives and their acolytes from embracing their flawed policies the next time around, even when they can easily be shown to be disastrous.

Given these failures time and time again, it's only right to wonder

how it is that progressive leaders and voters continue to cling to policies and programs that so plainly don't work. Are progressive leaders
such masters of lying and deception that their followers can be easily
fooled, even in the face of undeniable evidence? Or is it rather that
followers of progressivism are so eager to be lied to that they willfully
ignore facts and reason?

As we'll find out together in this book, the answer is both.

We all know what progressives want to do. We all know how
easily they lie and how easily adherents allow themselves to be lied to.
But what has rarely been asked or discussed is the more fundamental
question: Why? Where does the urge originate from, and how does
it hold so much power over the human mind? How does this impulse
to build institutions and pass laws that dictate the behavior of others,
stamping out individual choice in favor of the collective, overtake
logic and sound thinking so often?

Each of us is born a unique, individual being, possessing free will
and a mind capable of making rational choices. We're capable of caring
for both our loved ones and ourselves. But devotees of progressivism
reject their free will and rational capacity. What makes people adopt
a philosophy that is so fundamentally incompatible with their natural
birthright as free and independent beings who are able to determine
their own future?

The answer brings us back to the saber-toothed cat and to the
fear-hope dynamic buried deep within all of us.

Human beings are creatures of the natural world, following natural laws that govern all species on earth. Like that of our primate
ancestors and all other mammals, our DNA is filled with millions of
years of collective experience. The stories of their survival and our
evolution are written in organic matter such as proteins and nucleic
acids that form vast ribbons of DNA. As much as they are indicative
of our past, these strands of DNA also, in many ways, determine our
future—whether we're prone to cancer, whether our children will

have light skin or dark skin, whether we'll have a thick head of hair or be bald.

Our genetic sequencing also, it turns out, has a large effect on our political future.

Here's the short version. Our ancestors, among all creatures that have ever existed, were endowed by their creator with something unique in the animal kingdom, something that sets us apart from every other living organism: an awareness of our unavoidable death. It is the fundamental difference between human beings and every other advanced mammal. No other species except for humans has both the inherent desire to live *plus* the foreknowledge that we won't.

The awareness of death exists both consciously and unconsciously at the same time. Like members of all species, we experience fear as an inherent defense mechanism when faced with the danger of death or harm. That is the natural tool we are given to help us survive. But human beings are aware and afraid not only of immediate potential threats, as other creatures are, but also of future inevitable dangers, outside our control and perception, as other creatures are not. Human beings, therefore, more than any other living organisms, live in a constant state of terror over the danger of death. For some of us, the certainty of our death can create a sense of hopelessness. Each of us, and those we love and care about, will die. Eventually, no matter how many individual fights we might win against beasts from the under-brush, one of them will get us.

As we've evolved, the higher brain functions that enabled self-awareness, imagination, and reason had to create a counterbal-ance to the constant state of terror that came from foreknowledge of our own death. Psychologists identify this as a sort of coping mech-anism that helps us get out of bed each day and march forward with life. This is the other quintessentially human psychological trait: hope. Hope is what empowers us to defy fear, to arm ourselves and fight against the saber-toothed cat. Hope is what enables inherently irrational action against impossible odds, fighting each battle, while knowing that the war will eventually be lost.

Dr. Jerome Groopman, a Harvard Medical School professor who has spent years studying the science of hope, discovered that the brain releases chemicals that cause a hopeful sensation after a traumatizing experience. "Hope helps us overcome hurdles that we otherwise could not scale," he wrote, "and it moves us forward to a place where healing can occur."

These chemicals create an effect almost identical to that of morphine: a calming, peaceful sensation. The feeling of succumbing to fears and then transcending them with hope becomes addictive. It's why we love horror movies and Halloween. It's why amusement parks strive to build the tallest, fastest roller coasters every year. It's why adrenaline junkies jump out of airplanes and off bridges. It's why tens of thousands flock to endurance events like triathlons and Ironman races. It's why Navy SEALs and Army Rangers love the thrill of combat and why they continually subject themselves to grueling tests beforehand.

Progressivism works at both levels of the unique duality of the human psyche. Progressives first succumb to their own fear, and then they utilize that fear by instilling it in others. They helpfully identify the saber-toothed cats—the things that threaten us and will ultimately lead to our demise—hoping to export their fears to the rest of the herd so that others can be more easily controlled.

The pattern is always the same. First, they construct elaborate enemies that they say will kill us: overpopulation, global warming, gun violence, pornography, public health epidemics, bullying, SUVs, recreational drug use, or even masculinity itself. These are the saber-toothed cats. Then, having convinced us that we should be afraid of the predator in the brush, thereby filling our brains with adrenaline, anxiety, and stress, they offer us the "solution" that will allegedly kill the beast before it can kill us.

It's a never-ending cycle by progressives: introduce fear; exploit it; introduce hope; exploit it.

◆

This book will present a clear, concise, and documented picture of progressives as they really are: eugenicists, racists, misogynists, terrorists, and authoritarian tyrants. We'll dig through their own words, most of which have been airbrushed out of the official histories by liberal historians who'd rather we not know the truth about their intellectual forebears and the men and women they hold up in our children's classrooms as heroes of democracy. We'll unveil the progressives' methods. We'll puncture their lies, both the ones they tell us and the ones they tell themselves.

But more than that, I want you to walk away with the *why* and the *how* that animate the sordid history of progressivism and the perils it presents to a free people. Understanding this is vital to understanding the roots of the progressive impulse, seeing it for what it is, and freeing yourself from it.

Political movements—particularly the most pernicious ones—have always used fear as a selling point. Hitler used fear of the Jews. Hitler and Mussolini whipped up fear of the Communists in Russia, citing Mongolian-tainted blood. The Communists told their followers to fear the Fascists, the church, God, and capitalism. The progressives we'll study aren't all that different.

But wait, you say, there *are* differences. There was, for example, no racial component to how progressives employed fear to sell their program.

Think again.

Progressives used fear of nonwhites as a big part of their own particular "fear factor."

Exhibit A: Margaret Sanger, founder of Planned Parenthood. She advocated contraception as a tool to control inferior populations, whether African-Americans ("We do not want the word to get out that we want to exterminate the Negro") or lower-class whites.

The eugenics movement—a major component of the early-twentieth-century progressive movement—did much the same thing. "The emergency problem of segregation and sterilization must be faced immediately," Sanger warned in 1922. "Every feeble-minded girl or woman of the hereditary type, especially of the moron class, should be segregated during the reproductive period. Otherwise, she is almost certain to bear imbecile children, who in turn are just as certain to breed other defectives."

Nah, no fear-mongering here!

But back to the outright racist elements of progressivism—and of its country cousin, populism. Woodrow Wilson was unfortunately only the tip of the iceberg. South Carolina's Senator "Pitchfork Ben" Tillman, Georgia's Senator Tom Watson, Mississippi's Senator James K. "The Great White Chief" Vardaman ("The only effect of Negro education is to spoil a good field hand and make an insolent cook"), and Mississippi's Governor Theodore Bilbo were populist/progressives and also racists, often advocating violence and lynchings.

Virginia's Senator Carter Glass, coauthor of the Glass-Steagall Act and Woodrow Wilson's secretary of the Treasury, boasted, "Discrimination! Why that is exactly what we propose, to remove every negro voter who can be gotten rid of, legally, without materially impairing the numerical strength of the white electorate."

Outside the South, Theodore Roosevelt's 1912 Progressive Party running mate, Hiram Johnson, played on anti-Japanese hysteria. In 1913, Johnson signed the California Alien Land Law, which effectively barred Japanese persons from owning land in the state. During World War II, California's progressive Republican governor Earl Warren helped implement Franklin Roosevelt's forced internment of Japanese-Americans.

Progressives stirred up incredible hysteria before, during, and after World War I. Theodore Roosevelt exploited anxieties over "hyphenated-Americans," largely Americans of German or Irish birth who didn't share his enthusiasm for American participation in the conflict. After the United States joined the Allied cause in April 1917, Roosevelt's progressive rival, Woodrow Wilson, further stoked the fires of fear by banning certain publications from the U.S. Mail and imprisoning numerous antiwar figures, including Socialist Party presidential nominee Eugene V. Debs. Under Wilson's Espionage and Sedition Acts, even mainstream outlets were suppressed or outright banned.

Of course, there was a lot more to the progressive and populist fear factor than racism, xenophobia, and wartime crackdowns on free expression. A few decades ago, scholars Nathaniel Weyl and William Marina provided a pretty succinct summary of what the populists were peddling. It bears repeating:

> In terms of ideological characteristics, Populism was not merely a mode of organized political expression, but a mood and an attitude of mind. It covers a broad spectrum of movements, ideas and writings, characterized, to a greater or lesser extent, by common views and preconceptions about American society. Among these was the conviction that history was a conspiracy of rich against poor, of idlers and parasites against productive businessmen, farmers and workers, of bloodsucking finance capital against creative agricultural and agrarian capital, of sinister, subtle, sophisticated English and Jewish manipulators of world power against simple, upright American ordinary folk. The Populists tended to believe that the two great political parties of their country were a sham, essentially identical, both corrupt tools of the interests, engaged in loud but spurious battles as a means of diverting the attention of productive America from the fact that it had been deprived of its political birthright.

Sound familiar?

Progressives, meanwhile, were filling in whatever gaps existed in the fear factor game: food and drug safety (were you being poisoned?), workplace safety (were the bosses deliberately working women and children to death? would workers lose limbs or even their lives?), economic security (would the unemployed or the elderly starve?), big business (were the big guys squeezing out the little guys and jacking up your prices?), big-city corruption (what were those Irish saloon keepers up to in the political back rooms?).

It's no accident that among the most memorable phrases in all American rhetoric is Franklin Roosevelt's "The only thing we have to fear is fear itself—nameless, unreasoning, unjustified terror."

FDR may not have been a great economist, but he was a *brilliant* politician. Most politicians will subtly (or maybe not so subtly) play upon your fears. But in Roosevelt's case, he laid it all on the line:

> *You're scared silly. You're afraid of losing your jobs, your savings, your homes. You're scared of empty pots and starving children. I will save you from hunger. I will save you from bankers. I will save you from the saber-toothed cat! Just hand over your gold and your future income, and let me plan your retirement for you.*

And so, before a terrified America even knew it, FDR (who was soon about to frighten radio audiences with talk of "high finance" and the "malefactors of great wealth") produced the CCC, the AAA, the WPA, the PWA, the NYA, the NLRB, Social Security, Medicare, and on and on and on.

Fear + Progressives = Government Control.

The progressive cure to *your* problems always involves giving more power to *them*. Always. They are the experts. They know best. They know just how big a business should be allowed to get before it becomes dangerous. They will write regulations and collect taxes and generate debt to pay for their programs. They know just how much of your income you should be allowed to keep. The free market, the *free individual*, operates recklessly and wastefully, creates imbalances and unfairness. Freedom of choice should be feared because some people, most people, will choose badly. *They* will run things scientifically, nonideologically. And whatever their new programs might cost, somehow they will all magically cost less—and even more magically, *someone else* will pay for them.

Trust them. They're from the government, and they're here to help.

Or maybe not. More than a century later, after more than a hundred years of progressive "solutions" (Square Deal, New Freedom, New Deal, Fair Deal, New Frontier, Great Society, Hope/Change), progressives are still sounding the alarm about basically the very same fears. We've moved from Upton Sinclair's *The Jungle* to genetically modified foods, from outlawing booze to banning Big Gulps, from the Sixteenth Amendment to bashing the one percent. From banning the word *sauerkraut* in World War I to censoring "offensive" speech on today's college campuses. It never ends, the same cycle of fear on the one hand and salvation-can-be-yours on the other.

The three parts of this book will present progressives, from the left and the right, and help you understand them—their stories, experiences, and motivations—more deeply and completely than any book has done before.

Part I discusses the history of the progressive movement in America from the early days of William Jennings Bryan through four pivotal "waves" of progressivism led by Woodrow Wilson, Franklin Roosevelt, Lyndon Johnson, and Barack Obama. It also includes profiles of some key figures during those eras who adopted the damaging progressive mindset as a means to protect themselves from personal traumas. For example, you'll see how the deep depression and losses that Eleanor Roosevelt suffered as a child emboldened her to support a movement that hoped to bequeath to all Americans the parents she never had.

Part II examines some of the lies that progressives like to tell would-be recruits, for example, that progressivism means being open-minded and supporting freedom and diversity.

Part III discusses the future of the progressive movement while also laying bare its playbook. Most important, it gives us a road map for how to finally wake people up and convince them that fear is their friend. It doesn't need to be defeated—especially by lying, power-hungry politicians—it needs to be harnessed.

The saber-toothed cat may look a lot different today from how it looked seven million years ago, but it can still be defeated in the same way: not by cowering in our caves but by pledging our lives, fortunes, and sacred honor to one another. Reliance on our creator, ourselves, our families, and our communities is what's kept people safe and hopeful and happy since the beginning of time. Putting your faith in government and politicians instead is chasing fool's gold.

I hope that by the end of this book, you'll realize that FDR was mostly right but he left one important thing out. There is nothing to fear except fear itself . . . and the progressives who exploit it.

1

Roots:

Hegel, Marx, and the Making of Heaven on Earth

Looking into the future we can contemplate a society . . . in which men shall work together for a common purpose, and in which the wholesale cooperation shall take place largely through government.

We have reason to believe that we shall yet see great national undertakings with the property of the nation, and managed by the nation, through agents who appreciate the glory of true public service, and feel that it is God's work which they are doing, because church and state are as one.

—EARLY AMERICAN PROGRESSIVE RICHARD T. ELY, 1894

Chicago Coliseum
July 9, 1896

Moses ascended the mountaintop.
    Mount Sinai was the podium rising above a sea of delegates. The two stone tablets decreed that the U.S. government's monetary supply be backed with reserves of silver instead of gold, along with a zealous commitment to heal the wounds that America's "one

percent" had inflicted on everyone else. Greedy idolaters had wor-
shipped capitalism's golden calf for far too long.

That's why God, in his infinite mercy and wisdom, had finally
sent a prophet.

Thirty-six years old, his name was William Jennings Bryan.

The seething mass of humanity inside Chicago's enormous,
brand-new coliseum looked up at Bryan, the Democratic Party's
nomination for President of the United States, whose imposing
height, massive head, aquiline nose, and piercing brown eyes made
him a striking figure. As Bryan held forth on the Democrats'
proposed national platform, they shouted and cheered, frantically
waving red bandanas in a sign of solidarity with the global workers'
movement that had been sweeping Europe for decades.

For the first time at this convention the delegates saw a man of
presidential timber on the stage above them.

And, for the first time in generations, they saw a savior.

The sweltering Chicago heat and the stench of thousands of
sweating bodies inside the convention hall threatened to overcome
him, but Bryan steadied himself for his moment atop Sinai. His
knuckles turned white as he grabbed the sides of the lectern. He had
never lacked for confidence, so now that thousands of eyes among
the party faithful were upon him, now that reporters were furiously
scribbling his every word in their notebooks, now that the moment
he'd been waiting for all his life was upon him, William Jennings
Bryan knew he would not falter.

Bryan had arrived in Chicago uncertain of his chances of becom-
ing his party's presidential nominee. But as his speech progressed he
became convinced that victory was his. A new monetary policy based
on the coinage of silver—"free silver"—had proven to be an even
more enticing message than he'd expected. The new supply of money
would relieve crippling debts for the farmers and other impoverished
voters Bryan sought to mobilize.

As he neared the climax of his remarks he mustered every last ounce of energy he could and unleashed some of the most famous lines in American political rhetoric. "If they dare to come out in the open field," he thundered, "and defend the gold standard as a good thing, we shall fight them to the uttermost, having behind us the producing masses of the nation and the world. Having behind us the commercial interests and the laboring interests and all the toiling masses."

Bryan paused, raised his hands above his head, and continued, "We shall answer their demands for a gold standard by saying to them: you shall not press down upon the brow of labor this crown of thorns."

He brought his hands down around his head, as if he were placing an imaginary crown on top. Then he stretched his arms out to his sides, palms toward the delegates, took a deep breath, and bellowed, "You shall not crucify mankind upon a cross of gold!"

Moses had now morphed into Jesus, and the multitude assembled thought they were witnessing the Second Coming. Their shouts thundered through the coliseum, shaking its steel girders and echoing down city blocks in every direction. "Bedlam broke loose," exclaimed a stunned Washington Post *correspondent. "Delirium reigned supreme. In the spoken word of the orator thousands of great men had heard the unexpressed sentiments and hopes of their own inmost souls."*

With that speech, William Jennings Bryan—"The Great Commoner"— ignited the first progressive moment in American history. His speech transformed Thomas Jefferson's and Andrew Jackson's Democratic Party—a party famously skeptical of the federal government—into a vehicle for massively expanding the state and making it responsible for redistributing wealth, breaking up businesses, assailing private property, and providing all manner of aid to the poor.

Bryan was America's first prophet of progressivism, an ideology that would go on to redefine the Democratic Party for generations and ultimately destroy the experiment in limited government that had begun with the founding of the Republic.

But Bryan's progressivism, while new to Americans and antithetical to the American system, was not a new movement at all. In fact, it originated from the very place the Founders had fled: the authoritarian-ruled nations of Europe.

GEORG HEGEL: THE BIRTH OF "PROGRESS"

Ninety years before William Jennings Bryan's rapturous reception in Chicago, a German university professor cast his eyes on an emperor. Maybe it was because the commanding figure on horseback contrasted so starkly with his own bent and bookish posture, but the image impressed Georg Wilhelm Friedrich Hegel more than anything he had ever seen.

It was October 1806, and Napoleon Bonaparte, the self-declared emperor of France, was on his way to battle outside Jena, where Professor Hegel taught. Napoleon's forces slaughtered tens of thousands of Hegel's Prussian countrymen, defeating their kingdom's army once and for all. But his nation's humiliation hardly lessened Hegel's admiration for the French tyrant. If anything, it increased it.

Napoleon sought to build an empire, a vast, ambitious government of planners and administrators. He was, in Hegel's view, an energetic man bringing progress—bloodstained progress, perhaps, but progress nonetheless—to a land that desperately needed it. He believed this was the kind of strong, forward-thinking leader Europe had been waiting for.

FEAR AND SELF-LOATHING

The boy lay trembling in his bed, the sheets around him damp with sweat. Near his head, a cool cloth meant to provide relief from the fever had long ago fallen away as he lay half-dreaming.

He woke with a start. The room was dimly lit, with the fingers of dawn creeping through the curtains. The house was quiet, eerily so. He wondered if he might still be dreaming. At his bedside sat a bedpan and an untouched cup of tea from the night before. Wearily, he tried to sit up, his body weak, fever still sapping his strength.

He willed himself up, sitting on the edge of his bed for a moment to steady himself. "Mother?" he said softly into the darkness of the hallway. No answer, just the silence. The boy stood, shaky on his feet. A chill ran through him as he gathered his bedclothes in fists at his sides. He took a few timid steps, his vision blurry in the pale light. Down the hall, he saw the doorway to his parents' bedroom was open.

"Mother?" he tried again. Silence again rebuffed him. He slowly worked his way down the hall, occasionally reaching out to the wall for balance.

He reached the doorway and peered in. The window was open, curtains swayed slightly in a gentle breeze, but otherwise the room was silent. "Mother?" The query was louder this time, as the form of his parents still under blankets annoyed him. "Father?" No movement.

He stepped into the room and took a few steps toward the bed. Steadying himself for a moment, he shook the bedpost to wake them. He walked around the edge of the bed and reached up to touch his mother's shoulder.

"Mother?"

The coldness of her skin jolted him. He stepped back from

the bed, his breath stuck in his throat. Fear washed over him, freezing him in place for a moment. Then he stepped forward and shook her roughly.

"Mother! Mother!"

His cries were raspy but loud. He was desperate to wake her, even though he already knew she would never wake up. Fever had claimed her in the night, just as it had claimed so many others in their village and throughout Germany.

Fear turned to nausea and ran through him. He cried and ran around the bed to the other side, where his father lay just as silent. He reached out in terror, tears starting to blur his vision. He touched his father's cheek, expecting the same coldness from the grayish skin. But as he touched him, his father stirred with a slight moan.

He was still alive.

Georg Wilhelm Friedrich Hegel, thirteen years old, sank his head into the blanket, relief overwhelming him. He and his father had both survived the fever—but barely. His relief soon gave way to anger, however. Why had God abandoned them? The priest had put a blessing on their house. Georg had prayed every single day, pleading with God to spare his family.

But God hadn't listened. Or maybe he had listened but couldn't do anything about it.

Either way, it didn't matter. Georg decided then and there that no other family should have to go through that. If God couldn't help, then he would.

The French Revolution that culminated in Napoleon's reign differed wildly from the American Revolution that preceded it by a mere thirteen years. The colonists who challenged an empire were rebelling against the way things had been done for centuries. They were tossing out monarchs who claimed to have a "divine right," a mandate from God to rule their citizens. Their movement championed the inalienable rights of the individual over the government. It defended the governed against their governors. Americans had created a government of elections and the rule of law: classical liberalism. The French preached democracy and liberty, but they birthed something else entirely: a reign of terror, culminating with an emperor who wielded near-total power.

How did these two revolutions meet such vastly different ends? Perhaps because, in the Americans' case, the Framers of the Constitution were keen observers of human nature. As a result, they enacted checks against one man and one party amassing too much power, a careful balance of forces that trusted individuals more than it trusted the state and protected the people from too much centralized control. The architects of this new government possessed no illusions that they were creating a utopia ruled by perfect people—just the opposite, in fact. They believed man had fallen because he was naturally too self-interested and sinful.

Across the Atlantic, a growing movement of philosophers and academics had different ideas about the nature of man and what the future held, most notably the young university professor so entranced by the sight of Napoleon's majesty: Hegel, the father of the progressive movement.

Hegel, whose own father was a senior government official working for one of Germany's dukes, understood the importance of administrators from a very early age. As he worked on his PhD, Hegel found a new way of looking at history and mankind's role in it by drawing on the writings of Jakob Böhme, a German Christian mystic, and Jean-Jacques Rousseau, a French writer.

Böhme believed that the fall of Adam and Eve was a first necessary stage so that mankind could achieve self-awareness. Man was separated from God, but through evolution over centuries, he could eventually achieve perfect knowledge with science and education. Rousseau, on the other hand, coined a concept he dubbed the "general will" of the people as a whole. The will of the individual, he proclaimed, was far less important than that of the collective. It was the government's responsibility to identify and carry out that collective will.

Hegel believed that the history of humankind was the story of man becoming more and more rational and "achieving consciousness." To "perfect" humanity, all that was needed was a government that tamed the impulses of human nature for the greater good. This was Hegel's revolutionary idea of progress.

Like many progressives who followed in his wake, Hegel also dabbled in race theory to explain why some societies seemed to "progress" better or faster than others. According to Hegel, it was "the German nations" who "were the first to attain the consciousness that man, as man, is free." Inferior genes, he believed, were the only way to explain why other parts of the world remained economically backward.

Hegel concluded that the world now stood at one of the most advanced stages of human history and that experts and knowledgeable persons should rule with the most perfect government and unlimited authority over the individual. Through the state and its rulers, in Hegel's "philosophy of history," man essentially became God on earth. This was the foundational principle of what eventually became known as progressivism.

With his belief in scientific training, Hegel helped create the modern research university system. Modeling this on the Prussian style of education, he envisioned universities that churned out administrators trained in the science of governing men and women—an idea they called "social science." Prussian education reforms extended down to young children as well, with the establishment of free, compulsory education by the state, starting with a mandatory "kindergarten" and national tests to track childhood learning. Hegel believed that this "scientific" approach to governance and progressive reforms would ultimately lead to a well-managed administrative state of experts.

If there was a good example of what an "unreformed" society looked like in Hegel's estimation, it was the United States. He saw America in the 1820s and 1830s as a wild and open nation, a vast unsettled frontier land with a primitive government. There was nothing progressive about it. It was a land with too much individual liberty, too much protection for private property, and too many greedy, ambitious people trying to build their individual fortunes. America, Hegel thought, was in dire need of progressive reform.

Hegel became Germany's most renowned academic, eventually attracting followers around the world, even in America. But one follower in particular was far more consequential than the others. This disciple was a fellow Prussian philosopher, a university student who was a generation younger but just as ambitious and intent on making his mark on the world by proving that mankind could establish a progressive utopia here on earth.

His name was Karl Marx.

MARX: NO COMPASSION, NO EXCUSES

Europe was on fire.

The previous year had brought turmoil and upheaval to the continent, punctuated by uprisings against its faltering ancient monarchies, particularly in Germany. That was why, in April 1848, Karl Marx and his comrade Friedrich Engels took the great risk of returning to their native land to publish the *Neue Rheinische Zeitung*—the "New Rheinish Newspaper"—in the city of Cologne.

The paper was going to be their contribution to this great struggle, their way of fanning the flames of change, not just in Germany but in France, Hungary, Poland, and Italy and across the continent. And in large measure, they were already succeeding. Across central Europe, the masses demanded reform and social justice. Finally, thought Marx, revolution was in the air—and in the streets.

Of course, the revolution was not as "pure" as Marx and Engels would have liked. The proletariat working class had not yet emerged as the driving force, but there was time yet. First, thrones and crowns had to go. Then, even if the selfish bourgeoisie took over from the kings, the working classes could, soon enough, be roused in turn to dislodge the new bourgeois oppressors—and Marx's ideal society could be born.

Although riots and protests had broken out in most capital cities, the Cologne offices of the paper were eerily quiet. There were no shouts of celebration. The presses weren't running. There was no frantic pounding of feet as copy boys with rolled-up sleeves darted to and fro carrying last-second edits. The proudly inflammatory *NRZ* proclaimed itself on its masthead to be "The Organ of Democracy," but in May 1849, that organ had seemingly gone silent.

Standing over his desk, one fist turning slowly, grinding into the battered wood of its surface, Marx, the paper's editor in chief, was seething. This was it. The reactionaries had him cornered—again. With anger boiling inside him, the newspaperman-revolutionary reread the note from the Royal Police:

> *The tendency of the* Neue Rheinische Zeitung *to provoke in its readers contempt for the present government, and incite them to violent revolutions and the setting up of a social republic has become stronger in its latest pieces. The right of hospitality, which he so disgracefully abused, is therefore to be withdrawn from its Editor-in-Chief, Dr. Karl Marx, and since he has not obtained permission to prolong his stay in these states he is ordered to leave them*

within 24 hours. If he should not comply with this demand, he is to
be conveyed across the border.

The authorities had struck once again. Marx was being forced to leave Cologne, just as he'd been ousted from Prussia, Paris, and Brussels. His revolutionary ideas had landed him in trouble everywhere he went. The pressure had only become more intense since he and Engels had published *The Communist Manifesto* two years earlier from the relative safety of London.

Marx, however, was a fighter. When he was a student, his philosophical scuffling with classmates was equaled only by (and often intertwined with) his drunken carousing. He'd even fought in a duel and been wounded above the eye by an arrogant Prussian blue blood. But the more important struggles at that time had been raging within his mind, and much of his sparring had been over the ideas of his favorite intellectual: Georg Wilhelm Friedrich Hegel.

Marx plunged deeply into Hegel's ideas while at university in Berlin. He'd even fallen in with a group of like-minded philosophers who called themselves the Young Hegelians. They debated the views and legacy of the recently deceased thinker, speculating how Hegel's ideas about man's increased consciousness would influence the course of history. Marx later rejected much of Hegelian philosophy, but one principle lodged itself firmly in young Marx's mind and never left: the dialectic.

Hegel saw history as a constant clash of ideas, and Marx agreed. Ideas had to be tested by constantly pitting them against one another. Only through this grueling, perhaps even bloody, struggle could society advance. Survival of the fittest ideas—it was the only way. And survival usually required fighting.

The meek didn't inherit the earth, Marx thought, they were swept from it.

From his newspaper office in Cologne, Marx knew that Hegel had been right: 1848's round of revolutions was the very manifestation of this struggle of ideas, old feudalism against new socialism. Although he was forced to shutter his newspaper and leave the city, Marx wasn't out of the fight. He had to make sure his ideas triumphed in the struggle to come.

He sat down at his desk, which was strewn with books, papers, pens, and inkwells. He cleared a space and began to sketch out the final edition of the *Neue Rheinische Zeitung*. He decided not only to print the note from the Cologne police forcing him to leave town but to add a scathing commentary. He ended with an ominous threat that would ring through the decades: "We have no compassion and we ask no compassion from you. When our turn comes, we shall not make excuses for the terror."

The socialism Marx outlined in his *Communist Manifesto* was not identical to progressivism, but it shared ideological roots in Hegel and the idea that mankind would evolve—or "progress"—toward a more scientific and better-administered future where governments would drive and implement change. Not until the Bolshevik Revolution of October 1917 would the world see a truly socialist government, but Marx and Hegel fueled social movements around the world that demanded reform.

In the mid-nineteenth century, Hegel's ideas found a powerful—and unlikely—adherent in Germany's first chancellor, Prince Otto von Bismarck. "The Iron Chancellor," through war and diplomacy, forged Germany's patchwork of decentralized, independent states together into a single nation under Prussian control. Armed with administrators churned out by Hegel's Prussian academy, Bismarck built the world's first welfare state, a series of paternalistic government programs that sought to gain the support of the working class.

Although Bismarck fashioned himself a conservative fighting against radical firebrands like Marx, he thought the only way to defeat socialism was to adopt some of it. "My idea was to bribe the working class, or shall I say, to win them over, to regard the state as a social institution existing for their sake and interested in their welfare," he confided to a fellow progressive. Bismarck's government, with the blessing of Germany's first kaiser, would become the most enlightened in the entire world.

Frederic Howe, an American evangelist of this German system, explained in 1915 how this worked. From the "cradle to the grave," the German worker's "education, his health, and his working efficiency are matters of constant concern" to the government. The individual would be taken care of in return for his unswerving loyalty to the state.

This was reform. This was progress.

And it was only the beginning.

SOCIALISM COMES TO AMERICA

Progressivism was not a natural fit for America. The idea that mankind was evolving to a higher consciousness, or a more moral, perfect state, seemed incompatible with the sinful view of man and the "hellfire and brimstone" sermons taught from pulpits across colonial America.

By and large, Americans venerated the Founders as wise students of human nature who'd been inspired by the classical Greek notion of permanent principles and truths. One of those ancient truths is that human beings have dark impulses. "There is a degree of depravity in mankind," James Madison wrote in the *Federalist Papers*, "which requires a certain degree of circumspection and distrust." No amount of Hegelian mumbo jumbo or advanced degrees from German universities could change that.

Early Americans were also deeply suspicious of federal power.

They had resisted it at every turn, whether from London or from a newly formed federal government in Philadelphia (and later in Washington, D.C.). Skepticism of government and of politicians who promised big things ran deep in the national DNA. People firmly believed in self-reliance, local control, and a strong civil society where neighbors volunteered to help one another when things got bad. The federal government was a remote, abstract idea that never impinged on daily lives.

Americans had also never been as class-conscious as their European ancestors. The idea that bankers and moneyed interests were manipulating and exploiting them just didn't add up. They raised families. They went to church. They tilled the soil with their plows, mined the coal from deep within the earth, worked on the factory floor, or ran a general store in town. And if they happened to falter or fail, a frontier rich in opportunity let them start again.

But that frontier was changing by the late nineteenth century. Some argued that it had even been closed altogether. Americans had spread west to the Pacific Coast of California. The Industrial Revolution was changing cities. If all of this was changing, many thought, so, too, must America's politics, along with its very identity.

In the three decades following the Civil War, a nation of mostly wilderness and backwaters had been transformed into an economic superpower. Railroad tracks crisscrossed the vast American continent. Booming industrial centers with billowing smokestacks sprang up in nearly every state. By 1883, commerce had grown at such a clip that a national standardized time system replaced hundreds of local clock conventions.

Between 1865 and 1900, the American economy quadrupled. And in this tumult, a rebellion against the American idea was brewing in the academy—a rebellion that would soon spread to the churches.

THE INFECTION OF CHURCH AND STATE

Baltimore's Johns Hopkins University was founded in 1876 as a new kind of research university. Johns Hopkins prided itself on being the first American institution to replicate the Prussian academic tradition of Heidelberg, Freiberg, Göttingen, and Berlin. It was animated by Hegel's view of progress and the need for a powerful administrative state guided by disinterested, expert social scientists.

German immigrants had come to America by the millions during the fifty years since Hegel's death, carrying with them ideas about progress and efficiency. Some even brought the more radical contentions of Marx's socialism and the notion that government could be an organizing mechanism for social, economic, and moral reform. American graduate students had also gone to Germany to study in its legendary universities, bringing back the Hegelian appreciation for expertise and the idea that properly trained experts could be social engineers of the future.

This new generation of German-trained academics also brought back a disdain for "English" economics and natural law, the classically liberal thinking of philosophers such as John Locke and Adam Smith that had influenced the American Founders. The tradition of natural rights and the Anglo-American belief in the dignity of the individual were being replaced by a new kind of thinking that prioritized society as a whole.

The most prominent of the first American progressives was Richard T. Ely, a professor of economics who came to Johns Hopkins in 1881, two years after receiving his doctorate at Heidelberg. Ely, who once wrote that "God works through the State in carrying out his purposes more universally than through any other institution," helped found the American Economic Association, which is dedicated to social science and social justice (and which still holds an annual lecture named for him).

Ely had grown up on a ninety-acre farm in upstate New York, where he worked with his father raising crops through young adulthood. He loved the sense of community in his small agrarian village, of working to trade milk for tools and cheese for grain in the local market. His mother was a member of a local women's club that took donations of wool and made clothing for orphans in nearby cities and towns.

When he went off to college at Columbia in Manhattan, he felt alienated in the big city and missed the community he had loved. He wrote to his family that New Yorkers seemed to lack the principal Christian virtue he had found so comforting in his small farming community: charity. It seemed to him that this virtue was absent from big-city morals, which were focused on personal achievement and wealth seeking, all of which Ely viewed as "sinful."

While in college, and later in graduate school at Johns Hopkins, he blended his study of economics with the study of "Christian morals." In order to help man reach a new level of happiness, he determined that the cold science and hard numbers of economics must be blended with the Christian principles of charity and giving. The goal was to "end the suffering and loneliness that so often impacts the lives" of our fellow human beings.

To succeed, all that was needed was organizing resources to ensure that there were enough for everyone. In his small township, that had seemingly occurred out of the goodness of the hearts of his family, friends, and neighbors. But in cities, more powerful organizing forces were clearly needed. Ely's overt mission was to "save mankind from himself."

In an 1894 text on socialism, Ely wrote:

> *Looking into the future we can contemplate a society . . . in which men shall work together for a common purpose, and in*

which the wholesale cooperation shall take place largely through government. . . . We have reason to believe that we shall yet see great national undertakings with the property of the nation, *and managed by the nation, through agents who appreciate the glory of true public service, and feel that it is God's work which they are doing, because church and state are as one. . . . We may anticipate an approximation of state and society as men improve and we may hope that men outside of government will freely and voluntarily act with trained officers and experts in the service of the government for the advancement of common interests.*

"The property of the nation" is the thesis at the very heart of the progressive movement: nothing belongs to the individual; it's all owned by the state. The arbitrary powers of government can seize and do what they see fit with our property as long as government deems it good, right, and just for the broader society.

Ely rejected the socialist dictum of shared, collective property ownership. His family farm wasn't collectively owned, so depriving families of land ownership was a bridge too far. He did, however, believe that the production of that property, the goods and crops, could be proportionally shared with those less fortunate. A balanced, hunger-free society was within reach.

And thus, charity by force was born.

Like Hegel and other progressives seeking the "perfect" society, Ely also held an unsavory view of minorities, especially African-Americans. He complained that "the negro race, while endowed with a splendid physique and with great power for work, is neither progressive nor inclined to submit to regularity of toil, such as an industrial civilization demands." He campaigned to bar immigrants into the United States who were judged by elites to be "hereditary inferiors."

From the movement's earliest days, some progressives wavered between fully embracing socialism and keeping their distance. But for most, the two ideologies routinely intermingled—and for good reason: they shared a common ideological root. The marriage of progressivism and socialism was born of convenience as much as it was about shared goals. Progressives embraced the socialist movement because socialist theory enabled the use of government to further their reform agenda. Socialists embraced progressivism because it carried with it seemingly uncontroversial and popular causes such as protecting children, improving food quality and health standards, improving living standards, and protecting workers.

Ely believed that Marx's socialist theology and themes of class warfare—things he had studied in Germany—would be too alien and radical for Americans if unleashed to be absorbed all at once. Instead, he preferred "a socialism of spirit that would replace laissez-faire from within men's hearts." Americans had grown too selfish, Ely maintained. His job was to instill a sense of communal goals and to do so through training a new generation of social scientists. He believed that these disinterested, nonpartisan, scientific, and civic-minded people could regulate and manage the world's fastest-growing economy and compensate for those being left behind. This was the administrative state. *Everything* could be improved, as the prominent social reformer Jane Addams said.

Over time, Ely trained hundreds of social scientists in progressivism and his views about the "perfectibility" of society and man, but two of his disciples stood out: Woodrow Wilson and John Dewey.

When they first became attracted to Ely's ideas, Dewey was teaching high school and Wilson was working as a lawyer. Later, as students together at Johns Hopkins, where Ely was a professor, the two men even squared off against each other in a debate over a rather telling topic: "Whether the U.S. government ought to pay to educate the Negro." Dewey argued in favor, Wilson against.

Dewey went on to become a career academic and progressive educational reformer, arguing that only a far larger governmental appara-

THE GRUESOME SCIENCE

If mankind could be perfected over time, one of the best ways to do so, the theory went, would be by weeding out defective and less desirable genes from the pool. It had been a fantasy for millennia, dating back to at least as early as when Socrates speculated that humans could be bred like livestock, with only the best being allowed to reproduce. The rest of us could be sterilized, aborted, prevented from marrying or mixing with people of other races, or forced to use birth control to guarantee that our genetic material wasn't passed on to pollute future generations.

Modern eugenics—its name derived from the Greek for "well born"—sprang up in the mid-nineteenth century among progressive thinkers and scientists. It was coined by a British scientist and a cousin of Charles Darwin named Francis Galston, who mused, "If a twentieth part of the cost and pains were spent in measures for the improvement of the human race that is spent on the improvement of the breed of horses and cattle, what a galaxy of genius might we not create!"

Darwin took his cousin's theories on natural selection and not only applied them to humans but also argued that humans could manipulate this selection process themselves to create a kind of superrace.

Progressives like Ely would champion forced sterilization and social science to examine differences among races. A "Race Betterment Foundation" for the promotion of eugenics was launched, as was *American Breeders Magazine*. An International Eugenics Congress in London began under the leadership of Major Leonard Darwin, Charles Darwin's son, with "undesirables" being the target of its campaign to perfect the human species. The Anglo-Saxon race was considered the epitome of humanity.

One of the leading eugenic theorists was Madison Grant, an avid conservationist who also had some interesting ideas about how to "conserve" the Nordic race. In his book, *The Passing of the Great Race*, Grant proposed a plan that included the outright elimination of "the least desirable, let us say, ten percent of the community," which he described as "unemployed and unemployable human residuum" and a "great mass of crime, poverty, alcoholism, and feeble-mindedness." After that, he called for "restricting the perpetuation"—sterilization—"of the then remaining least valuable types" among those that remained. "By this method," Grant argued, "mankind might ultimately become sufficiently intelligent to deliberately choose the most vital and intellectual strains to carry on the race."

Two men in particular were greatly affected by Grant's writing. One was a friend from conservationist circles, a man named Teddy Roosevelt, who praised Grant for writing "a capital book; in purpose, in vision, in grasp of the facts of our people most need to realize . . . and all Americans should be sincerely grateful to you for writing it."

Half a world away, Grant's ideas also inspired a young German. He was a veteran of the World War I and a failed artist whose own radical ideas on race were starting to take shape while he was in prison in the 1920s. He called Grant's work his "Bible"—and very soon the world would come to know Adolf Hitler's name.

tus could cure the social ills of the twentieth century. He argued that freedom was not "something that individuals have as a ready-made possession"; it was "something to be achieved." In this view, freedom was not a gift from God or nature; it was a product of human making, a gift from the state. He emphasized state influence on early-childhood education in order to spread the progressive doctrine to children as early as possible, no matter what views they were exposed to at home.

Progressive academics such as Dewey and Wilson, who eventually left the legal profession to teach (first at Cornell and Bryn Mawr and then at Princeton), had an ally in American Protestantism. Most social scientists such as Ely and Wilson were devout Christians themselves and open about their desire as Christian missionaries to build a kingdom of heaven on earth. This was the "social gospel," a vision of Hegel's and Ely's progressivism that sought economic and social improvement by applying Christian ethics. Clergymen made up nearly half of the American Economic Association's charter members. Preachers from pulpits across America railed against capitalism as selfish. The solution was a new kind of Christian socialism that encouraged more labor unions and cooperative economics.

The "social gospel" organizers mobilized millions on behalf of their cause for reform. One of the first mass organizations was the Woman's Christian Temperance Union, founded in 1873. Its goal was to create a "sober and pure world" by encouraging abstinence, sexual purity, and devotion to Christian doctrine (as the organization's members defined it). Other groups also sprouted up—such as the YMCA and the Industrial Workers of the World—which marched, petitioned, and organized on behalf of progressive, and sometimes outright radical, reform.

By now, progressivism had captured the allegiance of a new generation of academics in campuses across America, along with thousands of pastors now evangelizing their flocks regarding the importance of social reform.

What progressivism needed next was a national leader to bring it all together and sell it to the masses.

BRYAN AND THE PROGRESSIVE PRAIRIE FIRE

Until 1896, progressivism in America had been confined to churches and campuses. But with one stirring speech, William Jennings Bryan changed all that.

Though a relative newcomer to the political scene, Bryan had a keen sense of how the winds were blowing in American politics. He positioned himself as a new kind of Democrat, the leader of a prairie insurgency against the Eastern elites. He thundered that Washington needed to "suppress" the business trusts and give debt relief by coining silver. He also supported the first peacetime income tax passed by Congress, although it was subsequently declared unconstitutional by the U.S. Supreme Court.

At that time, there was just one federal social-welfare program: the Pension Office, which dispensed funds to Civil War veterans. Government was almost exclusively a state and local affair. Bryan had little in common with the bespectacled social scientists of Johns Hopkins and the University of Wisconsin, but he was a devout believer in the social gospel that had captured Christianity in the late nineteenth century.

Bryan's populist campaign came as the Democratic Party warred against itself, torn between Eastern business interests supporting the Democrat incumbent Grover Cleveland's hands-off approach to the economy and the Southern farmers and Western mining interests hit hardest by the calamitous Panic of 1893. The haves, said the progressives and the populists, had given themselves everything, and therefore they thrived even when the economy was in a depression. Now the have-nots were going to exact their revenge—and as the next president of the United States, William Jennings Bryan would be the one to do it.

Bryan was a true believer, an idealist of the most innocent kind.

He knew that this new populism could propel him to the presidency, but he also believed in it deeply. So did millions of others who raged at the "robber barons," such as John D. Rockefeller, Andrew Carnegie, and J. P. Morgan. Bryan was channeling the mistrust and confusion generated by the rapid pace of change during the Industrial Revolution. Bryan and his followers wanted the federal government to step in and level the playing field for the working masses. Grover Cleveland represented the old Democratic Party of Thomas Jefferson and Andrew Jackson, skeptical of federal power. But now, aligned against Cleveland and the "robber barons," was a new party, one that had been bubbling up in local and state elections for a few years but had little presence nationally: the "People's Party" or "Populists."

Dubbed "hayseeds" and "anarchists" by their opponents and derided for their wispy beards and unkempt appearances, they embodied the first progressive movement in America. Through twenty-first-century lenses, nothing seems very radical about the demands of the People's Party. They called for massive public-works projects to reduce unemployment. They demanded federal relief for poverty-stricken farmers, particularly cotton farmers in the South and wheat farmers in the West. They wanted strict limits on and disclosure requirements of political campaign contributions, the registration of lobbyists, and the recording and publication of congressional committee proceedings. They urged states to adopt measures for "direct democracy," including recall elections, referendums where citizens could decide on a law by popular vote, and initiatives where citizens could even propose a law by petition and popular vote. They wanted social initiatives, such as a national health service including all existing government medical agencies, social insurance, limited injunctions in strikes, a minimum-wage law for women, an eight-hour workday, a federal securities commission, an inheritance tax, and a constitutional amendment to allow a federal income tax.

Eventually, the political initiatives of the People's Party also included women's suffrage, direct election of senators, primary elections for state and federal nominations, the recall of judges, and new rights for labor unions. As I said, not very radical. But most of all, the People's Party wanted silver.

The gold standard—the idea that American paper currency was backed by actual stockpiles of gold—had been in place since what some called the Crime of '73, the 1873 Fourth Coinage Act that demonetized silver. People's Party adherents saw gold as the money of "exploitation" and "oppression" by the Eastern financial establishment. The "free coinage of silver" would inflate the currency, decreasing its value and aiding those who had fallen destitute and in debt in the Panic of 1893. Wealth would be more equitably distributed from the wealthy Eastern elites to the struggling lower classes—not to mention to the special interests such as the silver-mine owners who stood to profit handsomely.

In Chicago's marbled Palmer House hotel, the silver lobbyists had plotted for days in advance of 1896's Democratic National Convention. They had found a sympathetic ear in Bryan, who promised to voice their concerns when he addressed the delegates. The silver-mine owners of Nevada and California were particularly keen to have the federal government suddenly purchasing vast reserves of silver, which would increase the price of the metal and boost their already hefty fortunes. As the "boy orator from the Platte," referring to his home state of Nebraska, he had been ostentatious in refusing any money from the big trusts and lobbyists. His honesty became legendary. He fashioned himself a man of the people.

Yet Bryan and his key supporters in the Democratic Party were intimately connected with their own big-business trusts, which represented the real one percent of America at the time. Prominent among them were Senator James Jones of Arkansas, the head of the Democratic National Committee, and Richard Croker, the boss of New York City's Tammany Hall Democratic machine. Croker had become ensnared in a major corruption probe, which revealed how he and his wife had profited to the tune of hundreds of thousands of dollars for protecting a monopoly on the ice trade, a booming business on the eastern seaboard. There was also John D. Clarke, a lawyer and lobbyist for the silver-mining interests, who were making millions from their mines in Nevada and California and stood to make millions more if only the U.S. government allowed its currency to be backed by silver as well as gold.

Not all of these interests shared the progressives' entire worldview, but they were all certainly ready to back "free silver." They understood that federal power brought with it the opportunity to make millions of dollars. If they pushed for Bryan, then he and his progressive allies could pick winners and losers. The winners would be anyone with a stake in silver.

With the influence of these moneyed interests, the election of 1896 fused together a populist progressive platform that radically redefined the Democratic Party. From the days of Thomas Jefferson and Andrew Jackson to the end of the Grover Cleveland administration, Democrats had believed in a small government. No more.

Bryan would go on to lose the 1896 election to Republican William McKinley, but he would boost the fortunes of his backers who successfully lobbied his fellow politicians at the local, state, and federal level. More important, Bryan would leave an indelible imprint on the Democratic Party. The new party of Jefferson and Jackson embarked on a far more radical course, one that would have an impact on the United States for generations to come and forever change how Americans viewed their rights, responsibilities, and relationships with government.

||||||||||||||||||||||||||||||||||||||||||||||||||||||||||||||||||||||||||||||||||||||||||||||||||||||||||||||||||||||

PROFILE IN FEAR:
MARGARET SANGER AND THE WAR ON "UNDESIRABLES"

Corning, New York

November 1892

The vagrants' collars are pulled high around their necks, a futile defense against the cold, slushy rain. As they rap on the door of the house before them, the two men stamp their feet to keep warm.

The door opens, and the warmth of a coal-fired stove pours over them. Light from candles and a lantern on the table reflect in the ice crystals that have formed in their dark, grizzled beards.

At first, the matronly woman in her early forties steps back to allow the visitors inside. But after scrutinizing the men, she has second thoughts and quickly moves to block their entry. There is an instant of silence, cut only by the splash of sleet on the stepping stones outside.

Behind the woman, the curious eyes of several children on the steps probe silently.

"Is the boss in?" one of the men asks.

"No, but I'm looking for him any minute."

"We want something to eat," the man says expectantly.

Not wavering in her command of the threshold, the woman stands for a moment longer, considering but silent. She is accustomed to these types of visitors: tramps and vagabonds, the "knights of the open road" who travel between New York City and odd jobs in the country.

Over the years, hundreds of men and dozens of children have found sanctuary in the house, with free access to food, milk, and warm beds, as well as glasses of whiskey always favored by their host. Anne has always borne it patiently, quiet in the wisdom that, despite having eleven children of their own, the Christian upbringing of her husband—which has evolved into the open adoption of socialism in the waves of reform sweeping the Eastern seaboard—simply wouldn't allow him to turn away the needy.

They are living, breathing adherents of the social gospel. Jesus, they believe, has commanded them to share their property. That includes their home on a cold night like this. Were her husband here and not out of town on business, Anne knows he would admonish her for having second thoughts about inviting them in with a smile. Yet every instinct tells her to turn these men away.

Sensing the hesitation, and without further ceremony, the men push past Anne and into the house, heading toward the kitchen. On the stairs, one of the family dogs barks, and Margaret, the eldest of the children, strains to hold the hound back from its protective instinct.

Leaving the door open, Anne bristles and moves defensively toward the foot of the stairs, declaring crossly, "How dare you come into this house!"

Ignoring her, the men begin searching for food. One throws open cupboards while the other stuffs rolls into the pockets of his trench coat. On a small desk near the stairs, Anne notices her husband's tools—a hammer and a chisel.

She looks up at little Margaret on the steps, takes a deep breath, and turns back to the men. "Toss! Beauty!" she shouts, beckoning the two dogs to come to her side. Hearing the fear in her voice, the dogs bark and snarl, leaping down the steps, lunging past the children and onto the backs of the men ransacking the cupboards.

Anne turns toward the stairs with a stern, desperate message. "Margaret, you keep those children there, no matter what occurs."

The children watch their mother charge forward to chase the men away. The dogs snarl and bite; the men throw punches, food, and utensils to fend them off. Anne swings the hammer at one of them, landing a blow on his cheek, only to have him smash her across the face with the back of his clenched fist. She falls hard to the floor, just as the other man lands a kick in her side.

The children cry out from the stairs, "No, Mother!" One of the dogs is felled with a blow from the hammer that Anne drops. The other retreats to the corner and barks and growls as the men grab what food they can and scamper out the door.

For an instant after they leave, it is impossibly silent. Snow and sleet splash in through the open door and onto the floor, mixing with spatters of blood and milk that spilled during the fracas.

On the stairs, the children cry quietly. Following orders, Margaret comforts them but doesn't allow any to venture down, even to see if their mother is still alive. Time passes. The lone candle burns down and dies out.

As he approaches the home, Michael notices there are no lights in the windows. He sees the front door hanging open and immediately senses that something is very wrong.

He runs and lunges through the door, slipping to the floor in his haste. On his knees, he crawls to his wife, who is lying in a pool of blood.

Her breathing is raspy, and her body is cold to the touch, but she is alive.

"Margaret!" he yells toward the stairs. His daughter leaves her post at the top landing and crouches next to him.

She fetches a wet cloth from the sink, and they begin to clean Anne's wounds. Michael shakes his wife lightly, trying to wake her. "Get the whiskey," he instructs his daughter. She obeys and brings the bottle from a drawer in his desk.

Margaret helps to hold her mother's mouth open as her father pours a dram into it. For a second, nothing happens. Then Anne coughs and gurgles and opens her eyes. She shivers in his arms as he holds her.

Anne developed a case of severe pneumonia over the ensuing days, turning a lifelong battle with tuberculosis into a crisis. From that day forward, she often had to lean against a wall or a counter to battle frequent bouts of coughing and labored breathing, and she endured seasonal cases of pneumonia, forcing bed rest off and on for the rest of her life. In the years that followed, vagrants coming to the Higgins household would only be served at the door and only if Michael was home.

Margaret acted as full-time nursemaid to her mother until Anne eventually died a few years later. Throughout those years of bringing her mother food and water, changing her bedclothes, and holding her while she was wracked with coughing fits, Margaret never forgot the lowly, evil men who had brought her mother to this state. The fear she endured that night had turned into hatred. And then into a blinding rage. She never forgave them. And she eventually dedicated her life to making sure that people like them—and anyone who, in her judgment, shared any of their undesirable traits—would be driven out of existence.

Victims of rape or violent assault often experience lifelong post-traumatic stress disorder (PTSD), a form of psychological panic that closes off part of the human brain where reason is processed. Margaret Sanger's experiences as a child, witnessing the attack on her mother and encountering hundreds of other vagrants who had boarded in her own home because her father believed it to be a moral duty to help, are classic examples of events that trigger

PTSD. The consequences can be varied, but they almost always include a powerful combination of ongoing shame, fear, and guilt.

The fear comes from not having control or the power to stop the event from recurring, and the shame and guilt come from not being able to stop it.

Sanger's own description of the attack against her mother is surprisingly short, but it is told in the first person, so we know that she was at home and personally witnessed it. Absent from the short narrative, however, is any mention that Margaret herself stepped in to stop it or to help her mother in any way, even after the attack was over and her mother lay unconscious and bleeding on the ground. It wasn't until her father returned home that Margaret had dared to come downstairs.

Perhaps unsurprisingly, Sanger became a passionate advocate for abortion, eugenics, and forced sterilization of both men and women (with particular focus on minorities, such as African-Americans and Chinese immigrants). Her desire to rid the world of what she saw as troublesome underclasses that produced violent vagrants is probably a direct result of her childhood experiences and the shame she must have felt over her inaction.

Merriam-Webster defines *eugenics* as "a science that tries to improve the human race by controlling which people become parents." Eugenics research, funded by America's elite industrialists, was carried out by scientists dedicated to the perfection of the human race. Their work influenced a generation of progressives and socialists—including Adolf Hitler, Woodrow Wilson, and, of course, Margaret Sanger.

As Sanger grew older, she became an early and earnest supporter of this diabolical science, a field that formed a pillar of the early progressive movement in its fixation on manipulating genetics to "perfect" humanity. In words that might well be approved by Hitler or David Duke, she wrote this about her plans for humanity:

> *The first step would thus be to control the intake and output of morons, mental defectives, epileptics. The second step would be to take an inventory of the secondary group such as illiterates, paupers, unemployables, criminals, prostitutes, dope-fiends; classify them in special departments under government medical protection and segregate.*

Sanger believed in a policy of "race improvement," once saying that it was necessary to create a "race of thoroughbreds." In 1926, she even saw fit to present her views before a women's chapter of the Ku Klux Klan, which led to "a dozen invitations to speak to similar groups."

Sanger also believed that families with too many children (remember, she was one of eleven kids) posed an unnecessary hardship on the rest of society. "The most merciful thing that the large family does to one of its members," she wrote in 1920, "is to kill it." (It's worth noting that Planned Parenthood claims that this quote is out of context, that it is really about the rising infant death rate among large families at the time. Let's assume they're right—does that make this statement OK? It's merciful to have a child and then kill it just because there is some percentage chance that it might die anyway?)

Sanger is perhaps best known as an early, staunch advocate of birth control, including abortion, and as the founder of the organization that would eventually grow into Planned Parenthood (its original name was more honest: the American Birth Control League). But the reasoning behind her zeal was deeper and darker than simply a disregard for individual human lives. Sanger believed that contraception, especially preventing birth among certain undesirables, was better for the human race as a whole.

In 1922, she wrote:

> *Those least fit to carry on the race are increasing most rapidly. People who cannot support their own offspring are encouraged by Church and State to produce large families. Many of the children thus begotten are diseased or feeble minded. Many become criminals. . . . Funds that should be used to raise the standard of our civilization are diverted to the maintenance of those who should never have been born.*

Despite these radical views, Sanger is, to this day, a progressive hero.

In 2009, Hillary Clinton proudly accepted the Margaret Sanger Award from Planned Parenthood. "Now, I have to tell you that it was a great privilege when I was told that I would receive this award," Clinton said. "I admire Margaret Sanger enormously, her courage, her tenacity, her vision."

For a singular moment, Clinton told the truth. She admires—as she said in her own words—this racist, bigoted, self-appointed deity who saw fit to decide who should get the gift of life.

2

First Wave:

Wilson, the Philosopher President

The difference between democracy and socialism is not an essential difference, but only a practical difference.

—WOODROW WILSON

The North Atlantic
April 19, 1912

For four excruciating days, a lone ship plowed the waves through fog, darkness, and rough, freezing seas. It sped toward a cursed patch of icy sea four hundred miles south of Newfoundland that had recently echoed with the desperate screams of twenty-two hundred souls.

The CS Mackay-Bennett, a two-thousand-ton cable-repair ship berthed in Halifax, Nova Scotia, had been overhauling a communications cable linking Canada and France when it received the White Star Line's desperate plea for aid. It embarked immediately after its macabre cargo—embalming supplies for hundreds of floating corpses and a hundred empty coffins—was aboard. This time, there *was no cable line in need of urgent repair. This was a mission of recovery and retrieval. This was a search for death.*

The April 15 sinking of the British luxury liner RMS had claimed more than fifteen hundred passengers and crew, chiefly because the Titanic, *this grand, state-of-the-art vessel, sumptuously appointed with all manner of luxuries and modern conveniences—from a squash court to a lending library to a Turkish bath—had simply not carried enough lifeboats for everyone on board.*

The dead who wore life vests bobbed on the ocean like human buoys. The Mackay–Bennett *recovered 306 corpses, far more than the number of caskets it carried. The bodies included that of a nineteen-month-old English boy named Sidney Leslie Goodwin; Isidor Straus, the seventy-seven-year-old owner of Macy's Department Store (his wife's body was never found); and a well-dressed, light-haired, fifty-year-old man whose shirt collar and gold belt buckle bore the initials J.J.A.*

He was, the crew later learned, John Jacob Astor IV, the richest man aboard the Titanic and, *in death, the richest man now aboard the* Mackay–Bennett.

As the elegant Titanic *capsized, Colonel Astor, a Spanish-American War veteran, had ensured that his pregnant eighteen-year-old second wife, Madeleine, her nurse, and their maid had safely boarded a lifeboat. "Might I be allowed to go with her?" the multimillionaire had asked a ship's officer. "She is in a delicate condition."*

"No, sir," the officer had replied. "No man is allowed on this boat or any of the boats until the ladies are off."

"Well, tell me," Astor had asked, "what is the number of this boat so I may find her afterwards?"

"Number four."

Astor had kissed his wife on the cheek and watched her boat

*being lowered to the choppy sea. He had known he would never see
her again, nor would he ever get to lay eyes on his unborn child.**
He'd asked for the lifeboat's number simply to calm her fears.

ONE DISASTER FORETELLS ANOTHER

In the three decades that preceded the sinking of the *Titanic*, the
public in both America and Britain had been gripped by a fear of
oceanic sailing. The waters of the North Atlantic, which were the
most transited in the world—and arguably the most dangerous—
claimed hundreds of lives each year. A young woman named Eleanor
Roosevelt herself was on the White Star Line steamship *Britannic*
when it nearly sank after colliding with another ship. Dozens of men
who had boarded a lifeboat before realizing that the ship was not actually sinking sheepishly returned to the scornful eyes of passengers
and crew.

In the twelve years leading up to the sailing of the *Titanic*, there
was at least one major maritime disaster per year, with more than
six thousand passengers lost at sea. While the fear of oceanic travel
among the public hadn't quite reached the level of a clinical phobia
yet (thalassophobia, fear of the sea, however, is a real clinical disorder),
the general mood in the United States and in Europe was that trans-
oceanic sailing was, in fact, a dangerous proposition. The White Star
Line was so anxious to allay public fear of ocean crossings that the
Titanic was built and marketed as "unsinkable" as early as 1909, two
full years before its steel hull ever touched water.

---

* Madeleine Astor would receive only five million dollars of her husband's huge estate. Sixty-nine
million dollars would go to his son from his first marriage, Vincent, who would become one of Franklin
Roosevelt's closest personal friends.

The marketing campaign worked brilliantly. The *Titanic*'s maiden voyage sold out in mere days, and White Star had bookings as far out as a year in advance. The *Titanic* and White Star Line's "unsinkable" campaign provided relief, giving the public an antidote to the fear that had been building with the stories of so many lives lost to the waves.

At long last, the public had hope.

That hope was quickly dashed when an iceberg ripped through the "unsinkable" vessel. News of the *Titanic*'s tragedy flashed across a horrified world, although one famed historian could not resist dark-humor parallels to another, larger tragedy about to befall America. Henry Adams, who had booked passage on the doomed liner's return voyage to Europe, wrote a longtime female friend, "I do not know whether Taft or the *Titanic* is likely to be the furthest-reaching disaster."

Incumbent Republican President William Howard Taft faced the fight of his life against both Theodore Roosevelt, his old friend and immediate predecessor, and that year's Democratic nominee, former Princeton University President Woodrow Wilson. Both Roosevelt and Wilson ran as passionate progressives—a term that had entered the lexicon thanks to Democrat William Jennings Bryan and was later adopted by Republican Roosevelt during his "trust-busting" presidency.

Teddy Roosevelt was the first chief executive to endorse a federal income tax and a national health-insurance program. He also waged war against big business, and he almost single-handedly transformed the presidency from its nineteenth-century practice of quietly administrating government, taking its lead from Congress, to making it the center of all power in the nation's capital.

In 1910, Roosevelt declared, "The absence of effective State, and, especially, national, restraint upon unfair money-getting has tended to create a small class of enormously wealthy and economically powerful men, whose chief object is to hold and increase their power." He also said that the government "should permit [their fortunes] to be gained only so long as the gaining represents benefit to the community."

This was a Republican essentially saying that private wealth is only allowable to the extent that it benefits the greater good. Roosevelt also argued that accumulated property is "subject to the general right of the community to regulate its use to whatever degree the public welfare may require it." He advocated concentrating power in the presidency to make this system work. "This New Nationalism," he said, "regards the executive power as the steward of the public welfare."

By 1912, Roosevelt labeled Taft, his designated heir, insufficiently progressive and unsuccessfully challenged him in the Republican primaries and at the hotly contested convention. In the general election, Roosevelt bolted from the GOP to run on a radical Progressive (or "Bull Moose") third-party ticket. The Roosevelt-Taft split guaranteed the election of Woodrow Wilson, the most radical Democrat in U.S. history. Wilson garnered a mere 41.8 percent of the popular vote but received 435 electoral votes to Roosevelt's 88 and Taft's minuscule 8.

Just a month after the *Mackay-Bennett* completed its grim recovery operation, the hatchet-faced Wilson addressed the prestigious Economic Club of New York at a hotel bearing the name of one of the *Titanic*'s most prominent victims. Speaking to business leaders at Times Square's Hotel Astor, Wilson pushed back against complaints that his ideas opposed the free-enterprise system. He believed that wealthy families such as the Astors had turned the American republic into their own fiefdom. The rich, he said, had to be reined in, their wealth confiscated for the public good, if necessary.

"The very thing that government cannot let alone is business," Wilson blustered. "Government cannot take its hands off business.

Government must regulate business because that is the foundation of every other relationship."

The tragic sinking of the *Titanic*, a ship that its owners boasted was unsinkable, was the consequence of hubristic, humanist assumptions about man's ability to control natural law and defy the will of God.

And so was the candidacy of Woodrow Wilson.

LIBERAL IDOL . . . AND BLIND SPOT

If you've listened to me on radio or TV, you probably know that I'm not a member in good standing of the Woodrow Wilson fan club. What you might not know, however, is that neither is the American public. Not a single recent public-opinion survey lists Wilson as among the greatest U.S. presidents. Even Jimmy Carter is more popular.

Yes, even Jimmy Carter.

Unfortunately, the people who write history haven't quite figured out just how awful a president (not to mention a person) Wilson actually was. In fact, few former presidents are held in such high esteem by modern liberals. Historians, most of them progressives themselves, routinely rank Wilson among the top ten of the nation's chief executives. In fact, two polls conducted by Arthur Schlesinger Jr. both rated Wilson behind only Lincoln, Washington, and (big surprise) Franklin Roosevelt.

How can that be explained? Here's Howard University historian Edna Medford's attempt: "How we rank our presidents is, to a large extent, influenced by our own times. Today's concerns shape our views of the past, be it in the area of foreign policy, managing the economy, or human rights."

If that's true, well, it only makes the liberal academic fetish for Wilson even more bizarre. Few presidents displayed such open contempt for the Constitution they swore to preserve, protect, and defend. Even fewer had such a severe disdain for women, minorities, and anyone else who deviated from Wilson's view of the "perfect citizen."

Some modern progressives have mixed emotions about Wilson. Embarrassed by his blatant prejudices, a few have demanded that his name be stripped from Princeton's elite Woodrow Wilson School of Government.* Yet most still seem to excuse him, in much the same way they excuse the abhorrent behavior of people like Bill Clinton, Donald Trump, or Robert Byrd simply because these people represent an ideology they support.

Never is this more apparent than in the case of Wilson. Here, for example, is an all-too-typical description of him from the "nonpartisan" University of Virginia's Miller Center:

> Woodrow Wilson was one of America's greatest Presidents. His domestic program expanded the role of the federal government in managing the economy and protecting the interests of citizens. His foreign policy established a new vision of America's role in the world. And he helped to make the White House the center of power in Washington. Most historians rank him among the five most important American Presidents, along with Washington, Lincoln, and the two Roosevelts.

Note how the Miller Center folks call him one of the "greatest"—not the "most consequential," which might actually be accurate—and also note how they directly tie his "greatness" to expanding the role of the federal government and to the creation of an imperial presidency.

It's not just academics like those at the Miller Center who display a fawning love for Wilson. A 2002 episode of the PBS series *Amer-*

---

* There's no demand, though, from modern progressives to rename a building just a few blocks away: the Paul Robeson Center for the Arts, named for an ardent Stalinist.

ican Experience glowingly "explores the transformation of a history professor into one of America's greatest presidents." Radical Liberal Prime Minister David Lloyd George, who in many ways was Britain's version of Wilson, once even likened him to Jesus Christ.

In the 1960s, President Lyndon Baines Johnson—another Wilson acolyte—spearheaded the formation of Washington, D.C.'s Woodrow Wilson Center. In announcing the project, Johnson proclaimed that there "could be no more fitting monument to the memory of Woodrow Wilson than an institution devoted to the highest ideals of scholarship and international understanding."

In November 2015, *Washington Post* columnist Richard Cohen even penned an article titled "Woodrow Wilson Was Racist, but He Deserves Our Understanding." Why does Wilson deserve our understanding when others do not? Is it because he was a "transformational progressive" who supported liberal causes such as the Federal Reserve system, the Federal Trade Commission, the implementation of the federal income tax, and the creation of the world government League of Nations?

You bet it is.

Wilson's presidency was the beginning of the end for the radical experiment in individual liberty that the Founders had fought for. How did it happen? Well, much like the case of the *Titanic*, the story of how something goes from mighty, brave, and unsinkable to slowly breaking apart and becoming a footnote in history requires the same relentless forces of humanity that the Founders tried so hard to protect citizens from: hubris, greed, and, most of all, fear.

YOUNG, CAREFREE, AND POWER-MAD

Thomas Woodrow Wilson was a proud son of the South. Born in Staunton, Virginia, in the calamitous decade preceding the Civil

War, he grew up mostly in Georgia and South Carolina. His father, a transplanted Ohio Yankee, was a passionately devoted secessionist and a Presbyterian minister.

Among Wilson's earliest memories was the searing sight of Union soldiers marching through his small town in the deep South at the end of the Civil War. They were Yankee invaders, a victorious occupying force, who wanted to make life as miserable as possible for Confederates like the Wilsons.

As an eight-year-old boy in Augusta, Georgia, he watched in horror as Union troops led the captured Confederate ex-President Jefferson Davis through the streets in chains. He recalled his mother tending to wounded Confederate soldiers, victims of the barbaric Northern aggressors. Although he would later hide it, he had severe contempt for the Union, for Abraham Lincoln, and for African-Americans. All of them had stood in the way of creating an elite Southern society that would prosper on the backs of slaves.

Most likely dyslexic, Wilson did not learn to read or write until he was nearly ten years old. But despite the slow start, he turned into an ivory-tower academic for his whole life. Whatever his official job title, he always remained an elitist "intellectual" who believed that experts (like him!) should be in charge of, well, just about everything.

Wilson came to define the nihilist, humanist philosophy that drives institutions of "higher" learning to this day. There is a sweet irony in the fact that the virulently racist Wilson was the prime mover in a progressive movement that is directly responsible for the hypersensitive, multicultural, and "trigger-warned" college campuses of today.

While he's had some competition through the years, Wilson remains the most "academic" of any U.S. president. After a short stint at North Carolina's Davidson College, Wilson enrolled at the College of New Jersey (now Princeton), where he graduated in 1879. He also briefly attended the University of Virginia Law School but soon abandoned practicing law. In 1883, he received his doctorate in political science and history from the recently formed Johns Hopkins University.

Wilson had been a student for more than a decade, so it was surely time to leave academia behind for the world of business, right? Of course not. Instead, he went into teaching, bouncing from Cornell to Bryn Mawr to Wesleyan and then finally back to Princeton as a professor and, eventually, as its president.

It wasn't until 1910, when he was in his fifties, that Wilson eventually got his first "real" job—if you consider being governor of New Jersey a real job (after Jon Corzine and Chris Christie, I have my doubts). Just two years later, a man who had spent more than three decades with his head in the academic clouds (and not one day in private enterprise) became president of the United States.

But let's be clear on something: Wilson defied the absentminded-professor stereotype. He was no bookish wallflower. Quite the contrary, he was a powerful speaker with a rich baritone voice. His students worshipped him. But he was also cold, calculating, and power-hungry from a very early age. (As a child, he printed up calling cards reading "Woodrow Wilson, United States Senator from Virginia.")

Wilson didn't spend decades in academia simply to learn. To him, higher education was a tool to hone a new philosophy of American government led by Hegelian experts focusing on the collective instead of the individual, an elite cadre of intellectuals at the helm working to perfect society. Wilson plotted to be the captain of that ship.

His time at Johns Hopkins only helped cement his big-government attitudes. Many of that university's early professors were German-trained. Through them—particularly the influential early progressive economist Richard Ely—Wilson lapped up an admiration for Prince Otto von Bismarck and the powerful new authoritarian German welfare state. He also imbibed a belief in Darwinism, concluding that a more powerful, centralized government was critical to society's evolution.

It all added up to an absolute infatuation with governmental power. "If any trait bubbles up in all one reads about Wilson," observed historian Walter McDougall, "it is this: he loved, craved, and in a sense glorified power."

Wilson was passionate and ambitious—and also quite arrogant. In 1886, as a young Bryn Mawr professor, he wrote, "[A]ll the country needs is a new and sincere body of thought in politics." Wilson had earlier made a "solemn covenant" with a friend in which the co-conspirators swore "that we would school all our powers and passions for the work of establishing the principles we held in common; that we would acquire knowledge that we might have power; and that we would drill ourselves in all the arts of persuasion . . . that we might have facility in leading others into our ways of thinking and enlisting them in our purposes."

These new "sentiments" and "ways of thinking" amounted to an entire rejection of the American experiment in limited government and classical liberalism. According to historian Charles R. Kesler, as "an undergraduate, graduate student, professor, and university president, Wilson spent three decades in the academy contemplating the failings of the old American constitutional system, testing his critique of it, and preparing the rhetorical case for its transformation." Even before finalizing his education, Wilson had already embraced "a new theory of the presidency and of the whole political system."

ORDAINED BY GOD

Y ou might not always like a politician's policies or ideology, but up close and personal, you sometimes discover that he or she is actually a very kind person.

That is not the case with Woodrow Wilson.

He was, of course, intensely ambitious and convinced that he was meant for great things. Beyond that, he often exhibited what he proudly called his Scotch-Irish fighting streak. This made him a tough, unbending, unforgiving enemy.

His closest political ally was probably Texas power broker Colonel Edward Mandel House. House once explained that the best way to convince Wilson of something was to "[d]iscover a common hate, exploit it, get the president warmed up, and then start your business."

Wilson eventually broke with House, just as he broke from almost every person who aided his rise from Princeton to the New Jersey State House to 1600 Pennsylvania Avenue. House was a strong personality, but most of the time, Wilson simply loved the sound of people saying yes to him, telling him just how wonderful he was. He had many followers but few close friends.

"Wilson," progressive journalist William Allen White once explained, "in his gayest hours, in his times of greatest happiness, stood always aloof, distrusting men instinctively. It was this suspicion of men, founded upon ignorance of men, which led Wilson always to question the strong, to fraternize with the meek, and to break ruthlessly and irrevocably, without defense or explanation, any friendship which threatened his own prestige."

When Wilson captured the White House in 1912, his arrogance was already so great that he reprimanded one supporter with these incredible words: "I wish it to be clearly understood that I owe you nothing. Remember that God ordained that I should be the next president of the United States. Neither you nor any other mortal could have prevented that."

Yes, Wilson would let nothing stand between him and power. The 1912 Democratic platform had demanded a one-term limit on the presidency, but Wilson violated his party's pledge and ran again in 1916. Even crippled by a major stroke, he angled for a third term in 1920.

Death was the only force with the power to fully silence his ambition.

MORE POWER FOR FEWER PEOPLE

Woodrow Wilson believed that "the State" was everything and that individual rights basically meant nothing. He even went so far as to claim that "the State of today may be regarded as in an important sense only an enlarged Family: 'State' is 'Family' writ large."

The State he had believed in for most of his youth was the Confederacy of the old South, run by a patrician elite. It didn't matter that African-Americans had no part in the State except to generate revenue in the form of cotton exports; in Wilson's eyes, they weren't really citizens.

Prior to Wilson and his progressive allies, this concept was not only laughable but also insulting and dangerous to the most important human institution: the family. But family, faith, and the individual—not to mention the Constitution itself—weren't bedrock principles to him; they were mere hindrances to be overcome. In keeping with the progressive mind-set, he believed that men could not reach perfection on their own; only the forces of society—unleashed, administered, and monitored by the State—could do that for them.

Wilson believed that America's founding principles were outdated at best and distasteful at worst. He loathed "blind worship" of the Constitution and thought veneration of the Founders prevented Americans from appreciating a "more glorious time" to come. "Progress, development—those are modern words," he said. "The modern idea is to leave the past and press onward to something new."

Wilson's generation was the first to question the wisdom, efficacy, and relevance of the Constitution. And much like today's progressives, he looked across the Atlantic to Europe for guidance on how to do things "better"—to Britain's ancient Parliament and Germany's newfangled welfare state.

Perhaps most damning of all, Wilson is the father of the single biggest philosophical threat to the Constitution the country has ever faced, one that splits the U.S. Supreme Court to this day. Wilson believed, in violation of everything the Founders stood for, in a "living and breathing constitution" that can and should be "modified by its environment." These "living political constitutions must be Darwinian in structure and in practice," he wrote in 1908.

The Constitution was, in Wilson's mind, subject to the concept of "survival of the fittest"—not bedrock at all but more like shifting sands. In the Wilsonian view, the government had to keep evolving, changing to meet the needs of the environment around it. There was no such thing as natural rights endowed to us by our creator or immutable principles.

Wilson's scorn for the Constitution rings clear and strong. He even derided the U.S. system of checks and balances: "No living thing can have its organs offset against each other, as checks, and live." He ridiculed the idea of individual rights:

> *No doubt a great deal of nonsense has been talked about the inalienable rights of the individual, and a great deal that was mere vague sentiment and pleasing speculation has been put forward as funda-*

mental principle. [However, the] rights of man are easy to discourse of, [but] infinitely hard to translate into practice. [Such] theories are never "law"; no matter what the name or the formal authority of the document in which they are embodied.

In a 1912 campaign address titled "What Is Progress?" (a speech he later included in perhaps the most ironically titled book of the twentieth century, *The New Freedom*), Wilson laid out in the starkest terms the progressive approach to the Constitution: "All that progressives ask or desire is permission [in an] era when 'development,' 'evolution,' is the scientific word, [to] interpret the Constitution according to the Darwinian principle; all they ask is recognition of the fact that a nation is a living thing and not a machine."

Wilson was equally contemptuous of the Declaration of Independence, claiming, "If you want to understand the real Declaration of Independence, do not repeat the preface" (that is, that whole "all men are created equal . . . endowed by their Creator with certain unalienable Rights . . . Life, Liberty and the pursuit of Happiness" thing). To Wilson, the "question is not whether all men are born free and equal or not," because we all "know they are not."

Wilson argued that Americans "are not bound to adhere to the doctrines held by the signers of the Declaration of Independence," because we "are as free as they were to make and unmake governments." Americans, he said, should not "worship men or a document."

Unless, of course, that man was him.

COMMUNITIES ARE SUPREME OVER MEN

Like all progressives, Wilson had a barely concealed elitist's disdain for the regular Americans he allegedly wanted to help and protect. As governor of New Jersey and later as president of the United States,

Wilson rarely talked about socialism, but he was much less guarded during his years in academia.

Wilson's brand of socialism was something he called "state socialism." "The thesis of the state socialist," he wrote, "is that no line can be drawn between private and public affairs which the State may not cross at will; that omnipotence of legislation is the first postulate of all just political theory."

Wilsonian progressive thinking leaves no room for protection *from* the state, however. "Communities are supreme over men as individuals," Wilson said. "Limits of wisdom and convenience to the public control there may be: limits of principle there are, upon strict analysis, none."

Wilson is perhaps best known for urging America to make the world "safe for democracy." Yet his core values—his core *progressive* values—drove him to undermine the very essence of American democracy in favor of state socialism:

> *Democracy is bound by no principle of its own nature to say itself nay as to the exercise of any power. Here, then, lies the point. The difference between democracy and socialism is not an essential difference, but only a practical difference—[it] is a difference of organization and policy, not a difference of primary motive.*

Let's pause for a moment and consider the gravity of this statement, one made by a revered American president. He is saying that there is nothing exceptional about American democracy because, with just a few "practical" tweaks to "organization and policy," it can be transformed into socialism.

And people wonder why I have the front page of the newspaper declaring "Woodrow Wilson Is Dead" hanging in my office.

FIRST BLOOD: THE SIXTEENTH AMENDMENT

Wilson—who once referred to paying taxes as a "glorious privilege"—was instrumental in passing the Sixteenth Amendment, which authorized the previously unconstitutional* federal income tax: "The Congress shall have power to lay and collect taxes on incomes, from whatever source derived, without apportionment among the several states, and without regard to any census or enumeration."

The amendment, which took effect just a few weeks before his inauguration, was one of his "practical" tweaks that would erase the "essential difference" between America's capitalist, democratic system and the state socialism Wilson so admired.

Once in office, he embraced the amendment with alacrity, summoning a special session of Congress to pass the Revenue Act of 1913, which by our current standards seems pretty innocuous. Its lowest rate was a mere one percent. Its highest rate at the time was just seven percent, and that was only on annual incomes of more than five hundred thousand dollars.

Progressives initially framed federal income taxes as only focusing on corporations and the very wealthy—targets their political heirs still favor today—but of course, they didn't stop there. Progressives never stop demanding more. Within a couple of years, the lowest income-tax rate had doubled from one percent to two percent. The highest rate had skyrocketed from seven percent to thirteen percent. But this was nothing compared with what Wilson would soon hit taxpayers with: a top marginal income tax of seventy-three percent! (Franklin Roosevelt took the top bracket to ninety-four percent

* In May 1895, the U.S. Supreme Court ruled 5–4 that an 1894 income tax act violated Article I, Section 9, Clause 4 of the Constitution, a clause that prohibited direct federal taxes on individuals.

SOCIALISM:
AN AMERICAN MASS MOVEMENT

American socialism flourished in the early 1900s. The Socialist Party elected dozens of mayors (including the mayor of Milwaukee) and state legislators. In the 1912 presidential election, Socialist Eugene V. Debs garnered six percent of the vote. While that's a small percentage, it still amounted to more than nine hundred thousand American voters supporting the overt Socialist banner.

Despite personal differences between Debs and Wilson—Debs was actually sentenced to ten years in prison under Wilson's Sedition Act for speaking out against the World War I draft—many socialists saw a fellow traveler in Wilson (and supported his reelection in 1916), and more and more radical leftists were drawn to an increasingly extremist Democratic Party.

In 1934, author Upton Sinclair, a prominent ex-Socialist then running for governor of California as a Democrat, theorized about how this continued leftward drift would play out in America:

> The American people will take Socialism, but they won't take the label. . . . I certainly proved it. . . . Running on the Socialist ticket [in 1932] I got 60,000 votes, and running [two years later as a Democrat] on the slogan to "End Poverty in California" I got 879,000. . . . There is no use attacking it by a front attack, it is much better to outflank them.

It's ironic that it took a writer to understand the immense power of words. Change them, and you change everything—even if the meaning is identical. Of course, by the time Sinclair said this, Debs-style socialism under Franklin Roosevelt's New Deal was already well on its way to becoming reality.

during World War II, and it remained above seventy percent until Ronald Reagan took over.)

Obviously, the issue of taxes is not really one of economics; it's one of ideology and redistribution of capital. Building a massive central government is expensive. Without an income tax, all of the proposals for new programs and initiatives had no chance of being funded. But the Sixteenth Amendment made a constantly growing state encroaching into nearly every area of life nearly inevitable.

THE RACIST AND MISOGYNIST "WHITE PRIVILEGE" OF WOODROW WILSON

Wilson was white and essentially Southern, Scotch-Irish, and highly intellectual. And if you weren't a member of one of his various tribes, you would feel his wrath.

He served as president of Princeton University and later as governor of New Jersey, but it's impossible to overstate just how Southern (actually, Confederate) he really was.

Wilson never abandoned his Southern sympathies. His cabinet was full of Southerners. But he very carefully picked and chose which Southern values he retained. He junked any idea of separation of powers or limited government, yet he retained a rabid racism and a belief in the forced segregation of the races.

Even when he served as president of Princeton, Wilson's prejudices tainted his decisions. He once said that the "whole temper and tradition of [Princeton] are such that no negro has ever applied for admission, and it seems unlikely that the question will ever assume practical form." He turned away black applicants, deeming any need or desire for their education to be "unwarranted."

His racist policies continued while he was governor of New Jersey, yet he successfully employed vague promises of equality to capture a sizable portion of the traditionally Republican black vote in 1912. African-Americans, however, soon discovered Wilson's true racial attitudes: this "Father of Progressivism" was really a rank white supremacist who "brought Jim Crow to the North."

Just a month after his inauguration, Wilson resegregated parts of the federal workforce (including the Navy Department, where a young Franklin D. Roosevelt was serving as undersecretary). Demonstrating the coldness of character that defined so much of his human interactions, Wilson dismissively claimed that he had made "no promises in particular to Negroes, except to do them justice."

Blacks felt betrayed. With Boston newspaper editor and Harvard graduate William Monroe Trotter, African-American leaders came to the White House to protest his actions. An incensed Wilson lectured them that segregation wasn't "humiliating but a benefit." He later signed a law banning interracial marriage in the nation's capital, segregated the U.S. military and parts of the federal workforce, and deprived African-American soldiers, sailors, and Marines of the opportunity to fight for their country.

Wilson even championed the nineteenth-century terrorists the Ku Klux Klan. He wrote in 1903:

> The white men of the South were aroused by the mere instinct of self-preservation to rid themselves, by fair means or foul, of the intolerable burden of governments sustained by the votes of ignorant negroes and conducted in the interest of adventurers. . . . Every countryside wished to have its own Ku Klux Klan, founded in secrecy and mystery . . . until at last there had sprung into existence a great Ku Klux Klan, an "Invisible Empire of the South," bound together . . . to protect the Southern country from some of the ugliest hazards of a time of revolution.

WILSON AND THE KKK'S
TRIUMPH OF THE WILL

Perhaps Wilson's most egregious public racism was his embrace of D. W. Griffith's 1915 pro-Klan, pro-segregation film *The Birth of a Nation*, which was based on Thomas J. Dixon Sr.'s 1905 novel *The Clansman* (Dixon was Wilson's friend and Johns Hopkins classmate). This truly shameful film—which glorified the Ku Klux Klan—was sprinkled with racist quotes from Wilson's writings and featured white actors in blackface portraying racist stereotypes of African-Americans.

Wilson not only liked and supported *The Birth of a Nation*, but he even screened the movie at the White House. At the showing, some reports (which may be apocryphal) claimed, he stated that the film was "like writing history with lightning, and my only regret is that it is all so terribly true."

There's a saying that life imitates art. Race relations during Wilson's administration not only imitated *The Birth of a Nation*, but they far exceeded it—and in the most negative possible sense. May 1916 witnessed one of the most brutal lynchings in American history, that of Jesse Washington in Waco, Texas. The details are too horrific to repeat here; you can google it if you really want to read about what happened. I mention it only to highlight how Wilson reacted: he didn't. Even as brutal race riots rocked East St. Louis in 1917 and Chicago, Omaha, Knoxville, and Washington, D.C., in the summer of 1919, Wilson took no action.

This reaction from the top, along with his embrace of *The Birth of a Nation*, sparked a rebirth of the long-defunct Ku Klux Klan. And when it came back, it was meaner and more bigoted than ever, spreading its hatred beyond blacks to Jews and Catholics ("Kill the Kikes, Koons, and Katholics").

Wilson's dismal record on race was the precedent for more than a century of progressives taking advantage of African-Americans by promising the sky to get their votes and then not delivering. FDR followed in his footsteps (he didn't even bother to desegregate the armed forces or the District of Columbia), and the practice has not stopped since.

Wilson admired the Protestant peoples of the British Isles, either the English and the Scottish themselves or his own Scots-Irish kinsmen. He had little use, however, for the flood of immigrants arriving at Ellis Island from the non-Nordic portions of the European continent. In 1902, he committed these prejudices to writing:

> *Immigrants poured steadily in[to America] as before, but with an alteration of stock which students of affairs marked with uneasiness. Throughout the century men of the sturdy stocks of the north of Europe had made up the main strain of foreign blood which was every year added to the vital working force of the country, or men from the Latin-Gallic stocks of France and northern Italy; but now there came* **multitudes of men of the lowest class from the south of Italy and men of the meaner sort out of Hungary and Poland, men out of the ranks where there was neither skill nor energy nor any initiative of quick intelligence;** *and they came in numbers which increased from year to year, as if* **the countries of the south of Europe were disburdening themselves of the more sordid and hapless elements of their population,** *the men whose standards of life and of work were such as American workmen had never dreamed of hitherto.*

Again, through the miracle of rebranding and the reliance on short memories, progressives have somehow whitewashed this anti-immigrant past to become the group that supposedly stands with open arms and open borders toward all those who want to come here.

Wilson's firm belief in Anglo-Saxon superiority led him to embrace one of the most disgusting notions of his time: eugenics. He believed that the human race could be improved through selective breeding.

In 1907, Wilson supported Indiana legislation mandating the compulsory sterilization of criminals and the mentally retarded, the nation's first eugenics law. After becoming governor of New Jersey, he wasted little time in implementing similar legislation there, proudly signing into law a bill calling for the compulsory sterilization of the "Feeble-minded (including imbeciles, idiots and morons), Epileptics, and other defectives." (Fortunately, other people with more sense prevailed, and the bill was quickly overturned by the New Jersey Supreme Court.)

This overt disdain for whole classes of people was pretty typical stuff for Wilson-era progressives, but many eugenics laws were less obvious. Take the minimum wage, for example. Royal Meeker, a Princeton economist and Wilson's commissioner of labor statistics, explained how economics can easily be used for human engineering: "It is much better to enact a minimum-wage law even if it deprives these unfortunates of work . . . better that the state should support the inefficient wholly and prevent the multiplication of the breed than subsidize incompetence and unthrift, enabling them to bring forth more of their kind."

Wilson also seemed to despise women—or at least not to think of them as being equal to men. He was a late and very reluctant convert to the women's suffrage movement, and he characterized the female mind as a "vacuum." He professed to be "frustrated" when teaching at Bryn Mawr, a women's college, because those students never challenged him. In fact, Wilson felt women were not "the intellectual equal of men." If their weaker minds couldn't handle the weighty questions of politics, why should they receive the privilege of voting?

From the moment Wilson stepped off his train in Washington, D.C., on the day before his inauguration, the suffragists stole his thunder and made his life miserable. As protesters became more frustrated and more militant in their tactics—which included daily rallies outside the White House—Wilson grew more and more irritated.

Initially cordial, he soon became rude and then downright nasty. He was "repelled by the militant suffragists outside his gate." To him, "their methods were insulting, unfeminine, and unpatriotic." Eventually, many were jailed and beaten. Those who protested further by going on hunger strikes were force-fed.

Several years into his presidency, Wilson finally relented, if for no other reason than to stop the incessant shouting of protesters outside his bedroom window. The fact that women could also form a core constituency for a new U.S. war abroad also didn't go unnoticed. Wilson would grin and bear granting the "lesser sex" the right to vote if it would mean that he would now have political support for war.

For progressives, the ends always justify the means.

WILSON AND THE NEW WORLD ORDER

Wilson was really the first "internationalist president." As a young man, he fell in love with the British parliamentary system (a system with no checks and balances). In such a system, a prime minister and his or her ruling party call the shots, and if anyone disagrees, well, that's just too bad. When Wilson campaigned for governor of New Jersey, he even vowed to be an "unconstitutional governor," planning to run roughshod over the state's legislature.

His justification for this was pretty simple. He didn't believe that the wisdom of the Founders applied anymore. He didn't believe in American exceptionalism. That experiment, he felt, had grown outmoded and woefully out of touch with current conditions. Limited government, God-given rights, and more than a century of American political traditions meant less than nothing to Wilson.

THE FIRST FASCIST PRESIDENT AND THE ESPIONAGE AND SEDITION ACTS

Wilson's disdain for democracy was most aptly represented by his support for the Espionage Act of 1917 and the Sedition Act of 1918. These crypto-fascist laws, passed in the midst of World War I, played on the fear of German propaganda and sabotage and made "disloyalty and subversion" punishable offenses while barring the sending of "seditious" materials through the U.S. Mail.

Thousands were arrested as a result of these acts, and they led to a highly bigoted anti-German crusade. Numerous volunteer "security" organizations sprang up, such as the American Protective League, a quarter-million-strong body of semiofficial government spies in the guise of citizen patriots; the National Security League; and the Boy Spies of America. These were American brownshirts, plain and simple.

Instead of life, liberty, and the pursuit of happiness, Wilson sought to control the minds of the masses by effectively repealing the First Amendment and criminalizing antiadministration free speech. That's tyranny, plain and simple, and there is no greater insult to U.S. history or threat to the U.S. republic.

This elitism knew no borders—literally. Wilson's ultimate goal was not just to bend the United States to the will of his "benevolent" expert elites. He and his progressive allies fixed their eyes on a much larger goal: an all-encompassing progressive global government to rule all of humanity under a big-government yoke.

But to do so, Wilson had to get the United States—his base of power—to shake off its natural and historic hostility to foreign wars and engage in the great conflict raging across Europe: World War I.

Throughout the 1916 election, Wilson ran on the slogan "He kept us out of war." It helped him gain an eyelash victory, and he reiterated his supposed desire to stay out of the European conflagration during his March 4, 1917, inaugural address. "We stand firm," he declared from the Oval Office, "in armed neutrality."

Five weeks later, the United States declared war on Germany. It was a complete turnaround by Wilson, one that still puzzles many historians.

Wilson mobilized more than four million Americans to bear the brunt of his world-building ambitions. More than three hundred thousand were killed or injured, shattering not only their own lives but also those of millions of friends, family members, and loved ones.

Their sacrifice proved decisive. With the introduction of millions of fresh American troops, the Allies vanquished Berlin, opening the door for Wilson to carry out the next phase of his plan for global dominance: the creation of the League of Nations.

America—and the rest of the world—feared the mass bloodshed of future wars. But, like any good progressive, Wilson knew how to exploit that fear and bend it to his will. Wilson's League of Nations would ostensibly prevent future conflicts and keep the world safe for democracy, but it was much more than just a peacekeeping organization; it was a truly radical global governing body, the first of its kind. Wilson hoped the League would mature from a place of discussion and compromise into one of command and control.

In December 1918, he began a tradition of presidential globe-trotting, personally traveling to Europe to negotiate a peace treaty and secure his precious League. His imperious attitude won him few friends abroad ("I could not bear him," Britain's King George V complained), and his unwillingness to compromise won him few friends at home.

Returning from Versailles, Wilson refused to cooperate with Republicans to secure Senate ratification of his treaty. He stooped to insults and threats instead, attacking opponents of his new world government as "blind and little provincial people" with "pygmy minds" who should be "hanged on gibbets as high as heaven, but pointing in the opposite direction."

"Any man," Wilson proclaimed, "who resists the present tides that run in the world will find himself thrown upon a shore so high and barren that it will seem as if he had been separated from his human kind forever."

Wilson, like a future acolyte named Barack Obama, was handsomely rewarded for his globalist efforts by winning the highest honor in the progressive, globalist land: the Nobel Peace Prize.

The U.S. Senate wisely rejected Wilson's plea to join the League, but the damage was already done. Two and a half decades later, Wilson's protégé Franklin Roosevelt picked up the world-government mantle by helping to create the United Nations, while across the pond, the European Union has forced progressive internationalism on an entire continent.

Although the progressive effort to place elites in charge of society and redefine world governance is incomplete, it is still very much under way. As Christine Legarde—head of the International Monetary Fund, a key component of the progressive world order—stated in a 2011 speech (fittingly held at Washington's Woodrow Wilson Center):

> More than anyone else, it was Woodrow Wilson who championed the cause of multilateralism and global fraternity. The seeds he planted bore fruit in the postwar milieu that produced the IMF and its sister organizations. For at the heart of our mandate lies a simple but powerful idea—that cooperation can bestow not only economic stability, but a better future for all.

Wilson's quest for top-down governance and globalism has not died with the passing of time. In April 2012, the Wilson Center bestowed its Award for Public Service on none other than Hillary Clinton. During the ceremony, Clinton sang the praises of the Wilson Center, but she did not once mention the sordid chauvinism, elitism, and bigotry at the heart of Wilson's life and agenda.

Drawing on the progressive German influences of his studies at Johns Hopkins and his later writings that openly despised the Constitution, Wilson began the first wave of progressivism, a wave that would forever change the relationship between the federal government of the United States and its citizens.

In 1896, 1900, and 1908, Americans soundly rejected populist and progressive William Jennings Bryan for the White House, but by 1912, the public had become desensitized enough to elect Wilson president. (Wilson, in turn, appointed Bryan as secretary of State.)

No longer was progressivism confined to the universities and fringe candidates in American politics. It finally found a home at 1600 Pennsylvania Avenue. With sweeping constitutional amendments such as the Sixteenth, the Seventeenth (allowing direct election of senators), and the Eighteenth (banning the sale of alcohol), Wilson led a political revolution that forever changed Washington, D.C., and the ways it interacted with the daily lives of Americans.

In Washington, progressivism served as an ideal excuse for further seizing control of the nation. Leaders of both parties shrewdly embraced this new ideology as the best way to expand the federal government's authority (as well as their own, of course) under the guise of improving the lives of all citizens.

Progressive acolytes filled newsrooms, university faculty rosters, church pulpits, and newly opened government agencies and bureaus within walking distance from the White House. They proselytized with a missionary zeal that their movement could help the poor, end the scourge of alcohol, reform politics, remedy income inequality, battle special interests, improve working conditions and living standards, and create a kind of heaven on earth—if only the right people were in power. They were Republicans and Democrats. They were members of the House and the Senate. They were judges and government lawyers. They were unelected government officials and administrators.

But they all shared a commitment to "progress."

One of Wilson's greatest admirers was a tall, striking man with an irresistible smile and an infectious laugh. For years, he had labored in obscurity in the bowels of the Navy Department across the street from the White House. What the young man lacked in national prominence he would eventually make up for with his singular ambition and his already familiar last name: Roosevelt.

PROFILE IN FEAR:

THE DEVIL'S WATER

Trumbull County, Ohio
Circa 1885

Wayne Wheeler swung a newly sharpened scythe through the alfalfa grass that came up to his hips.

At five foot six and with a tidy mustache, he didn't very much look the part of an Ohio farmer. His father, Joseph, had insisted that his son become an educated man—go to college and become a lawyer or a doctor. Young Wayne had every intention on following through with his dad's wish—he loved his books—but he also loved the rough-and-tumble of farm life.

Every July, his father would summon him, his siblings, and a handful of farmhands from neighboring towns to the fields, where they would work days on end from sunup to sunset, cutting the season's supply of hay. Wayne liked the feel of calluses on his hand at the end of harvest season. He liked being around the farmhands who joked and cursed. Even now, as beads of sweat gathered on his upper lip in the sweltering Ohio sun, he found the musty, comforting smell of freshly cut grass wafting toward his nostrils intoxicating.

But with each passing summer, Wayne noticed something troubling about a number of the farmhands, a few tormented souls who staggered in each morning, eyes bloodshot and smelling of alcohol. They'd sneak sips of their favorite liquid from mason jars kept out of sight of his devout Congregationalist father.

One time, Wayne had been upstairs in his house when a drunken farmhand ran in from the fields in a maniacal rage, muttering in long, slurred sentences, "I'm a kill you two ladies! But I ain't gonna do a hideous thang like that 'til I have my way with you two beauties!"

His mother and sister were screaming for help. "Joseph!" they cried out. "Joseph!"

Wayne cowered under his bed, covering his ears with the palms of his hands. He was paralyzed by fear.

He heard the front door slam open, then the sounds of fists pummeling flesh and bone, thumps and cracks audible through the floorboards. He never saw or heard from the farmhand again, nor was the subject ever spoken about in the Wheeler household.

And then there was "Old Soak," the affable neighbor with a fondness for Kentucky bourbon and a knack for impressions of local town characters. As his nickname implied, Old Soak was harmless, even endearing, until he got hold of the bottle. Liquor made him belligerent and aggressive.

One drunken evening, Old Soak ambled up to the Wheelers' front porch to show off his impressions, but his kind face had transformed into a sneering picture of horror. Joseph Wheeler took the man's arm and walked him home. As Wayne watched the silhouette of his father and this pitiable, broken man amble off down the road, the young man promised himself he would never touch alcohol.

But none of those run-ins with drunkards compared to what happened one fateful July day.

Wayne had piled up bales of hay and was loading them into a wagon. The choreography of lifting a hundred-pound hay bale into the air and then onto a cart was something to behold. Wayne had worked out a fluid rhythm: his pitchfork plunged into the hay bale, up it went, and then it leaped forward in a graceful arc onto the back of the wagon. Once he got into a groove, Wayne could fork bales forever.

That was when he heard the voice. "Hey, boy!"

The call came from the other side of the wagon. He'd been so busy he hadn't noticed anyone approaching. Around the side staggered Hank, a new farmhand Wayne's father had hired for the season. Just a few years older than Wayne himself, Hank already had a deep, gravelly voice, a mustache, scraggly hair, and a deep tan earned from many seasons in the sun. Wayne knew he was one of the hands who drank, but he'd never caused any problems.

Wayne had never seen Hank drunk like this, though. He was staggering, leaning on his own pitchfork like a staff. Wayne could see the top of a glass flagon poking up from the pocket of Hank's coveralls. It swished and sloshed with every step the man took.

"Hey, boy!" Hank said again, advancing on Wayne. "Ol' man says we ga-go farster."

Wayne couldn't understand. "What's that?" he asked.

"Ga-go farster!" Hank repeated. "Farster!"

Was he saying "faster"? Wayne could barely understand his drunken gibberish.

"Farster!" thundered Hank, almost shouting.

With that, he took his pitchfork and tore into Wayne's bales of hay, flinging them about in a desperate, frenzied attempt to throw more of them onto the wagon. He was making a bad job of it; strands of hay and larger chunks were flying every which way. Wayne's hard work was on the verge of being ruined.

"Hank, stop!" Wayne implored.

Hank's arms were moving like pistons, pumping up and down as he shoved the pitchfork into the hay and brought up again, pointing in the general direction of the wagon but instead scattering the hay into the low Ohio wind.

"Stop, Hank, stop!"

Hank stood straight for a moment, a wild look in his eye.

Wayne froze. He could hear Hank's grunting breaths and smell the stink of liquor from his lips.

Then Hank lunged forward once again, unsteady on his feet, seemingly aiming to grab another chunk of hay with the pitchfork. Instead, the sharp metal prongs plunged deep into Wayne's leg.

The pain blinded Wayne for a moment. When he opened his eyes again, he was on the ground, surrounded by hay, the pitchfork still in his leg. Hank had backed away and was swaying where he stood, looking not at Wayne but around aimlessly at nothing in particular. Clearly, he had no conception of what he'd just done. And more important, he would be of no help.

Wayne looked toward the house and saw some figures running across the field, no doubt attracted by his scream. One of them looked to be a woman, her shawl trailing behind her in the breeze. His mother? His sister? He couldn't focus his reddened vision long enough to see. Closing his eyes to try to block some, any, measure of the pain, he began to crawl toward the house, his bleeding leg burning as the pitchfork tines shifted with every small movement.

He looked over his shoulder and saw Hank shuffling around the wagon, hands in his pockets, whistling an infuriating tune. The smell of liquor clung to the air.

It was a smell that would haunt Wayne Wheeler for the rest of his life.

By 1893, Reverend Howard Hyde Russell was one of the nation's leading crusaders against alcohol. He had founded the Anti-Saloon League, preaching against the perils of the demon drink, while a student at Oberlin College. Now, on a return visit to campus, he delivered a lecture on temperance that enthralled many of his listeners but none more so than the student in his early twenties who found the abolition of alcohol to be a mission from God.

Wayne Wheeler, who had followed his father's wishes and entered college at Oberlin, sought out Russell after his speech. The reverend was so impressed by Wheeler's passion and zeal that he offered the young man a job on the spot. He believed he'd found a worthy apprentice. He was right. In fact, he'd found someone who would take the Anti-Saloon League to heights few had imagined.

Wheeler got right to work. As one of only a handful of permanent employees of the Anti-Saloon League, he rode his bike around Cleveland, evangelizing the masses during visits to churches and temperance meetings. He later enrolled in law school, knowing full well that his legal training could only help the cause.

Haunted by the memories of a childhood torment, Wheeler believed that only the full-scale abolition of alcohol across America could bring safety and comfort. Men could not be counted on to restrain themselves from their vices; the perfect world required absolute control. Besides, he wasn't going to let any other children cower in fear under their beds, loathing their own helplessness, while the devil's water turned men into demonic savages.

Turning the tide of public opinion against the powerful liquor industry was not going to be easy. And it wasn't going to be pretty. But it had to be done, regardless of the cost.

Wheeler put together a temperance army that didn't care about party or ideological labels. The "drys" would support any candidate from either party who adopted temperance as his campaign platform. They would use leaflets, advertisements, letter-writing campaigns, and visits from temperance advocates to increase public pressure on wavering legislators. Wheeler even coined the term *pressure group* to explain the League's tactics. This pressure was justified, of course, because Wheeler knew what was best for the communities. The freedom to decide whether to drink alcohol responsibly didn't belong to individuals, because those decisions affected the collective. Only sobriety could cure men who tormented their communities, people like Old Soak and Hank.

The first target was Ohio's governor, Myron Herrick, who was hostile to the cause. If Wheeler could unseat the powerful sitting governor, he knew the Anti-Saloon League would demonstrate its political power and terrify other politicians into getting in line.

Wheeler, now head of the Ohio Anti-Saloon League chapter, began to encircle Herrick by slowly helping League allies get elected to the Ohio legislature. From this base of power, he built alliances to form a massive campaign against Herrick, finally defeating him in the 1905 election. Having enforced his will on Ohio, Wheeler then turned his gaze toward the rest of the country.

In 1915, he left behind his dry comrades in Ohio and went to Washington, D.C., to become the general counsel for the entire Anti-Saloon League of America. He scaled his pressure-group tactics up to a nationwide level and became one of the most effective lobbyists of his time.

In 1920, thanks in large part to Wheeler's efforts, the Eighteenth Amendment to the U.S. Constitution, which banned "the manufacture, sale, or transportation of intoxicating liquors" in the United States, went into effect. Prohibition was now in force across the nation. But instead of creating a new, perfect world, the law opened the door for bootleggers and organized crime to make millions from the distribution of liquor.

That was of little concern to Wheeler. The drunks and brutes who'd scared him when he was young would not be able to scare anyone else.

♠

3

Second Wave:

FDR, Wartime Progressive

The only thing we have to fear is fear itself—nameless, unreasoning, unjustified terror which paralyzes needed efforts to convert retreat into advance.

—FRANKLIN DELANO ROOSEVELT

Washington, D.C.
East Capitol Steps
March 4, 1933

It was a time for action. A time for vigor.

A time for mobilizing the power of the executive office in support of full-scale war.

The man in the morning coat and top hat sat rigid, his veins coursing with adrenaline, but his head never more clear. He—and, more important, his nation—had been waiting for this moment for decades. The reins of federal government had become dust-covered, untouched for far too long. They had to be grabbed and the slack wrung out on behalf of the people. And if a whip had to be taken to the concentrated powers and the princes of property to give the forgotten man his fair shake, so be it.

A wry smile crossed his lips.

No longer would the weak use federal power for piddling projects in the face of crisis while labor lay dormant. No longer would the strong businessmen of the great trusts and their lapdog money changers be left to shape society to their selfish whims.

The ship of state was his for the steering toward a more social, equitable, and fair system. Planning was to be the operative word of the day, rather than wasteful, oligarchic, haphazard individualism. Could the politicians who surrounded him continue to just stand there, dazed and daunted, in the face of the rot of laissez-faire lunacy? No. The invisible hand was to be brought into the light of day.

There was nothing to fear but fear itself. And, he knew, there was no one better equipped to fill the vacuum of incompetency and inaction than himself, the newly elected president of the United States of America.

Franklin Delano Roosevelt put his enamel cigarette holder to his lips, struck a match, and took a long drag, thick smoke twirling in the cool air like so many of the dreams he was about to fulfill.

In that moment, he thought back to his days as a student at Groton and the much richer boys who never respected him. He thought of the last laugh he was sure to get over the bankers, lawyers, and industrialists who had doubted his cunning and intellect at Harvard and then at Columbia Law. They thought they were powerful—just watch.

He thought of his late cousin Teddy and how it was time to finally make good on the bold progressive vision and vigorous executive power he had championed. He thought about how Teddy had commanded the bully pulpit and breathed life into the American people. He thought about how through sheer personality and grit, *he, too, could marshal the resources of the nation for more social ends, not to mention his own.*

He thought of Woodrow Wilson, who had appointed him assistant secretary of the Navy, just as President William McKinley had done decades earlier for Teddy. He knew he could take Wilson's revolutionary but academic critique of America and mold it into something practical and concrete, something truly useful for the little man. He knew that he'd not merely been pandering months earlier at the 1932 Democratic Convention when he said, "Let us feel that in everything we do there still lives with us, if not the body, the great indomitable, unquenchable, progressive soul of our Commander-in-Chief, Woodrow Wilson."

He thought back to his days at Hyde Park and his responsibility now to command a much larger estate.

He thought about how he had been preparing for this day his whole life.

Taking in the sea of people one last time from his chair, Roosevelt collected himself, clutched the arm of his son James, and gathered all the strength he could muster to ascend the steps to the podium. The steel braces dug into his sides, the pain nearly unbearable as he swung one leg in front of the other, the product of nearly a decade of determined rehabilitation to become somewhat mobile again. He had always been athletic, an embodiment of vivaciousness, much like Teddy, until one day, he woke up and couldn't feel his legs. But neither polio nor the attempt on his life mere weeks earlier could keep him from his rightful office.

Franklin raised his right hand and repeated after Chief Justice Charles Evan Hughes: "I, Franklin Delano Roosevelt, do solemnly swear that I will faithfully execute the Office of President of the United States, and will to the best of my ability, preserve, protect, and defend the Constitution of the United States."

Yes, he thought to himself, I can take this oath, with a

caveat: it's the Constitution as I understand it, flexible enough to meet any new problem of democracy. *He suspected the reactionaries on the Supreme Court might not go along with his plans, but such recriminations would have to wait for another day. Right now, it was time for hard facts.*

Roosevelt began his address with confidence and conviction. "This is preeminently the time to speak the truth, the whole truth, frankly and boldly," he said. "[L]et me assert my firm belief that the only thing we have to fear is fear itself—nameless, unreasoning, unjustified terror which paralyzes needed efforts to convert retreat into advance."

Fear had gripped the nation ever since the stock market crashed three years earlier. Proud Americans who had once owned the polished cars and opulent mansions on the Upper West Side of his youth were reduced to beggars living in shantytowns in Central Park. Survival was now foremost in their minds. Freedom was a fine principle, but when your day consisted of living hand-to-mouth in search of scraps of food to keep your family and yourself alive, it didn't much matter. What mattered was giving people hope, even if it meant surrendering to the loving arms of a federal government. That was what FDR promised to deliver.

His legs throbbing, Roosevelt ignored the pain and enumerated the economic strains under which the country languished, laying the Depression right at the feet of the "rulers of the exchange of mankind's goods," *who had* "failed through their own stubbornness and . . . incompetence." *The* "unscrupulous money changers" *had been discredited. Punctuating his point, FDR said that such men were merely* "self-seekers [with] no vision, and when there is no vision the people perish."

There it was, the thing mankind feared the most: death. It was no accident that he'd carefully worked it into his speech. Scare them with their own demise, and then show them how, by following you, they can avoid it or at least stave it off for as long as possible.

Roosevelt's vision wasn't merely talk, however; it required action. Men were to be put to work. "Redistribution" was to be achieved nationally. Supply and pricing imbalances were to be rectified. Foreclosures were to be halted. Government planning and supervision would rule the day. The greater good would reign.

The balance of power between the executive and legislative branches would have to be tilted in his favor. "I shall ask the Congress for the one remaining instrument to meet the crisis," he said. "Broad Executive power to wage a war against the emergency, as great as the power that would be given to me if we were in fact invaded by a foreign foe."

The crowd roared.

His wife, Eleanor, shuddered. She found the crowd's raucous reaction a bit terrifying.

But, just across the way, prominent progressive journalist Walter Lippmann didn't shudder; he smiled. A few days earlier, he'd advised FDR that the situation was critical and that the new president might have no alternative but to assume dictatorial power. Lippman had assumed that it would take a lot of coercing and pressure over the following months to get FDR to agree.

Little did he know that the newly minted president would need no cajoling.

THE MAKING OF A "LIBERAL"

What exactly did Franklin Roosevelt have in mind as he delivered his first inaugural address with America in the throes of the Depression?

Well, it's very likely the exact same sentiment that future Democratic operative Rahm Emanuel later expressed as "Never let a serious crisis go to waste."

In his 1932 Commonwealth Club address, the more tactful Roosevelt had said that the statesman's job was to redefine rights based on a "changing and growing social order." Conditions had changed during the Depression, he believed, and so government, as well as the rights it was charged with securing, would have to change, too.

Roosevelt's philosophy was perhaps best articulated by the man who helped author his first inaugural address. This little-known Columbia University professor, who would help form the inner intellectual sanctum of FDR's presidency—the "Brain Trust"—wrote of FDR:

> *He believed that government not only could, but should, achieve the subordination of private interests to collective interests, substitute co-operation for the mad scramble of selfish individualism. He had a profound feeling for the underdog, a real sense of the critical unbalance of economic life, a very keen awareness that political democracy could not exist side by side with economic plutocracy.*

The professor noted that, as with other "inglorious liberal[s]" in America, Roosevelt drew directly on the likes of Woodrow Wilson, Herbert Croly, and Walter Lippmann, among a who's who of other progressives.

But, perhaps learning from the progressive titans before him, FDR knew he had a branding problem. The term *progressivism* was waning in the 1920s. The years between Wilson and FDR had witnessed America's return to its small-government roots under Presidents Harding and Coolidge. In foreign affairs, the horrors of World War I called into question the idealistic notion that mankind was becoming more humane and more perfect with each successive generation.

Progressivism was also being identified—rightly—with German philosophy, which had become far less appealing once the kaiser unleashed a calamitous war on the world. At home, the American economy was booming. So while Herbert Hoover had been technocratic (like George W. Bush preceding Barack Obama, he laid the ground-work for programs that Roosevelt would later expand in crisis), pro-gressivism receded.

All of this led to FDR's purposeful rebranding of the progressive ideology. During the 1932 Democratic National Convention, he ex-plained, "Ours must be a party of *liberal* thought, of planned action, of enlightened international outlook, and of the greatest good to the greatest number of our citizens."

FDR's new "liberalism" clearly betrayed the classical liberal thought of John Locke and Adam Smith, not to mention the men who signed the Declaration of Independence and the Constitution. It was a noble lie, a label cynically reappropriated to obscure the total break from an older meaning and tradition that progressive ideology represented. This new interpretation of American politics and gov-ernance that elevated the state above the individual had begun under Teddy Roosevelt and Wilson, but it accelerated under FDR. Rights no longer came from the individual, much less God, but directly from government. This was everything that classical liberals had come to reject about the "divine right" of monarchs and the tendency of the state to trample individual liberty.

Before the 1930s, *liberalism* hadn't been a term used to describe any political group in the United States. But FDR, above all else, was a good marketer. Progressivism was now too closely associated with Wilson and failed third-party efforts. Adopting liberalism would also deprive Republicans of their intellectual heritage while associating progressivism directly with the nation's founding.

Republican President Hoover had tried to describe his policies as "liberal" during his time in office, but FDR suggested a new word for Republicans: *conservatives*. At the time, the term sounded dis-tinctly un-American and out of the mainstream, something like *Tory*, vaguely monarchical and fascist. If FDR was liberal, by definition, his opponents were *illiberal*.

He explained this further in his 1932 nomination acceptance speech:

> There are two ways of viewing the Government's duty in matters affecting economic and social life. The first sees to it that a favored few are helped and hopes that some of their prosperity will leak through, sift through, to labor, to the farmer, to the small business-man. That theory belongs to the party of Toryism, and I had hoped that most of the Tories left this country in 1776. But it is not and never will be the theory of the Democratic Party.

John Dewey, the dean of progressive education, argued that the more politically expedient word was *liberalism*, snatching its use from *real* liberals—classical liberals who believed in individual freedom and limited government—in a bit of verbal jujitsu. Dewey argued in a 1934 speech that liberalism no longer signified natural rights, individual liberty, and a state subservient to the people (rather than their master). He instead contended that liberalism was "committed to the idea of historic relativity. It knows that the content of the individual and freedom change with time."

According to Dewey, what the Founders meant when they spoke about liberty was specific to their time and place. To help people achieve liberty *now* would require enlightened experimentation.

And with that, the transformation of the word *liberal* was virtually complete.

A nation run on scientific principles by intelligent men of goodwill was the engine powering the administrative state FDR was to build. At Oglethorpe University in May 1932, the president declared that the nation demanded "persistent experimentation."

And experiment he would, thanks to lots of help from Ivy League professors. As one FDR critic wrote of his "Brain Trust," "Here was

HERBERT HOOVER AND THE
GREAT MISSISSIPPI FLOOD

He stood at the edge of the waters, his entourage of engineers, military officers, and local businessmen yards
behind him, watching the portly man ankle-deep in mud. Fourteen percent of Arkansas was under as much as twenty-two
feet of water. More than twenty-seven thousand square miles
of the lower Mississippi delta was completely flooded, inca-
pacitating hundreds of thousands of Americans, most of them
farmers, sharecroppers, or black laborers. The rest of America
might have been roaring during the 1920s, but the flooding had
precipitated a humanitarian crisis that was dragging Arkansas
back into primitive times.

The great engineer charged with fixing the crisis had been
granted sweeping powers by the president to handle the emergency. Telegrams had been dispatched from the White House
to state governors, to Army generals, even local sheriffs and
bank managers, ordering them to comply with any orders he
might give them. There was no specific constitutional clause
that enabled this authority, but that had never stopped him
before. Ten years earlier, as America declared war on Germany
and entered the Great War, he'd been appointed to head the
U.S. Food Administration (USFA), an innocuous-sounding
agency responsible for ensuring that U.S. soldiers and refu-
gees in Europe didn't starve.

The USFA had created nationwide mandatory rationing
programs, combined with patriotic marketing campaigns
designed to inspire voluntary participation, since the agency
itself had limited legal authority to force civilians to comply.
His "Tomato Tuesdays" and "Potato Wednesdays" had largely
been successful, encouraging millions of American families to
set aside certain items on certain days in jars, cans, or bags to
be donated to local food banks.

Now, standing in the flood plain with his hands on his hips, looking at billions of gallons of soil-blackened water, Herbert Hoover had a new mission, along with a handful of executive orders granting him powers over local, state, and federal government authorities. Even the three-star general standing behind him was directly beholden to his command. He also had authority to conscript private property, equipment, and manpower by invoking eminent domain.

Hoover was a results-oriented, no-nonsense fellow. It wasn't *how* that mattered but only the outcomes. Over the coming months, he would conscript tens of thousands of men, mostly blacks, into forced-labor parties to dig ditches, fill sandbags, load boats, tear down homes, and clear debris. By the end of 1927, he had ordered the demolition of more than eight thousand damaged homes and businesses. He had claimed government ownership of thousands of square miles of riverbank and seized and slaughtered tens of thousands of farm animals, including horses, to be used to feed refuges.

When refugee camps became overfilled, Hoover struck deals with railroads to carry supplies into besieged areas and to help move tens of thousands of poor blacks out of the area, most to big cities such as Chicago, New York, Atlanta, and Pittsburgh. He ordered the U.S. military to dynamite and then rebuild more than twenty bridges or dams. He took over dozens of local hospitals and schools in Arkansas, Mississippi, and Louisiana, turning them into makeshift camps and local headquarters for the distribution of food, medical supplies, and blankets.

The Great Mississippi Flood of 1927 turned out to be a watershed for progressive idealism. Hoover demonstrated the efficiency of centralized, federalized power in the face of an emergency. The federal government had granted itself total authority over public, private, and military resources to respond to a crisis. All authority was vested in one man—with state

rights, private-property rights, and personal liberty subordi-
nate to him.

The quietest revolution in the history of the world, the Great
Mississippi Flood was a propaganda tool for Hoover to increase his national media profile a year before he would run for
the presidency in 1928.

Hoover swept the election over Democrat Al Smith with
nearly sixty percent of the popular vote and forty states. Three
states that didn't vote for Hoover were three states that experienced firsthand what it looked and felt like when one man
could wield total power over everything: Arkansas, Mississippi,
and Louisiana.

the Great Brain itself surrounded by all these bulging foreheads han-
dling easily the tough problems that had baffled the feeble intellects
of bankers, magnates, and politicos. Now in a new sense the real age
of reason had come. It was the Age of the Professors."

Their progressive policies would simply be a means to the most
important end for the opportunist FDR: power.

FDR TAKES OFFICE

The economy was bottoming out as FDR took office. Banks were
failing. Unemployment had risen to a peak of more than twenty-eight
percent. The Dow Jones Industrial Average was still hovering at the
lowest it would ever get during the Great Depression. International
trade had collapsed from the Smoot-Hawley–induced tariff war.

In the brief but devastating recession of 1920–21, government
shrank, and the economy healed on its own. Now, with another crisis
at hand, FDR had an opportunity to translate Wilson's theory into

practice. Roosevelt declared during his 1932 Commonwealth address that America had hit the end of economic progress and that the job of government now was to "equitably" redistribute its fruits. "The day of enlightened administration [of resources] has come," Roosevelt said. In the Industrial Age, the corporation had replaced the tyrannical role of repressive central government. The state was to create an "economic declaration of rights, an economic constitutional order," to tame business.

FDR used his first hundred days in office to seize power from "tyrannical" business in the name of getting the economy working, largely by executive order. The result was an alphabet soup of agencies designed to regulate and intervene in every aspect of American life.

Under the National Recovery Administration (NRA), Roosevelt created cartels controlled by big business in almost every industry, overseen by the federal government. These cooperatives fixed wages and controlled prices, production, quantities, qualities, and distribution methods under seven hundred competition-killing industrial codes. In its first year alone, the NRA released 2,998 administrative orders approving or modifying existing codes, along with 6,000 press releases, some of which served as legislation.

Understanding the value of propaganda, the administration promoted the NRA with a massive public-relations campaign. Trucks circled the streets blaring pro-NRA messages through megaphones. Businesses that complied with the NRA were adorned with "Blue Eagles" in their windows to reward their solidarity with the government. "In war in the gloom of night attack . . . soldiers wear a bright badge to be sure that comrades do not fire on comrades," FDR said. "Those who cooperate in this program must know each other at a glance. That bright badge is the Blue Eagle."

The NRA also strengthened labor unions with substantial collective-bargaining powers and compulsory membership, which caused prices to rise. Workers began to strike—there would be more than two thousand strikes during FDR's first term—and economic activity stagnated.

While all of this new regulation was awful, something more insidious occurred at the human level. Jack Magid, a tailor from New Jersey, was fined and jailed for the offense of pressing a suit for thirty-five cents, five cents less than the Tailors' Code commanded. Labor leader Sidney Hillman, who was responsible for the garment industry's codes, hired enforcement police. Within minutes, this force could take over a factory, interrogate its employees, and commandeer its books. Night work was made a crime, and these code-enforcement squads went on patrol looking for anyone who dared so much as sew pants after dark.

African-Americans were particularly hard hit by the NRA's labor codes. The newly empowered unions negotiated artificially high minimum wages that implicitly (and intentionally) discriminated against lower-skilled black laborers. It is estimated that five hundred thousand black workers lost their jobs as a result of NRA minimum wage laws alone.

Small businesses suffered acutely. In the case of *Schechter* v. *United States*, the Schechters, Jewish immigrants whose name is derived from the Yiddish word for "butcher," lived up to their name by operating a chain of Brooklyn slaughterhouses. Their lives were turned upside down when they were convicted of violating the FDR-authorized Live Poultry Code. Among other things, the Schechters had sold an "unfit" chicken—an egg was lodged inside it—and they allegedly sought to undercut competitors with their pricing.

The Schechters were fined $7,425, a substantial sum now but astronomical for the time. They were also sentenced to between one and three months in jail. They took their case to the Supreme Court, challenged the code, and won—a stunning blow that put the brakes on FDR's progressive runaway train.

The legislation that created the NRA was struck down by the Court (1) as a violation of the Commerce Clause of the Constitution (the code regulated commerce solely within the state of New York, not interstate commerce), and (2) on separation-of-powers grounds (the president could not legislate from the Oval Office).

For the unemployed, FDR's government became the default employer. Economist John Maynard Keynes later wrote that a nation could decrease unemployment and increase income by burying jars of money and having the public dig them up. Roosevelt anticipated him, funding a series of "stimulus projects" and relief programs purportedly to spur the economy. The government was essentially paying one group to dig holes and another group to fill them in.

The dirty secret was that putting billions of dollars in Roosevelt's hands politicized the spending. FDR doled out funds from the Works Progress Administration (WPA) specifically to states believed to be critical to the 1936 presidential election. In contested Pennsylvania, he increased WPA expenditures more than three thousand percent, the largest increase in any state in the nation. Patronage and politics made the government's make-work projects, which were paid for by tax increases and debt, twice as bad.

The Agricultural Adjustment Act (AAA) represented one of the cruelest and most unusual punishments of Roosevelt's "liberal" agenda. It was designed to decrease the agricultural supply to prop prices up. Arch-progressive Secretary of Agriculture Henry Wallace literally paid farmers to destroy produce while Americans starved.

As FDR critic John T. Flynn wrote:

We had men burning oats when we were importing oats from abroad on a huge scale, killing pigs while increasing our imports of lard, cutting corn production and importing 30 million bushels of corn from abroad . . . [and] while Wallace was paying out hundreds of millions to kill millions of hogs, burn oats, plow under cotton, the Depart-

ment of Agriculture issued a bulletin telling the nation that the great problem of our time was our failure to produce enough food to provide the people with a mere subsistence diet.

But while "restoring purchasing power" to farmers sounded noble, it was like trying to defy gravity. Prices are determined by supply and demand. Government was fighting markets that needed to adjust if a real recovery was ever to come about.

The NRA also propped up prices by letting unions require industries to pay above-market minimum wages. As another critic of the New Deal put it, "The theory here, embraced by FDR and his New Dealers . . . was that the depression was caused by falling wages, and if wages could be forced up, the depression would be cured." The flaw, of course, is that wages cannot be "forced up"; that's defying laws of nature. Nature always wins in the end. Always.

Compounding these problems was FDR's undermining of property and contractual rights. One of his earliest acts was to end banking in gold, expropriating privately owned gold and ordering the abolition of all contractual clauses calling for payment in it. The federal government itself reneged on these obligations.

FDR's reasoning was devious. According to Treasury Secretary Henry Morgenthau Jr., Roosevelt wanted to "keep things on an unsettled basis" until the Supreme Court ruled on the constitutionality of his gold legislation. The more chaos for the Court and financial markets, the greater the chance the public would throw up its hands and demand that FDR be given control over the currency.

Meanwhile, with the dollar off the gold standard, FDR could set the price himself, which he did, often over breakfast with Morgenthau. Just how arbitrary was this process (which was aimed at raising prices)? Morgenthau revealed that Roosevelt suggested a price increase from nineteen to twenty-one cents one morning because "It is a lucky number . . . because it's three times seven."

When FDR set the gold price to thirty-five dollars per ounce by law, he devalued the currency by more than forty percent, wiping out savings with a pen stroke.

FDR LOSES THE BATTLE BUT WINS THE WAR

Many of the most harmful of Roosevelt's policies were struck down by the Supreme Court, which was led by FDR's old friend, Chief Justice Charles Evans Hughes. But FDR wasn't about to take it lying down.

In February 1937, fresh off reelection, FDR proposed what would become known as the "court-packing" scheme. Alleging that the Court was flouting the will of the executive and legislative branches in its "activism," he chided the Court for "making law from the bench." He argued that modern conditions demanded action.

His plan called for federal judges to be given the option to resign and accept a pension upon reaching the age of seventy. If they refused, FDR would get to appoint additional judges. Since six judges on the Supreme Court were older than seventy, Roosevelt would have the power to potentially expand the Court to fifteen judges, thereby ensuring a favorable majority.

In spite of Democratic control of Congress, a series of events conspired to kill Roosevelt's bill, including a flurry of Court decisions upholding parts of the New Deal that hinged on the defection of one judge from the "conservative" side to the "liberal" side, the retirement of another judge, and a shift in public opinion against FDR.

Although Roosevelt lost this battle, he won the war. William Rehnquist, who became chief justice five decades later, argued that by breaking with the two-term tradition to win four terms in office, the power-hungry FDR was able to appoint eight Supreme Court justices, shaping decisions for decades to come.

MORE NEW DEAL NUISANCES

Court actions notwithstanding, much of FDR's agenda continued to surge ahead. He tripled taxes; created more government entities such as the Federal Communications Commission (FCC), the National Labor Relations Board (NLRB), and the Securities and Exchange Commission (SEC); created a new entitlement in Social Security; and doubled federal spending.

The FCC's regulation of the communications industry, designed to protect a limited resource, also gave it the power to regulate the content of communications. The FCC threatened anti-FDR stations with license revocation and restricted all "partisan" broadcasts, Roosevelt's own notwithstanding.

The NLRB "protected" labor by forcing employers to bargain collectively with unions and by mandating minimum-wage floors that dramatically increased unemployment. Strike activity doubled from fourteen million days to twenty-eight million days from 1936 to 1937. But FDR's "pro-labor" policies did have a positive political effect—at least, for him and future Democrats. Between 1933 and 1945, union membership grew to fourteen million from less than three million, most of them loyal FDR Democrats. By this time, union members now accounted for thirty percent of the entire labor force.

The SEC, designed to protect investors by regulating securities, imposed costly disclosure requirements on businesses, preventing them from raising more capital to expand and create new jobs. Studies showed that rates of return on stocks before and after the SEC's creation were indistinguishable, which should not have been the case if their job was actually to prevent frauds. The SEC mandated price fixing, sustaining a cartel of Wall Street firms. The little guy received the same investment returns but paid more for them.

Speaking of frauds, Social Security, which is, in effect, a legalized Ponzi scheme, has been on a path to insolvency since the day it was signed.

Roosevelt spent and regulated like a drunken sailor in spite of criticizing President Hoover on those very same grounds during the 1932 presidential race. And perhaps worst of all, he paid for it all by vastly expanding and steeping the tax code. What was only four hundred pages at the start of FDR's administration ballooned to more than eighty-two hundred pages by the end of it. While designed to make individuals and businesses pay their "fair share," it had the effect of stifling economic growth and completely reshaping the economic promise of America from one of individual achievement into one of redistributive equality.

FDR MAKES THE DEPRESSION GREAT

The New Deal was designed to relieve suffering and put America on a sustainable and equitable path. But *designed* is the key word there. The actual effect was something else entirely.

FDR, in fact, turned what would otherwise have been a Depression into a Great Depression through his attempts at social and financial engineering. From 1933 to 1940, the average annual unemployment rate averaged 18.6 percent. The economy went on a "capital strike," as private investment did not return to 1929 levels until 1941. FDR's constant "experimentation" created uncertainty, and there is nothing that private companies and stock markets hate more than that. Business was paralyzed as a result. In 1937 and 1938, after brief gains from the depths of the Great Depression, the economy collapsed into a double-dip recession. From 1937 to 1938, industrial production declined by thirty-three percent. National income hemorrhaged thirteen percent. Wages went down by thirty-five percent. All of this unsurprisingly added up to an unemployment rate that rose by roughly five percentage points. An estimated four million workers lost their jobs.

C. S. Lewis, in *God in the Dock*, could have been speaking for millions of demoralized Americans when he wrote:

> *Of all tyrannies, a tyranny sincerely exercised for the good of its victims may be the most oppressive . . . those who torment us for our own good will torment us without end for they do so with the approval of their own conscience. They may be more likely to go to Heaven yet at the same time likelier to make a Hell of earth.*

Treasury Secretary Henry Morgenthau Jr. may have summed it up best when he said that "after eight years of this administration we have just as much unemployment as when we started. . . . And an enormous debt to boot!"

Everyone seemed to be a loser, except for Roosevelt himself. After all, if his primary mission was to consolidate and retain power, his agenda would have to be deemed a rousing success.

But a simple rousing success was not what he had in mind. He wanted to be thought of as an all-time great.

And a world war would be exactly the thing to get him there.

FDR GOES TO WAR

In peacetime, spending and regulation were FDR's tonics for fixing what ailed America. But war provided him with an excuse to plan centrally on a far greater scale—the free world depended on it. If America didn't reform, it would be occupied by Hitler's storm troops. Hitler himself was known to fantasize about "the downfall of New York in towers of flames." In March 1942, before the United States had even entered the war, FDR warned journalists: "Nazi forces are not seeking mere modifications in colonial maps or in minor European boundaries. They openly seek the destruction of all elective systems of government on every continent, including our own."

Fear of Nazi occupation, of losing everything we loved. But of course, there was hope. We could avoid war if only we'd get our own economic house in order—which, in FDR's telling, meant giving more power to the federal government to regulate business and confiscate private property.

Given this context, it shouldn't be too surprising that FDR conferred upon himself unprecedented executive powers after Pearl Harbor, including the right to ignore tariffs, close radio stations, order the military to take over any plot of land, close financial exchanges, and alter labor regulations.

The federal bureaucracy boomed.

The War Production Board (WPB) was created to direct production and allocate materials and fuel. It converted civilian industries into wartime ones, rationed basic materials, and regulated everything down to even the quantity of fabrics used in dresses.

Vice President Henry Wallace—the former agriculture secretary who supervised the hog-slaughtering AAA—now headed the Board of Economic Welfare (BEW), which procured raw materials. Although the BEW spent $1.2 billion during the war, it was never authorized by law, nor did the Senate ever affirm Wallace's appointment to lead it.

Under the BEW, Wallace sought to kill two birds with one stone by internationalizing the New Deal in service of the war. For example, he built rubber plantations in Haiti and Brazil, while subsidizing the natives' "general welfare." This sounds great until you look at the math. Private industry produced rubber for $0.30 per pound; the rubber from Haiti cost $546 per pound.

Wallace was a progressive who was, at a minimum, a proud social-

HENRY WALLACE'S 1944 TRIP TO THE SOVIET UNION

He looked out over the plains of Kolyma toward the snow-capped mountains in the distance. The tall man from Iowa probably did not expect to find himself feeling at home in the stark landscape of northeastern Russia, yet Vice President Henry Wallace, visiting this remote corner of Soviet Siberia as part of a tour of the Far East in May 1944, sensed that he was visiting a land of bounty not so different from America's own heartland.

"The vast expanses of your country, her virgin forests, wide rivers and large lakes, all kinds of climate," he said to the Soviet officials who greeted him, "from tropical to polar—her inexhaustible wealth. It all reminds me of my homeland."

Among Wallace's official Soviet guides was Sergei Goglidze, who was introduced as a civil official. Wallace told Goglidze that he saw him as a very fine man and very understanding with people. In reality, however, Goglidze was the top commander of the Soviet foreign intelligence services in the region and had arranged for a number of his agents to be placed among Wallace's welcoming committee.

Shepherded by Goglidze and other Soviet handlers, Wallace spent several weeks visiting the region's farms, mines, and factories. He chatted amiably with the seemingly cheerful workers he met along the way.

Of course, it was all a ruse. They were literal Potemkin villages to charm and impress credulous visitors like the American vice president.

What Wallace was actually touring was a massive prison complex where hundreds of thousands of political prisoners from all over the Soviet Union and beyond labored as slaves of Stalin. The gulag archipelago of Siberia stretched for thou-

sands of miles in each direction. Wallace would have had no
way of knowing. Soviet officials had seen to that. According to
Elinor Lipper, a prisoner in the camp who was originally from
Switzerland and was later released, "in honor of Mr. Wallace
the wooden watchtowers were razed in a single night."

Also hidden away were the prisoners themselves, who were
prohibited from even venturing into the camp yard during Wallace's visit. Instead, guards, other camp staff, and members of
local Communist youth groups were corralled into masquerading as miners, farmers, and workers for Wallace to meet with.

The charade worked. Wallace went home and two years
later published an enthusiastic account of the trip, describing
the efficient, prosperous workforce he had encountered. But
back in Siberia, in the words of Lipper, "the watchtowers were
put up again, the prisoners sent out to work again."

"Wallace," she said, "saw nothing at all of this frozen hell
with its hundreds of thousands of the damned."

ist. Many argued that he was actually an outright Communist. Like
so many others in FDR's employ, Wallace hired Communists, dupes,
and useful idiots under him. (Thirty-five BEW Reds were later identified by the House Committee on Un-American Activities.)

Wallace fancied himself an expert on Russia. He had studied Marx
and Lenin and even taught himself the language. In 1944, he traveled
to Siberia as FDR's vice president. When it became clear that Soviet
dictator Joseph Stalin had less-than-peaceful plans in eastern Europe
and elsewhere, Wallace steadfastly argued for appeasement, offering
to relinquish the atomic bomb in exchange for a deal with the tyrant.

Roosevelt created the Office of Price Administration (OPA) to
fight price inflation. The OPA could freeze rents and set prices for
goods and commodities. Rationing soon followed. Labor unions,
however, did not see their wages frozen, nor did FDR take action to

break up strikes. (It's probably not a coincidence that union members were a key source of Roosevelt votes.)

All of this central planning only made the economic dislocations of war worse. Aside from the rationing, price inflation and mass shortages of basic goods such as rubber and flour also followed.

The distorted war marketplace created labor shortages resulting in a job freeze of twenty-seven million workers issued in April 1943. Strikes that year numbered 3,752, including those in vital war industries like steel and coal. This amounted to thirteen million man-days of labor lost at a time when the country couldn't afford any.

Historians Burton and Anita Folsom wrote that the OPA "issued more than 600 rent and price regulations on more than 8 million articles, with 3,100 investigators and 700 attorneys, plus support staff" by 1945. "Snoopers" submitted hundreds of thousands of cases to the courts alleging illegal black-market transactions.

Economic liberty wasn't the only thing languishing.

The Office of War Information (OWI) published and distributed pro-FDR propaganda worldwide and promoted the efforts of the Soviet Communist "ally" in Europe. In addition to the politicized messaging in its hundreds of radio programs, daily cables, recordings, and movie shorts, OWI also printed millions of pro-FDR pamphlets in the run-up to the 1944 election. News that might have reflected poorly on Roosevelt was often suppressed.

The FCC and OWI took control of foreign-language radio, often installing un-vetted immigrants with "questionable" (read: Leftist) political views to broadcast to millions of people. The OWI, in conjunction with the FCC, forced out those whose views did not comport with theirs. Eugene L. Carey, a member of the Congressional Select Committee Investigating the FCC, noted that "a real Gestapo was created and a lawless enterprise was launched." OWI also worked with Treasury to use the airwaves to emphasize the patriotic duty of paying taxes. The theme? "Taxes to beat the Axis."

More chilling was Roosevelt's use of illegal wiretapping. Under cover of war, the president authorized agents to bug the phones of not just aliens who threatened national security but also "potential political enemies" and even "political friends." Roosevelt's spying targets included former President Herbert Hoover, 1940 Republican presidential opponent Wendell Willkie, and critical journalists.

FDR asked Treasury Secretary Morgenthau to run a tax audit on the *New York Times*, among other IRS investigations FDR ordered on behalf of actual opponents. He also sicced the heads of various agencies, including the FBI and the Department of Justice, on several newspaper publishers in a failed witch hunt for evidence of Nazi ties.

FDR's internment of almost one hundred twenty thousand Japanese, most of whom were American, was particularly brazen. It violated the rights of habeas corpus, protection against search and seizure, and protection of property. Meanwhile, Germans and Italians—the latter of whom consisted of six hundred thousand noncitizens—were never interned en masse.

Roosevelt, however, was really just following the progressive playbook, responding to his innate fear of people different from himself. Consistent with the progressive eugenicists who came before him and held disdain for "inferior" peoples, Roosevelt had historically argued that Japanese immigrants were inassimilable on a biological basis. The Germans could be excused—Wilson had, after all, praised the "Teutonic race"—but not the Japanese. The distinction was made based purely on race. Roosevelt's irrational fear led to the rounding up and unjust imprisonment of tens of thousands of loyal Americans who happened to come from a different background. This is the price of progressive fear in high places.

FDR'S LAST PROGRESSIVE HURRAH

....

As World War II wound toward its end in 1944, FDR proposed a "Second Bill of Rights." The first was apparently insufficient for him. In that year's State of the Union address, he argued: "True individual freedom cannot exist without economic security and independence. 'Necessitous men are not free men.' People who are hungry and out of a job are the stuff of which dictatorships are made."

Roosevelt claimed that government had to secure Americans' fundamental right to a job; a decent living; trade without "unfair competition"; a fine home; sufficient health care; financial support in old age, poor health, or unemployment; and a solid education—all to prevent tyranny.

He may have originally claimed that all we had to fear was fear itself, but the reality was that he wanted Americans to fear a whole host of things, from Japanese-Americans to those who didn't have enough to eat. Fear, after all, opened doors to all sorts of things that people wouldn't otherwise think possible.

In addition to fear, Roosevelt also appealed to pride and patriotism. He noted that the nation must not be allowed to slide back into 1920s "normalcy." Were that to happen, he said, "even though we shall have conquered our enemies on the battlefields abroad, we shall have yielded to the spirit of Fascism here at home."

In other words, FDR argued that if Americans let his wartime reforms go away, then they might as well have just lost the war in the first place. It sounds incredible, but it's a strategy employed by progressives in government over and over again. Legislation passed during a crisis lives on like a cockroach, able to survive even in the worst of conditions. It was a crisis, after all, that gave birth to the Patriot Act, a law that continues to be used to invade Americans' privacy long after September 11, 2001.

In FDR's wartime America, "rights" were to be granted no longer by our creator but by the federal government. "Security" was to trump liberty. And if you disagreed with any of that, you were a Nazi or at least someone who didn't much care for American values.

Earlier in this chapter, I mentioned a professor who was instrumental in drafting FDR's first inaugural address. This man, Raymond Moley, went on to work for Roosevelt for several years before eventually breaking with him as FDR's policies bore their poisonous fruit. In his 1952 book *How to Keep Our Liberty*, Moley wrote:

> It was no secret that a great number of . . . reformers [in Roosevelt's bureaucracy] were admirers of the "great Soviet experiment." And some . . . were secret agents of Communism.
>
> In my opinion, there is a greater danger in collectivists than in the betrayal of our secrets to foreign powers. The danger lies in what can be done to a nation by public officials who do not believe in a free economy. In Roosevelt's day there were many people working for the government who regarded his reforms as a mere prelude to revolution.
>
> America has been fortunate to avoid such a fate so far, but Roosevelt's revolution not only accomplished more than Wilson and the other progressives who came before him had ever dreamed possible, but it also set the stage for what was to come next.
>
> A New Deal and a Second Bill of Rights were terrific starts, but what America really needed was someone who could pull all of the disparate pieces together. Someone who could appeal to all races and creeds and make Americans believe that they could achieve what no one before them had, that it was their duty to work toward something bigger than themselves, something he called a Great Society.

PROFILE IN FEAR:
ELEANOR'S DOLLHOUSE

This was his last chance. For most of his life, Teddy Roosevelt had tried to help his younger brother, Elliott. He'd tried to get him to live a vigorous life, to take advantage of their family's wealth, his good looks, and his easy charm and to contribute something useful to the world.

Instead, Elliott was a reprobate. A spendthrift. A philandering drunk. A dangerous maniac.

Elliott's latest embarrassment—knocking up one of the servants—had left the family in a state of utter dismay. It only underscored Teddy's wisdom in filing the lawsuit in the first place.

With his distraught sister-in-law's approval, he filed to have Elliott judged mentally incapacitated and to take control of his fortune before he spent it all on women, booze, or other passing fancies. The suit did have some negative repercussions—"Elliott Roosevelt Insane" was a headline in one of the New York papers in 1891—but the hope was that the shock of the lawsuit and the likelihood that he might be committed to an asylum (yet again) might finally straighten him out.

It had the opposite effect.

From Paris, where his family had demanded he go in exile, Elliott vowed to fight.

Teddy boarded a ship bound for Europe. It had been several months since the Roosevelts had seen Elliott in America, and they were relieved that he was no longer causing disastrous headlines and embarrassing the family. Now Teddy was prepared to offer his brother yet another Faustian bargain, hoping to finally bring him around. As Elliott's anxious family awaited a report, Teddy went to work on his brother.

A few weeks later, the Roosevelt family received a letter from Teddy that filled them with hope. "Won!" the letter read. "Thank Heaven I went over."

Teddy reported that his brother was "utterly broken, submissive, and repentant." Elliott had agreed to sign over two-thirds of his property to his wife and to return home and try to make amends with his family, which included his beloved daughter, Eleanor, who still worshipped him.

Unfortunately, Elliott's experiment with sobriety did not last. Later that year, his wife, Anna, contracted diphtheria, a form of the croup, and passed away. Their son, Elliott Jr., died of the same disease the following year. A distraught Elliott returned to the safety of the bottle and the madness it brought. Not long after, drunk and delirious, he fell from a window and suffered a seizure.

He was dead at thirty-four.

Teddy later wrote that Elliott was pursued by "the most terrible demons that ever entered a man's body and soul." But the devastation was most acute in the sorrow of his adoring daughter. In two short years, young Eleanor had lost her mother, her brother, and now her father. She was now, at just nine years old, an orphan.

The loss of her father—"the love of my life when I was a child"—undoubtedly hit her the hardest. She could never completely come to terms with his raging illness, his selfishness, his neglect. She kept the few letters he had written to her like treasures. And for the rest of her life, she clung to the memory of a sainted man who had never truly existed.

Shipped off to her grandmother and living a sheltered existence, young Eleanor had a childhood of depression and panic. She never had the family life she wanted, and she yearned for the safety and security of one. But what she lacked in her personal life she tried to make up for in her ideological views, turning to a belief system that allowed her total control. It was an ideology that promised to heal wounds, those seen and unseen, and to remake the world in her own image. The perfect world she had always wanted.

All of which brings us to a small town in West Virginia.

Authoritarians love to build monuments to themselves. In the 1930s, the fad was to build model cities that demonstrated an ideology's glory and greatness. Stalin built the town of Magadan in the wilds of Siberia. Hitler built Ramersdorft. And Eleanor Roosevelt built the town of Arthurdale.

Organizing it to respond to the plight of West Virginia coal miners, Eleanor Roosevelt persuaded her husband to make construction of this new city a federal priority. Arthurdale was designed to be a city for the future, a city in which all of its inhabitants would show the wisdom and value of the progressive way of life.

The project was managed by the Division of Subsistence Homesteads (DSH), whose aim was to "build 'a new American man' and 'a new social order' in which 'the common good' would replace 'selfish motives.'" Author C. J. Maloney wrote that these homesteads were to make up small, semi-independent towns under a centrally planned industrial policy designed to decentralize American industry.

Eleanor Roosevelt made it her pet project, overseeing budgets, contacting potential employers who might locate in the city, and raising money for the program in Congress. She'd fix the despair and fear that the miners' families had experienced in a way that no one had been able to fix her own.

The vision of Arthurdale was nothing short of a worker's paradise, a place where citizens would spend half of their days working at a factory and the other half tending their own five-acre plots. Industries would flock to the town. It would become a model for cities across America.

Eleanor Roosevelt would visit the town frequently as first lady, attending dances and graduations and frequently talking about its future course. She offered extensive input on the design of new homes, complete with indoor plumbing. Arthurdale was her own real-life dollhouse.

And it was a failure from the start.

The first houses sent to West Virginia had come from Cape Cod and were not very well suited for mountain winters. They also didn't fit the existing foundations constructed by Arthurdale residents. Fixing this error—along with the many amenities that Eleanor Roosevelt had insisted on—made the homes three hundred percent more expensive than typical American houses.

As one author summarized it: "The planners of Arthurdale, when conjuring an entire town out of scratch, forgot one of the most basic lessons of real-estate investing: location is everything. Arthurdale's location was less than ideal; in fact, it was in the middle of nowhere."

Its remoteness made it almost impossible for manufacturers to want to locate there. Various companies, often at the federal government's urging, set up shop there for a time but eventually folded. Eleanor Roosevelt had personally persuaded General Electric to open a facility there, but it too quickly shut down. What was meant as a project to show how the government could create a self-sustaining city run by empowered individuals turned out to be an embarrassing and very expensive flop as the costs far exceeded expectations. By 1940, nearly every single citizen of Arthurdale was dependent on a government job.

From the acquisition of the land, through the management of the community, to its collapse in 1948, Arthurdale demonstrated an utter failure of collectivism. All of the town's holdings were eventually sold off at steep discounts.

Arthurdale was a fitting tribute to FDR progressivism, but it was an even more fitting tribute to how powerful emotions, like the fear of families falling apart, can result in big government projects that offer hope but deliver nothing.

♠

4

Third Wave:

LBJ and the Power of Envy

If only I could take the next step and become dictator of the whole world, then I could really make things happen. Every hungry person would be fed, every ignorant child educated, every jobless man employed.

—LYNDON JOHNSON

Love Field
Dallas
November 22, 1963

Blood was everywhere. The dark, red liquid stained his waking thoughts and haunted him when he closed his eyes. It decorated the leather interior of the limousine that sped toward Parkland Memorial. It was on the gurney that carried his shattered friend. And it was splattered over the pink dress of the dazed woman who stood beside him.

It was a baptism by blood.

Like the state he loved, Lyndon Baines Johnson was large and imposing. His head, his ears, his hands, his voice—they all seemed to overwhelm those around him, traits that helped him make deals with timid, cowering colleagues. But now, in the two hours since he'd first heard those loud pops, the new president of the United States tried his very best to be small.

At 2:28 P.M., aboard a hot and crowded compartment on Air Force One, Johnson raised his massive right hand, placed the other on a Bible, and swore "to preserve, protect, and defend the Constitution of the United States." John F. Kennedy's casket lay next to him, the lifeless body having been rushed to the plane in a hearse within minutes of the president being declared dead. Amid tears and trauma and blood, so much blood, the Kennedy era—what would soon by christened "Camelot"—had come to a violent end.

Unlike others in the administration, it was fair to say that LBJ's love for his fallen leader was not total. It was hard for a man of destiny and greatness—as Johnson had long seen himself—to surrender his powerful Senate seat in order to play second fiddle to a young man from Harvard who'd probably never worked one hard day in his life.

As vice president, LBJ was largely powerless, mostly marginalized. He knew the Kennedy boys made fun of him. Jackie, who now stood humbly at his side, privately referred to him and his wife, Lady Bird, as "Uncle Cornpone and his little porkchop." Her deceased husband hadn't been much kinder, once asking her rhetorically, "Oh, God, can you ever imagine what would happen to the country if Lyndon was president?"

But there was no doubt. Lyndon needed them now, all of them. He needed Jackie, the family, the Cabinet, even his nemesis, Bobby, if he had any hope of leading a nation that didn't know him and of leading a party that had chosen someone else just three years earlier.

LBJ paced restlessly about the aircraft, avoiding eye contact with the grieving widow. He bit his oversized lower lip as he pondered the task before him. How could he claim the Kennedy mantle when, truth be told, he thought the Kennedy agenda was far too cautious and timid?

He took his seat as the hulking aircraft taxied to the runway. Its four engines soon roared, and the plane shot forward and then up, as if on the trajectory of a rocket. He closed his eyes and relished the blackness.

When he finally opened them a few minutes later, he peered out the window at the endless miles of fluffy clouds beneath him. There, at the top of the world, he decided that the Kennedy presidency would need to be remodeled.

Fortunately, he wouldn't have to spend much time thinking about whom to model it on. His two idols, Woodrow Wilson and Franklin Roosevelt, had already created the template.

Now Lyndon Baines Johnson just had to fill in the blanks.

THE POWER OF ENVY

Lyndon Johnson came from nothing, lived with nothing, and was expected to amount to nothing. His family had helped settle the great state of Texas, a place where people thought big and dreamed big, and his father had served as a state representative.

After their family farm went bust, Lyndon's dad struggled to pay off his crippling debt for much of the rest of his life. The result was that Lyndon never had much money growing up, not like all the rich folks in the big cities or the people he saw on TV. Most of his neighbors and friends didn't have money, either. It all seemed so unfair.

Lyndon was never much of a student, but he did have the gift of gab and the rugged adventurism of the American Southwest. He once described himself to reporters as "a cross between a roughneck cowboy and a Baptist preacher."

Johnson caught the political bug at an early age and pounced at the chance to serve as an aide to Congressman Richard Kleberg. He arrived at the U.S. capital in the 1930s at an exciting time in Washington, D.C.: a new president named Franklin D. Roosevelt had taken over the reins, and he just so happened to be Lyndon Johnson's lifelong hero.

Johnson spent several years in Kleberg's office getting a crash course in how to get things done—or not done—in Congress. The wheeling and dealing. The backslapping. The late-night heavy drinking. The fondling of the pretty young women who orbited every member of Congress.

He found all the trappings of the political world to be intoxicating, but he also knew that he could do his boss's job ten times better. The only thing standing in his way was the small inconvenience of actually having to win an election.

After a failed attempt at a Georgetown University law degree, lightning struck. Johnson was plucked from obscurity and tapped by the Roosevelt administration to run the Texas division of the National Youth Administration (NYA), one of the dozens of "progressive" programs that Roosevelt promulgated in the 1930s.

Johnson was a true commissar at the NYA, a program that ostensibly provided "education, jobs, recreation, and counseling" for teens and young adults, as well as "financial assistance to students in exchange for part-time jobs as clerks or maintenance workers." It sounds admirable, but in reality, it was a giant taxpayer-subsidized welfare program that created jobs that weren't needed. The program also "put non-students to work on public projects such as highways and roadside parks, playgrounds and schools, recreational parks, and public buildings all over Texas."

It was at the NYA that Johnson got his most effective training in how to squeeze the most largesse out of a government program—and how someone could use it to get large groups of people (e.g., demographic groups, industries, political factions) to do exactly what he wanted. Both of these lessons became key ingredients in Johnson's future success.

In 1937, Johnson got his next big break when a vacancy occurred in the Tenth Congressional District of Texas. He ran for election in a large field of hopefuls as the most Roosevelt-infatuated candidate. "I support Franklin Roosevelt the full way," he said. "All the way, every day. That's what I intend to do when elected as your representative in Congress."

Johnson's campaign motto was "Franklin D. and Lyndon B."—and he tied his own successful election directly to the president's agenda. "This is not a personal triumph," he said. "This is but approval of the president's program . . . the people of the 10th district [of Texas] are sending to Washington the message that they are . . . as strong as horse radish for Roosevelt."

During the time between 1937 and 1945, Johnson met with the president no fewer than twenty-three times (at least officially; the unofficial number is likely significantly higher). And when Johnson was scolded for being Roosevelt's "water boy" on Capitol Hill, he claimed he would "be glad to carry a bucket of water to the Commander in Chief any time his thirsty throat or his thirsty soul needed support."

FDR was like a second father to Johnson, so Roosevelt's death in 1945 left him devastated. "He was just like a daddy to me always," Johnson said. "He always talked to me just that way. I don't know that I'd ever have come to Congress if it hadn't been for him. But I do know I got my first great desire for public office because of him."

Once in the House, LBJ quickly became a protégé of Texas-born and all-powerful Speaker of the House Sam Rayburn. From Rayburn, he learned how to wield absolute power, but, unlike "gentleman Sam," Johnson was, for most of his adult life, a crude and grotesque monster. When you got past the suit and tie, LBJ was nothing more than a bully who threatened and intimidated people who didn't agree with him, a sexual predator who would paw people right in front of his wife, and a graceless oaf who sometimes made staffers meet with him while he sat on the toilet.

Lady Bird Johnson was his long-suffering spouse; her husband's philandering was not just notorious, it was legendary. Biographer Robert Dallek called Johnson a "competitive womanizer" and noted that "when people mentioned Kennedy's many affairs, Johnson would bang the table and declare that he had more women by accident than Kennedy ever had on purpose."

LBJ wasn't even particularly discreet about his womanizing. At a NATO meeting in Paris in 1960, LBJ, Lady Bird, and others were having dinner. The vice president got drunk and ended up with a diplomat's wife sitting in his lap, "groping" her. Lady Bird just had to deal with it. When he wasn't cheating on her, he was treating her as if she was invisible in public, berating her, or speaking ill about her cooking, housekeeping, or clothes.

Johnson's philandering was evidence of his deep-seated need to dominate and humiliate people through bullying, cajoling, or outright humiliation. This need both informed and fed his disdain for others, including those in his Secret Service detail who had pledged their lives to protect him. Johnson reportedly once "asked a Secret Serviceman to shield him while he peed outside," and then he "purposely peed on the agent's trouser leg." When "the agent mentioned how gross that was," Johnson was unapologetic. "I know," he said. "That's my prerogative." Dealing with the president's bodily functions was just a part of life in the Johnson administration. Speechwriter Richard Goodwin was once summoned to Johnson's bathroom for a "meeting." "I remained standing," Goodwin remembered, because "Johnson had the only seat in the room." The president was sitting on the toilet.

Johnson quickly established himself as a D.C. natural, but it wasn't until he was elected to Congress's upper chamber in 1949 that his legend as "Master of the Senate" began. In this, the world's most "elite club," Johnson thrived as he perfected the bullying tactics and overbearing style that would win him so many battles—and help usher in countless progressive programs.

LBJ's main aspiration was power. Control. He would improve the lives of his fellow sad sacks in the failed farmlands of Texas by running things from Washington with a massive federal government that would build a better America. How he'd obtain that power was simple. He'd prey on the American people's fear while harnessing his own. He'd leverage his own personal childhood anxiety about being destitute, broke, abandoned, and alone to make sure others felt those same powerful emotions.

Modern society, with its "vast wasteland" of televisions, dreary office cubicles, and the constant threat of nuclear war with the Soviet Union, could be scary. What everyone needed was a "daddy" (as FDR had been to him) in their lives. Someone to smile. Someone to reassure them. Someone to take them by the hand and tell them that they're from the government and they're here to help.

Always looking for a bigger desk—and more influence—Johnson ran for the Democratic presidential nomination in 1960. He lost, but despite misgivings, John F. Kennedy asked Johnson to be his running mate. Kennedy, an Irish-Catholic from Massachusetts, believed he needed support from Southern Democrats to win what was projected to be a close race between himself and sitting vice president Richard Nixon. Kennedy's instincts were right. Their ticket barely beat Nixon (it was the type of election where dead people voted for the Democrats in Chicago) and took over the White House in 1961.

After Kennedy's assassination, LBJ finally had the chance to live up to the legacy of his second daddy and make the spirit of Roosevelt proud. He "had a specific objective in mind that guided his presidency from the start," one reporter noted. "To out-do Franklin D. Roosevelt as the champion of everyday Americans."

He would be the next generation's FDR. He would be their daddy. Whether they liked it or not.

What Wilson had done to organize progressivism as a political force in the first place and what FDR had done to build new progressive economic institutions during the crisis of the Great Depression and World War II, LBJ would now do by spreading progressivism into the mainstream at a time of similar tumult and disorder. And in doing so, he would set in motion the destructive forces of nihilism, hedonism, and blasphemy that marked the 1960s, a decade that would change America forever.

THE NOT-SO-GREAT SOCIETY

Johnson's presidency is primarily remembered for two things, both of them massive failures: the Vietnam War and the Great Society. Both exacted a horrific human toll on America. The war scarred an entire generation, and its consequences can be measured in lives lost or irreparably destroyed. The Great Society, however, left its mark on several generations, pushed America farther toward progressivism, and can only be measured in lives ruined.

For progressives like Johnson, issues such as poverty, education, women's rights, and jobs are simply tools to be used in a continual effort to consolidate power and control. To understand how this works, we have to get into a bit of psychology. By stoking the fear of failure, disorder, and the unknown, progressives manipulate our most primal instincts. They hold out the collective—or the herd—as the solution to those fears and the way to alleviate our insecurities. Let's face it, solving our own problems is hard. Self-reliance takes work, pain, sacrifice, and, often, failure. Putting your trust in someone else to solve your problems is a lot easier.

Scared of being poor? Don't be. Poverty can be solved; we just have to declare war on it. Scared your kid isn't doing well in school? It's probably not his or her fault; we just need to put more taxpayer money into public education. Scared about losing your job? Plenty more can be created if the rich would just pay their fair share. Women can achieve equality if only we provide them with government-subsidized contraceptives and health care. The environment can be saved if only we would enact sweeping regulations and new taxes that punish polluters. And on and on and on.

Every problem has a big-government solution, and these were cornerstones of the Great Society, LBJ's ultimate promise of hope and happiness to a fearful American public. Like Wilson and Roosevelt before him, Johnson had no qualms about sacrificing the rights and personal liberty of individuals at the altar of the state. The Great Society—much like Wilson's New Freedom and Roosevelt's New Deal—was meant to further transform American society and government from individualism to collectivism.

In addition to being fearmongers, progressives also tend to be elitists and narcissists. LBJ had both of these traits in abundance. It takes an enormous amount of arrogance to believe that you and other "chosen" progressives know what is best for everyone else. Johnson was the apotheosis of this theory—both in terms of the personal and political contradictions at his core and in the resources, ability, and unique moral force he could deploy in its service in the wake of the JFK assassination. It's not much of a stretch to say that the Great Society would never have happened absent the Kennedy assassination. Not just because JFK himself wouldn't have pursued it but because it took Johnson's skillful exploitation of the nation's grief to get such a sweeping and radical agenda passed.

The vast scope of the Great Society speaks to the unbridled arrogance of the man who promulgated it. In championing his cause, Johnson claimed that through his leadership and expansive government powers, America could eliminate poverty, vastly improve education, create an urban renaissance, protect the environment, and produce (actual, not theoretical) equality for all.

LBJ pushed for a raft of new programs, all with FDR in mind. Cambridge University historian Anthony Badger, who wrote *FDR: The First Hundred Days*, described LBJ's near-obsession with FDR like this: "Throughout his presidency, Lyndon B. Johnson consistently measured his record against that of his political hero, FDR. In April 1965 he pressed his congressional liaison man, Larry O'Brien, to 'jerk out every damn little bill you can and get them down here by the 12th' because 'on the 12th you'll have the best Hundred Days. Better than he did!'"

By at least one estimate, the JFK-LBJ administration added 390 domestic social programs to the federal government. Prior to their time in office, the entire federal government had only 45 such programs. The Great Society was the New Deal on steroids, the most destructive, antidemocratic, and antientrepreneurial program of the twentieth century.

Johnson's vision was utopian, statist, and reckless, as any rational observer would have concluded. But the grief of a nation reeling from an assassinated president and a general sense that America was spiraling out of control, coupled with the fear of doing nothing—polluted rivers, impoverished cities, failing schools, and so on—spurred LBJ to act. Using these fears, he persuaded millions of Americans to abandon their traditional values of hard work and self-reliance in exchange for the soullessness of self-actualization. The message was simple: if you merely dream it, it will happen, and the Great Society will help you get there. As Johnson explained in a May 1964 speech at the University of Michigan:

> *Your imagination, your initiative, and your indignation will determine whether we build a society where progress is the servant of our needs, or a society where old values and new visions are buried under unbridled growth. For in your time we have the opportunity to move not only toward the rich society and the powerful society, but upward to the Great Society.*

Johnson went on to explain that the "purpose of protecting the life of our nation and preserving the liberty of our citizens is to pursue the happiness of our people." That pursuit no longer mattered if it was just one individual's happiness. Instead, the proper pursuit was now the happiness "of our people," or the collective as a whole. That was our nation's calling.

"[The] challenge of the next half century," LBJ continued, "is whether we have the wisdom to use that wealth to enrich and elevate our national life." Here's how we'd do it. The Great Society:

- "rests on abundance and liberty for all [and] demands an end to poverty and racial injustice."
- "is a place where every child can find knowledge to enrich his mind and to enlarge his talents, [where] leisure is a welcome chance to build and reflect, [where] the city of man serves not only the needs of the body and the demands of commerce but the desire for beauty and the hunger for community."
- "is a place where man can renew contact with nature, [which] honors creation for its own sake, [where] men are more concerned with the quality of their goals than the quantity of their goods."
- "is not a safe harbor, a resting place, a final objective, a finished work"; instead, it is "a challenge constantly renewed, beckoning us toward a destiny where the meaning of our lives matches the marvelous products of our labor."

This was not a policy speech, it was a collectivist fantasy that could have been written by Karl Marx himself.

Fittingly, the Great Society approach started with Johnson's disastrous "War on Poverty." In reality, this wasn't a war on poverty at all, it was a war *against* prosperity and success. Like all progressives, Johnson believed in economic leveling. Instead of lifting everyone up through commerce and capitalism, he wanted to force everyone into an economic purgatory where mediocrity was the norm and striving for greatness was discouraged.

Like all progressive scams, the Great Society sought to convince marginalized groups—especially minorities, the poor, immigrants, and so on—that their relationship with the government should be redefined from JFK's "Ask not what your country can do for you, but what you can do for your country" to the complete opposite. Had LBJ been as articulate as JFK he easily could've framed the Great Society as "ask not what you can do for your country, ask what your country can do for you."

LBJ pitched a simple deal to all those who felt aggrieved: the government will take away your fears and hardships, and you, in turn, will devote your life, including your paychecks, to the state.

In practice, the Great Society is an alphabet soup of government programs that cater to our every desire and complaint. If we want our children to be fed breakfast at school, there's a government program for that. If we want more art in our public buildings or ballet in our theaters, there are government programs for those things, too. Here's a short list of just some of the measures passed under LBJ to show how all of this paternal care was translated into big-government nonsense:

- Antipoverty programs such as the Economic Opportunity Act of 1964, an Omnibus Housing Act, and the creation of Job Corps.
- Education (and brainwashing) programs such as Head Start, the Elementary and Secondary Education Act, and the creation of Volunteers in Service to America (VISTA).
- Sweeping health-care "reforms" such as the creation of Medicare and Medicaid.

- The beginning of job-killing, reactionary environmental controls via the Wilderness Protection Act and the Air and Water Quality Acts.
- Creation of the federal-government-as-cultural-patron through programs such as the National Endowment for the Arts and Humanities.

Under LBJ, the nation witnessed the true creation of a welfare state based on massive entitlement programs and predicated on the government's ability to drive the populace to an ambition-destroying focus on "inner meaning" and "quality of life" instead of character, ambition, and success. This, in turn, created a crisis of conscience and confidence in people that made them both susceptible to undermining traditional norms and predisposed to reliance on the state to handle the things that were "too hard" for them.

LBJ laid the groundwork to create an environment for self-actualization through the government: conservation programs, federal patronage of the arts, and public broadcasting, to name a few. These were not meant to foster national elevation or celebrate American greatness; they were created as a corporate, secular replacement of religion as sources of spiritual fulfillment for the masses. Replace God with government, and you control not just people's minds but their hearts and souls as well.

Johnson's conclusion in his Ann Arbor speech that day in 1964 should be telling for anyone who's wondered how the Founders and their principles have become so marginalized over the last few decades: "Let us from this moment begin our work so that in the future men will look back and say: It was then, after a long and weary way, that man turned the exploits of his genius to the full enrichment of his life."

This "long and weary way" he refers to is, of course, the previous centuries of American history. Centuries in which our forefathers built the greatest and most free country in the history of the world. This is what Johnson wished man to turn "the exploits of his genius" away from.

It's no surprise that this speech by a gruff Texan reads like a self-help book. Johnson was more than just a daddy to the masses; he was also the father of the new powerful cultural trends that gave people the excuse to be selfish. The Me Generation would never have existed if Johnson hadn't set out to specifically engender self-obsession. True freedom didn't come from hard work or any kind of traditional definition of professional achievement, such as becoming a doctor or a lawyer. True freedom, Johnson argued, could only be obtained by pursuing whatever you personally found fulfilling, whether other people found it useful or not.

Johnson was not the only the proponent of this kind of progressivism. Half a century earlier, John Dewey had taught that a new, progressive social order would allow individuals more freedom because government would be there to back them up. In 1902, Dewey, along with the like-minded John Tufts, wrote:

> The more comprehensive and diversified the social order, the greater the responsibility and the freedom of the individual. His freedom is the greater, because the more numerous are the effective stimuli to action, and the more varied and the more certain the ways in which he may fulfill his powers. His responsibility is greater because there are more demands for considering the consequences of his acts; and more agencies for bringing home to him the recognition of consequences which affect not merely more persons individually, but which also influence the more remote and hidden social ties.

That is a perfect—if not somewhat opaque—summary of the spiritual and personal fulfillment that progressives believe is achievable through reliance on an all-powerful State.

LADY BIRD'S GOOD FORTUNE

Inherent in the progressive mind-set is the belief that most
rules don't really apply to them.

After all, progressives believe themselves to be more enlightened than the rest of us. It follows, therefore, that they
have every right to tell others what to do, even if they don't do
those things themselves.

Do as I say, not as I do.

LBJ was a perfect embodiment of this philosophy.

Johnson had always been known as a wheeler-dealer, with
implications of the kind of quid pro quo approach to politics
that skirts the line of legality and morality. But corruption in
the Johnson White House, not to mention in his own personal
household, ran deep. He was no stranger to scandal, corruption, and graft.

The *New York Times* obituary for Lady Bird Johnson, who
died in 2007, states that the Johnsons came to Washington, D.C., in 1934, and that by the time Lyndon became president, Lady Bird had become "a successful businesswoman,"
especially through the purchase in 1942 of a small Austin,
Texas, radio station, KTBC.

The *Times* notes that although "the station was bought
in Mrs. Johnson's name," her husband's political influence
"helped in acquiring the license from the Federal Communications Commission." Afterward, Lyndon Johnson "became the
commission's champion at a time when Congress was about
to cut its budget," and Lady Bird's "application was speedily
approved."

Lady Bird's *Washington Post* obituary told a similar story.
The station's "previous owners had been unable to obtain
approval from the Federal Communications Commission for a
power increase, but Mrs. Johnson was granted approval within

a month." Critics "concluded that her husband's close connection to Franklin D. Roosevelt had made the difference."

The *Post* also notes that while Mrs. Johnson was president
of her company, "it was her husband who negotiated an affilia-
tion with the CBS radio network," which "dramatically boosted
advertising revenue and made the Johnsons millionaires."

Johnson often used Lady Bird as his financial vessel, purchasing businesses and stock in her name while peddling influence to increase the value of these holdings. During the twenty
years after the purchase of KTBC, the Johnsons would amass
something of a telecommunications empire, with the purchase
of numerous affiliates, a television station, and "cable interests," as well ranches, real estate, and a bank.

Much of the corruption during the Johnson years revolved
around the Vietnam War. For example, soon after Johnson
became president, the fortunes of one of his closest corporate associates, Texas construction firm Brown & Root (now
known as KBR and a onetime subsidiary of Halliburton), magically and dramatically improved.

National Public Radio, an outlet hardly known for being
critical toward progressives, reported that Brown & Root
"won contracts for huge construction projects for the federal
government" during the Johnson administration, which, by the
mid-1960s, had the press and political opposition suggesting
"that the company's good luck was tied to its sizable contributions to Johnson's political campaign."

Brown & Root was also part of the notorious "Vietnam
Builders" consortium of companies hired by the U.S. government under Johnson to build the military and logistical infrastructure for the United States' rapidly growing role in South
Vietnam.

In 1966, a young congressman from Illinois named
Donald H. Rumsfeld charged the Johnson administration with
allowing contracts that were "illegal by statute" and "urged

investigation into the relationship" between Johnson and the Vietnam Builders, particularly the "infamous 'President's Club,' to which Brown & Root, one of the principal Vietnam contractors, had given tens of thousands of dollars in campaign contributions."

Johnson also showed incredible favoritism and provided significant largesse to another company with which he also had close ties: a helicopter manufacturer named Bell Corporation. After Bell supported Johnson in his 1948 U.S. Senate campaign, the company went on to make huge profits from the Vietnam War. These profits were shared with one of the company's big shareholders. You guessed it: Lady Bird Johnson.

Some analysts and historians believe that Johnson's escalation of the Vietnam conflict was driven at least in part by his desire to "pay back" supporters in both the defense industry and the military itself. Before winning reelection in 1964, Johnson promised these groups that if he was victorious, "you'll get your war."

If it sounds like corruption, that's because it is. But progressives don't view it that way. They justify the self-dealing and cronyism because it provides resources for them to serve the country and the "greater good." It's an age-old "ends justify the means" argument; the Johnsons' millions in side deals were a small price to pay for building the Great Society.

Dewey (whom Johnson affectionately referred to as "Dr. Johnny") was the intellectual godfather of cultural progressivism; Johnson was the ambitious architect who brought his ideas to life.

All of this came at great cost to the country. Not simply in the way that Americans' relationship with the Founders was forever changed but in actual dollars. According to a Heritage Foundation analysis, President Johnson's agenda led to the government "expanding the non-defense budget by 14 percent per year," and "tax increases and economic stagnation followed."

In the end, the Great Society has cost American taxpayers more than $22 trillion in today's dollars. That's "three times the amount of money that the government has spent on all military wars in its history, from the Revolutionary War to present," according to the Heritage Foundation's Robert Rector. Each year, we add another $1 trillion to the costs of the Great Society, with more than eighty federal programs doling out dollars to fight the "War on Poverty."

But costs hardly matter to progressives; the ends always justify the means.

THE CIVIL RIGHTS MYTH

History books say that Johnson played a pivotal role in the enactment of the Civil Rights Act of 1964. No argument here—he was definitely pivotal. But the real story is far more complicated, interesting, and revealing about the progressive mind-set than anything you'll read in a history book.

Like his idol Wilson before him, Johnson was an abhorrent bigot and sexist. And at the heart of his bigotry and misogyny was his own overweening sense of self, his elitism and narcissism, which drove Johnson's political and societal views. This is all in keeping with progressive ideology, which envisions the creation of the perfect human, a human who, in progressives' minds, clearly doesn't include anyone with dark skin.

Johnson's Herculean sense of personal entitlement—like an overgrown, spoiled teenager—only exacerbated his legendary racism. Johnson deployed the term "nigger" on a near-daily basis. In fact, according to MSNBC reporter Adam Serwer, he was something of a "connoisseur of the word." Preeminent Johnson biographer Robert

Caro explained that LBJ would "calibrate his pronunciations by region, using 'nigra' with some southern legislators and 'negra' with others."

Johnson's racism, which was not confined to African-Americans (he once described East Asians as "hordes of barbaric yellow dwarves"), was the perfect combination of his personal cruelty with his racial disdain. He once asked his African-American chauffeur Robert Parker if he would prefer to be called by his name rather than some pejorative term such as "boy," "nigger," or "chief." When Parker had the temerity to say he preferred to be called by his own name, Johnson reportedly responded: "As long as you are black, and you're gonna be black till the day you die, no one's gonna call you by your goddamn name. So no matter what you are called, nigger, you just let it roll off your back like water, and you'll make it. Just pretend you're a goddamn piece of furniture."

Johnson's devotion to civil rights was, to put it mildly, tepid. Really, it was just a matter of political expediency. He saw the way the winds of history were blowing, and he wanted to smell good when he was upwind of future historians. His hostile views toward racial equality make sense once you remember that he spent most of his career as part of the segregationist Southern bloc of Democrats. Caro wrote that Johnson, until 1957, "had never supported civil rights legislation—any civil rights legislation."

In fact, it's not just that Johnson didn't support civil rights legislation; he abhorred it, referring to the 1964 Civil Rights Act and its predecessors as "the nigger bill." When he appointed African-American jurist Thurgood Marshall to the Supreme Court, he reportedly told an aide, "Son, when I appoint a nigger to the court, I want everyone to know he's a nigger." Even while making history in race-equality efforts, Johnson couldn't help his racism.

Speaking of making history, perhaps the most important side note from the entire 1964 Civil Rights Act saga, one that seems to have been lost by history, is that the only reason the act passed into law was that it had the overwhelming support of Republicans in Congress.

According to CNN, "more Republicans voted in favor of the Civil Rights Act than Democrats." Progressives, as we'll soon see, make a great deal of noise over their supposedly exclusive advocacy on behalf of minorities, but the truth is that issues around equality (whether race, sex, or anything else) don't seem to matter much to them unless they also happen to advance a political agenda.

Johnson's support for civil rights should be seen for what it really was: an opportunistic game of high-stakes identity politics. All progressives don't share Johnson's overt racism, but they do all support policies that ultimately take a paternalistic view of racial minorities as groups of people who can't make it on their own.

After consistently blocking civil rights legislation as a member of the U.S. House of Representatives and the Senate—and then, as vice president, strongly urging Kennedy to slow down his planned actions on civil rights—Johnson did an about-face when he became president himself.

While his reasons for doing so are complicated, they boil down to one tactic in support of two goals: to secure the far-left wing of the Democratic Party so that he could both escalate the war in Vietnam and prevent Robert F. Kennedy—brother of and attorney general to the late president (and heir presumptive to the Kennedy legacy)—from running for the Democratic nomination in 1964.

Johnson, who was ultimately successful in both endeavors, also wanted to secure his own presidential legacy, but there was a complicating factor between his newfound dedication to civil rights and his ardent desire to keep the Oval Office and fight a major war in Vietnam: Dr. Martin Luther King, Jr. Although Johnson and King would be forced to work together on civil rights, King was an ardent opponent of the U.S. presence in Vietnam in general and especially of escalating America's role in the conflict.

LBJ figured that King, like his chauffeur, had to be reminded of his place in society—and that place wasn't to be publicly challenging a sitting commander in chief. Given his obvious lack of consideration of ethics or morals, it's no surprise that LBJ chose to send his message to King by wiretapping and extorting the civil rights leader.

Johnson's partner in wiretapping crime was FBI chief J. Edgar Hoover. During the Johnson administration, the FBI spent enormous resources following, photographing, and wiretapping King and other antiwar activists, including gathering evidence of his marital infidelities. (All of this was despite the fact that Johnson had publicly declared his opposition to wiretapping American citizens except on the basis of "national security." Johnson ordered broader surveillance of civil rights advocates at the 1964 Democratic National Convention.)

The Johnson FBI was not hesitant to put the fruits of these efforts into coercing King into submission. They used the information from wiretaps to try to split King from his wife, and they also sent him an unsigned letter claiming that the writer would expose King's unfaithfulness unless he committed suicide:

> No person can overcome the facts, not even a fraud like yourself. Lend your sexually psychotic ear to the enclosure. You will find yourself and in all your dirt, filth, evil and moronic talk exposed on the record for all time. . . . Listen to yourself, you filthy, abnormal animal. You are on the record. . . . King, there is only one thing left for you to do. You know what it is. You have just 34 days in which to do it (this exact number has been selected for a specific reason, it has definite practical significance). You are done. There is but one way out for you. You better take it before your filthy, abnormal fraudulent self is bared to the nation.

King wasn't the only person the Johnson administration (or the FBI) wiretapped and harassed in its efforts to increase and secure

LBJ AND THE PROGRESSIVE VISION FOR NATIONAL HEALTH CARE

In July 1965, President Johnson flew from Washington, D.C., to Independence, Missouri, home of the Harry S. Truman Library. There, with the bespectacled Truman looking on proudly, LBJ signed legislation enacting Medicare into law. Truman had been the first president to endorse a national health insurance program, although Teddy Roosevelt included government-backed health care in his 1912 "Bull Moose" platform.

"It all started with the man from Independence," Johnson said in his thick Texas drawl. He had "planted the seeds of compassion and duty" in the citizens of America.

Then, with one swipe of a pen, the near-century-long progressive dream of beginning the nationalization of health care was realized. Covering the elderly would be the first step in expanding taxpayer-funded health care. Next would be the poor (Medicaid), children (the Children's Health Insurance Program, CHIP), and, eventually, everyone else (Obamacare).

Truman was the first person to receive a Medicare card, number one, and his wife, Bess, received card number two, thereby making the Trumans the first Americans to take part in the nation's greatest Ponzi scheme.

Here's how the scheme works: Because people are living longer than ever before, most Medicare recipients receive far more in benefits than they pay in during their lifetimes. In fact, over a lifetime, beneficiaries receive between two and six dollars in benefits for every dollar they pay in.

Free money, right? Of course not. The benefits paid to today's elderly are funded by those who are currently working and paying into the system. In 1965, six working-age people paid for one Medicare recipient. Today only four workers do, and it's projected to continue getting worse as the population ages and people live longer.

Medicare cannot be sustained, but that hasn't stopped most Republicans from embracing it as a permanent fixture of modern society. President George W. Bush, for example, didn't fight to make Medicare sustainable; he fought to expand it via Medicare Part D, a new prescription-drug benefit plan.

"If you're a low-income senior, the government's going to pick up a significant portion of your tab. . . . If you're an average-income senior, you're going to see your drug bills cut in half," Bush said.

What he didn't say was who would be picking up that tab. It isn't going to be you or me; it's going to be paid for by our children and grandchildren. And that tab is going to be at least $100 trillion, or about the price of some eighty Iraq wars. Your personal share of that $100 trillion comes out to about $330,000, or $1.3 million for a family of four. Perfectly manageable, right?

America's role in the Vietnam War. In 1967, Johnson ordered the CIA to undertake a domestic espionage campaign—Operation CHAOS—to spy on antiwar activists and other dissidents.

Eventually, CHAOS grew to include more than four thousand informers within the antiwar movement, leading to hundreds of thousands of U.S. citizens being placed on watch lists. Thousands of others had wide-ranging files collected on them by the government.

Other Johnson-era domestic spying efforts included the National Security Agency's monitoring of numerous American citizens—including King, as well as members of Congress, reporters, actress Jane Fonda, folksinger Joan Baez, and pediatrician Benjamin Spock. Johnson followed the progressive playbook by realizing that ultimate control had to be an essential element of his agenda—and that can only come with total information. It was the only way to keep the revolution on track.

THE RECKONING

One of the worst things about the progressive approach to governance is the improvisational manner in which massive societal changes are implemented. As the late Democratic iconoclast Senator Daniel Patrick Moynihan, who had a front-row seat to the Great Society as part of Johnson's administration, wrote in *Maximum Feasible Misunderstanding*: "A program was launched that was not understood, and not explained, and this brought about social losses that need not have occurred. . . . The government did not know what it was doing. It had a theory. Or, rather, a set of theories. Nothing more."

And what were the consequences of all this experimentation with our lives and bedrock principles? The counterculture of the 1960s, social breakdown, racial violence, corruption of youth, and cultural nihilism. Not to mention the creation of domestic terrorists, such as Barack Obama's friend Bill Ayers and his Weather Underground, which bombed public buildings in the name of communism and anti-imperialism.

Consider, for example, a young lady from Chicago named Hillary Rodham. In 1964, she was an honest-to-goodness "Goldwater Girl" who supported the Arizona senator against Lyndon Johnson. As late as 1968, she attended the Republican National Convention. But by 1972, she was on her way to being fully radicalized and working on George McGovern's disastrous presidential campaign.

What happened to Hillary? The same thing that happened to countless other promising young Americans in the 1960s: she went to college and learned that the Constitution was flawed, that America

CHILDREN OF THE SIXTIES

Bethel, New York
August 17, 1969

The crowd—dirty, tired, higher than the clouds. The ground—muddy, covered with garbage, and swimming with excrement. Food is scarce, water tainted, and bathrooms nearly nonexistent. The rains aren't cleansing; they just made the muck and feces fluid and easier to spread. Traffic getting in was awful; getting out would be almost impossible.

The "Aquarian Exposition: 3 Days of Peace & Music," otherwise known as Woodstock, was coming to an end. And with it two lives: one dead from a heroin overdose, one from being run over by a tractor.

Surveying the dwindling, dirty crowd late that Sunday morning, Jimi Hendrix wearily swayed with his guitar. He was nervous, and it showed. Despite his massive fame, he hated performing before large crowds.

But he did his job, giving the audience what it wanted, including a tortured, butchering solo guitar version of "The Star-Spangled Banner" that put the exclamation point on the end of the 1960s.

With the set over, Hendrix collapsed backstage, unable to hold himself up by his own power. Awake for nearly three days by that Sunday morning, he was exhausted.

Like the counterculture movement that had elevated him to nearly unprecedented fame, he was a spent force. His body desiccated by drug and alcohol abuse, his soul empty from meaningless sex, and his mind turned away from all that was good by both, his collapse signaled the end of an era.

He'd be dead a year later.

Woodstock was the embodiment of the hedonistic,

consequence-less, do-whatever-you-feel-like society that progressivism unleashed. It was sex in the mud, drugs, rock 'n' roll, no values, no morals, no rules.

The revolt against the old white men of our founding and their outdated, rigid rules and Constitution had morphed into a rebellion against all rules whatsoever. By the 1960s, academia had embraced moral relativism and rejected the classical ideas of virtue and right and wrong. Right and wrong were just abstract ideas; what was right for you was whatever you thought it was.

At the time, few saw the coming danger of this worldview. Most people just saw some crazy kids running around in the mud and the rain. "They'll grow out of it," they thought to themselves. The problem was, many never did.

The children of the sixties, kids who were shaped by this fundamental shift in American values, did not stay children forever. They grew up, and while they may have eventually put on suits and gotten jobs and embraced at least the trappings of mainstream society, their moral relativism never left.

When the members of the Woodstock generation came to inherit the world, they brought Woodstock ideals right along with them.

was evil, and that capitalism was the same thing as imperialism. She emerged—just like her country—as something her parents couldn't recognize anymore.

Of course, Hillary being Hillary, she also got her radical tutelage from leading lights of the progressive and radical Left, including pen pal Saul Alinsky, the godfather of "community organizing," who would prove to be an inspiration to both Obama and Hillary Rodham Clinton. This "community organizing"—a nice branding term for radicalism bordering on terrorism—would turn into the mayhem of riots, terrorism, and lawlessness that would come to define the 1960s.

On January 31, 1967, with his popularity beginning to fade, Lyndon Johnson accepted a portrait of FDR at the White House. He immodestly recalled that he was a "proud friend and follower of President Franklin Roosevelt," to whom "any likeness" is "an inspiration."

Almost three years earlier—on January 30, 1964—Johnson had made glowing remarks to celebrate the eighty-second anniversary of Roosevelt's birth:

> The place of Franklin Delano Roosevelt in our history and in the history of the human race grows steadily with time. Few men in history have served freedom so effectively and so nobly as did he, both in our own land and around the world. His liberal compassion towards his fellowman, together with his conservative respect for the institutions of our economy and society, guided this Nation past the shoals of radicalism and reaction. He provided our ship of state with both the ballast to hold a steady and stable course, and the sail to move us forward progressively toward the broader horizons of human hope.

Such was Johnson's devotion to Roosevelt that as his final act as president, on the morning of his last day in office, he signed a proclamation to create the Franklin Delano Roosevelt Memorial Park.

That was one of the only bright spots in an otherwise dreary end to the LBJ administration. The nation was embroiled in the Vietnam War and overcome with riots and protests by marijuana-smoking young people (the millennials of their time). School buses had been brought to the White House to act as barricades against the thousands of protesters who sang antiwar songs and held up peace signs day and night. The collective chants of "Hey, hey, LBJ, how many kids did you kill today?" could be heard in every room of the White House.

LBJ was leaving the presidency in disgrace, with anger over his failed policies in Vietnam threatening to consume any hope he had of a decent political legacy. Eventually, the man who had worked so hard to gain power had no choice but to walk away from it all. On March 31, 1968, he announced: "I shall not seek, and I will not accept, the nomination of my party for another term as your president."

None of this was what he had envisioned on that tarmac in Dallas just hours after JFK's assassination, but he did accomplish one thing he'd set out to do: he'd realized his Rooseveltian ambitions to remake the federal government and forever shift the popular culture to embrace progressivism.

He'd outdone his idol FDR, and the consequences for America would be far more disastrous.

PROFILE IN FEAR:
PHILIP BERRIGAN AND
THE ANTIWAR MOVEMENT

The Ardennes Forest
December 1944

The sun was just beginning to set when the trucks finally began to roll in.

Phil Berrigan heard them coming before they came into view. The young artilleryman from Minnesota stood next to his howitzer, along with the other men of his battery, and listened to the low rumble of the convoy of 2.5-ton, "deuce-and-a-half" Army trucks.

Berrigan knew their cargo: the trucks were bringing death.

Just a few hours earlier, Berrigan's ears had been assaulted by another rumbling, this one sharper, harsher, and far closer. It was the sound of his own guns. His artillery battery had been busy that afternoon, launching 105-millimeter shells toward the German lines, which, Berrigan knew, lay somewhere inside the tree line a few miles away. The Americans and their British allies elsewhere were launching a counteroffensive, pushing the Germans back through the massive "bulge" they had smashed in the Allied lines earlier in the month.

Berrigan and his comrades had loaded and fired shell after shell as men and trucks and tanks streamed past their position on the outskirts of a bombed-out town, crossing the snow-covered fields on their way to meet Hitler's forces. It was the artillery's job to "soften up" the enemy positions, but by the sounds of the subsequent fighting and the limited reports they'd received from the front lines, the infantry and armor had a real battle on their hands. Now, with the guns silent, the casualties of the day's action were starting to stream back toward the rear.

Berrigan heard a mechanical coughing and sputtering and turned to see another truck approaching from the opposite direction, back toward town. It pulled up to the battery, and a lieutenant poked his head out of the cab.

"Supply depot sent up some more ammo for you boys," he announced. "I need one man from each gun to unload."

Berrigan's gun crew looked at their sergeant, leaning against one of their gun's wheels, who curled his lip around the cigar clenched in his teeth. "Berrigan!" he barked. "You heard the lieutenant!"

"Yes, Sergeant," Berrigan responded, and shuffled toward the supply truck with the other men on the unloading detail. But inside he burned. He had known Sarge would pick him. He was always "randomly" chosen him for extra duties—digging the latrine, cleaning the gun axles, peeling potatoes. Sometimes Sarge would lose his head completely, and the whole gun crew would catch hell, but Berrigan got it the worst, and it made him burn with a fire he knew all too well.

His father, Tom Berrigan, had been like that, too. A man of quick temper, prone to violent mood swings, he ruled over his wife and six sons with impunity—"tyrannical," as Phil would later describe him. Raising his family amid the ravages of the Great Depression, he had young Phil working on the family farm by the age of five.

But Tom Berrigan was also a man of great passion. Always a proud union man—he'd worked on the railroad before losing his job—he eventually became a committed socialist. He raised his sons in his own Irish Catholic tradition but also subscribed to the progressive *Catholic Worker* newspaper, which highlighted the church's work in social justice. Phil's mother, Frida, was a believer in progressive causes, too, and the conversation around their house frequently questioned the established order of things, even of the Catholic Church itself.

The Berrigan boys inherited a complicated legacy from their parents. While Phil was inspired by his father's convictions, he chafed at the despotic manner in which Tom ran his own household. In some ways, Phil was an enhanced reflection of his father. He inherited his father's antiauthoritarian nature, but this was, in turn, amplified in Phil as he grew up under his father's strict rule.

Now, as his artillery unit advanced across Europe after the Normandy landings, Berrigan had already looked death in the eyes a thousand times over. He had seen the bodies of fellow soldiers, mutilated beyond recognition, eyes missing from their empty sockets, shredded muscles and shattered bones sticking out of lifeless torsos. He had seen whole towns destroyed. He had seen the aftermath of the indiscriminate bombings on civilians. Some lay dead in the streets of their villages; others wept over the charred rubble of their homes.

The images stalked his every waking moment. And they didn't leave him when he closed his eyes. The nightmares were intense and unrelenting.

Through it all, the demons in Phil Berrigan's head danced. They followed him and his comrades on the long march to Berlin, leading them on periodic side trips to hell. They coordinated every ambush and guided every sniper's aim. They inhabited the minds of his friends who'd gone stark raving mad under the pressures of combat. They sent artillery shells astray so they landed in the middle of friendly villages rather than on enemy positions. Berrigan had even seen American soldiers pour their fire into a body of troops, only to find out too late that their targets were Americans, too.

Who but demons could have orchestrated that?

And now came the latest pieces of their hellish handiwork. As Berrigan unloaded artillery shells, he had failed to notice that the trucks from the front had made it to his position. They were rumbling past now, into the village beyond, where a field hospital had been set up. Berrigan had seen these grim caravans before. The trucks carried some wounded, too crippled to walk, but mostly they carried the dead. The frozen corpses with rigid arms and legs bounced on tailgates as the truck tires ran over the cobblestones.

The walking wounded shuffled in the wake of the trucks. Those with lighter injuries, only one arm in a sling or a bandage around their heads, helped along their comrades who couldn't walk. Some leaned on their rifles for support. Here and there, a man was carried on a stretcher—the trucks had run out of room. The men were coughing, wheezing, moaning, cursing with every painful step. Cigarettes dangled from some lips, all unlit—not even the smallest fires stood a chance against this cold.

These were shells of soldiers, bearded and bedraggled, only shreds of clothing between them and the frigid wind. They reminded Berrigan of the vagrants who'd come begging at their door during the Depression. Those men would always get a meal from his mother, cooked with whatever she had to spare. But there was nothing Berrigan himself could do for the men who now passed by him.

As Berrigan looked up from his work, he saw that interspersed with the walking American wounded were German prisoners, many of them wounded themselves. They were carrying wounded Americans with M1 Garand rifles pointed at their backs every step of the way. As he looked at the worst of the German wounded—men with legs, arms, whole chunks of their bodies shot away—his insides began to twist themselves into knots. These weren't wounds made by bullets or even hand grenades, he realized.

LIARS

145

These were the victims of artillery shells, *his* shells. These were the men who'd been right under their initial "softening-up" barrage. Maybe the shells that had ripped their flesh had even been loaded by Berrigan and fired from his howitzer.

Yes, these were supposed to be his enemies, but they were men first, and he had harmed them. And for what? Because his cause was supposed to be more just than theirs? What was just about this violence, this brutality? What was just about killing any of God's creations?

As this macabre procession of broken men straggled by and these thoughts played in his mind, Berrigan and his comrades unloaded more and more shells. These shells would make more carnage, which would make more broken and dead men, who in their turn would straggle past Berrigan's artillery position later on. On and on it would go.

And suddenly, it all became too much. The fear of death and war consumed him. Carrying a 105-millimeter shell toward his gun, Berrigan closed his eyes to try to shut out the demons from his brain. He was shaking, his arms trembling under the weight of the shell and his anxiety about who else it might kill next. He lost his balance and tripped, falling to his knees in the snow. Sarge started barking immediately. Berrigan knew he had to get up, and he would. But now, finding himself kneeling down in this forsaken place, still cradling his weapon of war, he lifted his face to the cold, gray, and ever darkening sky.

"Never again," he vowed silently to the God he'd grown up worshipping. "Once I get through this, never again."

Then Phil Berrigan got to his feet and went back to war.

After World War II, Phil Berrigan followed his brother Daniel into the priesthood. His fear of death and his utter revulsion at

war never left him. He turned to Catholicism, but he embraced
the new kind that preached social justice and liberation from the
conservative orthodoxies that had dogged the church for centuries.

The terror he had felt on the battlefields of Europe compelled
Berrigan to begin a crusade to ensure that others never experienced the same. He was not able to eliminate war, as he had
hoped to do on that snowy evening in 1944, but the Berrigan
brothers did wage their own "war against war" through the latter
half of the twentieth century, with a militancy of method that was
surprising in such self-described pacifists.

While they first preached passive resistance in 1967, as the
Vietnam War protests grew, they declared themselves revolutionaries for peace and social justice and sought to achieve those ends
by any means necessary. With a group of other protesters who
would become known as the Catonsville Nine, they stole draft
records from a government office in Catonsville, Maryland, and
set them on fire using a concoction of their own design made to
resemble napalm.

Blood was another one of the Berrigans' weapons of choice.
They doused draft cards in it and threw them at the doors of the
Pentagon. In 1976, they picketed the home of then–Secretary of
Defense Donald Rumsfeld, whose young children had to walk to
school through a line of Phil Berrigan's shouting acolytes. They
were arrested only after they started digging a "grave" on the
Rumsfelds' lawn.

The Berrigans hatched plots to kidnap Henry Kissinger and plant
bombs under federal buildings in Washington. They also cycled
in and out of jail. By 1993, Phil Berrigan had been arrested one
hundred times and had spent about six years in prison.

♠

Berrigan tried for decades to fight his way past the traumas he'd experienced in World War II, but he failed to realize that no amount of blood sprayed, draft cards burned, or criminal plots concocted can change basic human nature, including its violent elements. Being human means that our worst tendencies and instincts will recur, no matter how idiotic they might seem to the "enlightened." As Rudyard Kipling wrote in *Gods of the Copybook Headings* after losing his son in World War I:

> *As it will be in the future, it was at the birth of Man—*
> *There are only four things certain since Social Progress began:—*
> *That the Dog returns to his Vomit and the Sow returns to her Mire,*
> *And the burnt Fool's bandaged finger goes wabbling back to the Fire.*

Human instinct, like that of dogs and sows, is impossible to change. No matter how many times we are burned, the fire still beckons for our hand once more. Most people understand these immutable ground rules of life.

Progressives do not.

5

Fourth Wave:

The Hope and Change of Barack Obama

We are five days away from fundamentally transforming the United States of America.

—BARACK OBAMA, 2008

Chicago, Illinois
July 1995

The future president of the United States stood in the living room of a domestic terrorist.

They were in Hyde Park, a Chicago neighborhood of tree-lined streets dotted with handsome old stone and brick houses. In this highly segregated city, Hyde Park stands out as a vibrant, racially diverse but monolithically leftist melting pot. There couldn't be a more fitting place for a future commander in chief to live, just mere blocks away from former domestic terrorists, not to mention Nation of Islam leader Louis Farrakhan.

Hyde Park is home to the prestigious University of Chicago, but venture just a few blocks outside the neighborhood, and you'll find yourself in the middle of Chicago's notorious South Side. The ivory tower of elitist academics looms over crippled communities riddled with drugs, gangs, and broken homes. The slums and Section 8 housing projects are home to some of the highest murder rates in the civilized world. The wreckage caused by decades of leftist rule iron-ically lies all around the progressive Hyde Park denizens, although they refuse to acknowledge it, let alone take any responsibility for it.

"Barry, if I have one lesson for you," Bill Ayers said, "it's this: if you really want to change things, you've got to drop the radical pose for the radical ends. You're a talented community organizer; politics is just community organizing on a larger scale. People project their hopes, dreams, and aspirations on you. They don't expect you to actually solve all of their problems, but they want you to say you'll try."

Barack Obama, a thirty-four-year-old aspiring politician, listened intently. "What matters more than what you say," Ayers continued, "is how you say it. You can play on fear, but ultimately you also have to give people the antidote, and that is hope. We lost a genera-tion of progress because we didn't understand that simple rule."

Obama grinned as he put out his cigarette, anticipating the arrival of his wife, Michelle, and Ayers's wife, Bernadine Dohrn, as well as many guests whom he would attempt to dazzle out of their money that night. The duo of Ayers and Dohrn was nothing if not dynamic. The two had spent almost eleven years on the run, fugitives from the law. In fact, Dohrn had achieved the distinction of making the FBI's Ten Most Wanted list, all the more impressive considering that only nine women have ever been listed there.

What were they running from? Ayers, Dohrn, and their Weather Underground coconspirators had sought to spark a full-on Communist revolution in the 1960s and '70s, by destroying prop-erty and killing those who got in the way. After the two grew tired of running and finally turned themselves in to authorities, only Dohrn faced charges, and they were minor.

Blessed with unexpected freedom, the two revolutionaries con-
tinued to adhere to their beliefs, never expressing remorse for their
crimes. Dohrn eventually landed at the prominent law firm Sidley
Austin—the same firm where Barack would later meet Michelle—
and she later served as a professor of law at Northwestern Uni-
versity. Ayers reinvented himself as a professor of education at the
University of Illinois, where he got to shape young minds on a daily
basis, this time without explosives.

As they finished their conversation, Obama, ever the shrewd
politician, asked one last question: "What do I tell people if they
ask about our relationship?"

Ayers displayed his characteristic mischievous smirk. "Just tell
them I was a guy in the neighborhood." Then he turned and opened
the front door to a stream of prospective Obama donors.

As it turned out, it was the opening of a door that would one
day lead right to the White House.

Looking back, as improbable as it may seem, the same system that Obama
would later claim was rigged had actually worked out quite well for
him. A man who grew up in a fractured home had ended up attending the greatest academic institutions in the world and was now on
the cusp of a meteoric rise in Illinois politics, an ideal place to cut
one's teeth and build a progressive power base.

In the middle of it all were these radicals–turned–educators who
had once led the Weathermen, an organization that was responsible
for twenty-five bombings on American soil, including attacks at
the U.S. Capitol, the Pentagon, and New York Police Department
headquarters. The group had murdered at least seven people, including three police officers, and they didn't seem to have a whole
lot of sympathy. "In a revolution," Ayers once told a Weathermen

colleague who'd become an FBI informant, "some people have to die."

And now this group of aging revolutionaries had found an ambitious young man with a zeal for politics and a strong progressive streak right in their own backyard.

He was the messenger they had been searching for.

THE MAKING OF A PROGRESSIVE

There have been all kinds of wild attacks leveled against Barack Obama: that he's a Third World sympathizer, a secret Islamic Manchurian candidate, a devotee of Saul Alinsky (OK, maybe this one is true), an undocumented Kenyan illegal immigrant, an avowed socialist, and so on. I'm wary of conspiracy theories like these because they assume a certain amount of forethought and malice. We cannot look into Obama's heart and know what he truly feels.

But we can certainly judge him by his words and actions.

Obama calls himself a progressive. He has spent his entire life proving his devotion to this cause; sacrificing Democratic majorities in both houses of Congress; lying to, alienating, and dividing millions of Americans; and endangering the nation by empowering its worst enemies to advance his agenda.

By background, association, words, and actions, President Obama's progressivism has pervaded almost every aspect of the man's life. His ability to seamlessly combine leftist ideology with community-organizing tactics designed to win over a nation demanding "change" in a time of crisis has helped to usher in a new wave of progressivism. In its short time, this wave has already eroded the limited government victories of the Reagan Revolution and of the moderates under Bill Clinton who'd seemingly accepted the new reality of smaller, more effective federal government. Obama has returned the Democratic

Party to the unapologetically liberal, government-expanding tradition of FDR and LBJ—and this wave may just be getting started.

Obama came from a progressive family in a progressive state. But unlike that of those who preceded him, elites such as the Roosevelts or even many of the leading leftist agitators of the '60s, Obama's broken background betrayed the fact that he was destined for prominence. He was born with no silver spoon in his mouth, no bourgeois upbringing to rebel against. He was a living product of the civil rights movement of the '60s, the son of a black Kenyan man who left him and his mother, Stanley Ann Dunham, a white woman from Kansas who later married an Indonesian.

Young Barack's early years were spent in exotic locales—Honolulu with his mother and Jakarta with his stepfather's family. For long stretches during his childhood, Dunham left young Barack to be taken care of by her parents.

A Norman Rockwell painting this was not.

The near-total absence of his biological father, combined with his mother's transience, could not have been easy on Barack. Yet Dunham proved to be a strong, if unconventional, influence. According to a profile by Tim Jones in Obama's hometown newspaper, the *Chicago Tribune*:

> [*T*]*he parental traits that would mold him [Obama]—a contrarian worldview, an initial rejection of organized religion, a questioning nature—were already taking shape years earlier in the nomadic and sometimes tempestuous Dunham family, where the only child was a curious and precocious daughter of a father who wanted a boy so badly that he named her Stanley—after himself.*

Politically, Dunham ran in leftist intellectual circles that questioned the capitalist system. Even as a student she was known to ask her teacher, "What's wrong with communism?" The church her family attended while she was growing up in Washington State was dubbed "The Little Red Church on the Hill" because of its radical ties.

Obama later described his mother as a "lonely witness for secular humanism, a soldier for New Deal, Peace Corps, position-paper liberalism." Dunham's political leanings are relevant here because Obama himself says they are. "The values she taught me," he said, "continue to be my touchstone when it comes to how I go about the world of politics."

Obama's father seemed to share a similar ideology to that of Dunham. One white paper drafted by Obama Sr. indicates that he felt there was nothing theoretically wrong with a one hundred percent tax rate and that nationalizing industries and economic redistribution were chief aims of government.

Young Obama's time in college further reflects the influences of those with whom he spent his youth. As he later wrote about his college years:

> To avoid being mistaken for a sellout, I chose my [college] friends carefully. The more politically active black students. The foreign students. The Chicanos. The Marxist professors and structural feminists and punk-rock performance poets. . . . At night in the dorms we discussed neocolonialism . . . [Franz] Fanon, Eurocentrism, and patriarchy . . . we were resisting bourgeois society's stifling constraints.

At Occidental College, Obama was known to hang out with the "kids most concerned with issues of social justice." John C. Drew, an Occidental classmate, has indicated that based on conversations with Obama during their college days, the future president was a "doctrinaire Marxist revolutionary, although perhaps—for the first time—considering conventional politics as a more practical road to socialism."

THE CLOWARD-PIVEN STRATEGY

In May 1966, two Columbia sociologists named Richard Cloward and Frances Fox Piven took to the pages of the iconic leftist magazine *The Nation* to pen an important essay titled "The Weight of the Poor: A Strategy to End Poverty."

The idea was astoundingly simple—and sinister: overload the public welfare system at the state and local levels to precipitate a debt crisis that would plunge America even further into poverty. Washington, D.C., would then have no choice but to act and implement a federally guaranteed minimum income level for every American.

"The ultimate objective of this strategy—to wipe out poverty by establishing a guaranteed annual income—will be questioned by some," they wrote. "Because the ideal of individual social and economic mobility has deep roots, even activists seem reluctant to call for national programs to eliminate poverty by the outright *redistribution of income*."

The Cloward-Piven strategy would overcome those pesky American ideas of individual and economic mobility through a sudden, cataclysmic economic collapse in which millions of people would be forced to become wards of the state, dependent on government for food stamps and basic income. A massive economic crisis would necessitate radical change.

Piven pitched a voter-registration strategy to "radicalize the Democratic Party and polarize the country along class lines," which would be accomplished through collaboration with community-organizing ally the Association of Community Organizations for Reform Now (ACORN), Project Vote, and others over the next two decades.

Cloward-Piven was a resounding success. Beginning with LBJ's "War on Poverty," the number of welfare recipients grew from 4.3 million to 10.8 million in the nine years from 1965 to

1974. Another 100 million Americans now collect some form of check from the government, totaling $1 trillion annually.

The Cloward-Piven strategy succeeded with the urban poor beyond anyone's wildest dreams. It's been accelerated with Obamacare and the addition of tens of millions of Americans to federally subsidized health-care programs that Americans can't afford. The next front very likely involves the country's southern border.

We wonder why progressive politicians have no objections to open borders and millions of illegals flooding the welfare rolls and driving up our debt. But we shouldn't wonder, because the answer was given to us by Cloward and Piven long ago. After all, an unsustainable federal government is only a bad thing if you believe in the current system.

After transferring to Columbia University, Obama says, he attended "socialist conferences." Author Stanley Kurtz places him at the 1983 Socialist Scholars Conference that celebrated the centenary of Karl Marx's death. Delivering the opening remarks at that conference was City University of New York professor Frances Fox Piven, a famed leftist sociologist and advocate of the Cloward-Piven strategy to crater the American economy and replace it with a socialist system.

Activists, slam poets, artists, ivory tower professors, amateur philosophers, social justice advocates—these were the people Obama had known for years. These were the people he felt most comfortable around. He loved the to-and-fro of debate in college seminars. He loved the adrenaline that came from knocking on doors, urging complete strangers to vote for causes. He was a proud activist.

In 1992, Obama directed Project Vote's Chicago voter-registration drive, helping to elect the socialist-linked Carol Mosely Braun to the U.S. Senate. While at Columbia, he published an editorial in the

Columbia Sundial in favor of disarmament, with the goal of a nuclear-free world. This position would later reappear in 2009, when, as president, Obama vowed that "the United States will take concrete steps towards a world without nuclear weapons."

Obama's community organizing in Chicago further reflected, and also likely reinforced, his progressive principles. "Community organizing" was what socialists had done for decades in an effort to hide their true socialist beliefs behind a facade of "populism." The idea was to push the country toward socialism gradually, under the guise of pragmatic "problem-solving."

Three of Obama's mentors studied at the Industrial Areas Foundation, an organization founded by Saul Alinsky that advocates a variety of leftist policies. Alinsky himself sought a socialist "future where the means of production will be owned by all the people instead of just a comparative handful." To achieve this end, he developed organizing strategies and tactics (most notably in his book *Rules for Radicals*) that provided the foundational playbook for Obama's political rise.

While it may have been self-serving, what Alinsky's own son wrote of Obama in a 2008 *Boston Globe* editorial is telling:

> Barack Obama's training in Chicago by the great community organizers is showing its effectiveness. It is an amazingly powerful format, and the method of my late father always works to get the message out and get the supporters on board. When executed meticulously and thoughtfully, it is a powerful strategy for initiating change. . . . Obama learned his lesson well.

Obama would continue to support these causes as a civil rights attorney when he practiced at Miner Barnhill & Galland, representing, among others, community organizers such as ACORN.

The friends and advisors Obama has surrounded himself with shared a similar progressive vision to his own. Consider, for example, that the man who had the greatest influence on Obama's faith, baptizing the future president and officiating at his wedding ceremony, was Reverend Jeremiah Wright. You'll recall that Wright yelled things like "God damn America," blamed 9/11 on American foreign policy, and accused whites of being endemically racist. But Wright also provided Obama with a first-class education in black liberation theology, a school of thought that added a religious tinge to the progressivism Obama had imbibed.

Obama would later speak of the need for fellow progressives to understand and internalize faith, both as a political imperative and because the values provided by faith would help make a progressive vision a reality.

Another close Obama friend was Columbia University professor Rashid Khalidi. Khalidi is an acolyte of Arabist and anti-Israel professor Edward Said, whose famous book *Orientalism* paints the West as the racist, imperialist, colonialist oppressor of the Islamic world. Israel is cast in this progressive dialectic as the "powerful" or "victimizer," against the "powerless" or "victim" Arabs. The small, formerly socialist Jewish nation surrounded by bloodthirsty enemies had morphed from David to Goliath in the Left's historical reading.

Khalidi has been an Obama ally since the 1990s, hosting him for social functions and organizing a fund-raiser during Obama's unsuccessful 2000 congressional bid. It also happens that Khalidi is a close friend of Ayers. He, like Ayers and Obama, lived in Hyde Park while teaching at the University of Chicago during the 1990s.

Why so much attention to Obama's friends? Simple. "Show me your friends, and I'll show you your future" is not just a popular saying, it's a fact. We've seen the president's friends . . . and now we're starting to see our own future.

THE MARKETING OF A PROGRESSIVE

Obama's background and associations were a toxic brew of progressivism that made him an easy political target, not just for conservatives but also for moderate Democrats who rejected the excesses of the 1960s leftists. Obama knew this, which is why—like most shrewd progressives who aspired to the highest elected office in the land, from Wilson to FDR to LBJ—Obama hid his more radical views under the cloak of "liberalism."

Obama's public rhetoric on many issues appears to be moderate and within the liberal mainstream. It is the kernels of progressivism embedded within his words and the broader narrative he crafts that reflect a symmetry between his life's work and associations and the beliefs to which he adheres. This tactical calculation is consistent with what he learned as a community organizer.

Here's how this works in practice. While a nonpolitician progressive (such as influential historian Howard Zinn, for example) will say that America's experiment has been immoral, Obama will rephrase that to say that the mistreatment of Native Americans and our original sin of slavery indicate that we have not always lived up to our values and that we must still be better.

Obama may not overtly attack the rich, but he will argue that they ought to pay their "fair share" and that at some point people have earned "enough."

He will not exhibit blatant hostility toward private business, but he will admit that he sides with labor and that regulations can help strengthen the economy while protecting the environment.

He will not claim that America is a racist nation, but he will say that there are issues of race that still have not been overcome and that minorities continue to have legitimate grievances.

He will not explicitly say that his framework is dialectical—that is, based on the Marxian vision of looking at the world through a prism of competing races, classes, and sexes, such as the oppressors versus the oppressed, the victimizer versus the victim—but he will admit to standing with the "powerless."

In Obama's book *The Audacity of Hope*, almost every argument is presented as follows: *Conservatives believe X. Liberals believe Y. While both sides have legitimate concerns, and we should respect conservatives for their beliefs, I stand with liberals.*

While Obama is quick to praise the free market, such praise is almost always followed with a "but." During a 2005 address, he said that "our greatness as a nation has depended . . . on a belief in the free market. But it has also depended on our sense of mutual regard for each other, the idea that everybody has a stake in the country, that we're all in it together."

"But." There's that word, when there really shouldn't be one. *I love our constitution, but . . .*

As he would later argue during a speech in Osawatomie, Kansas, the spot at which Teddy Roosevelt had delivered his famous "New Nationalism" address a century earlier, "We simply cannot return to this brand of 'you're on your own' economics if we're serious about rebuilding the middle class in this country."

Noting that Roosevelt's critics had called him a "socialist" and "even a communist" for his views, Obama said that "we are a richer nation and a strong democracy" for having fought for progressive goals such as "an eight-hour work day and a minimum wage for women . . . insurance for the unemployed . . . political reform and a progressive income tax." Progressivism trumps the caricature of free market economics.

While Obama purports to believe in individualism, he also argues that America can only be strong when it acts collectively. During his heralded keynote address at the 2004 Democratic National Convention, he said that "alongside our famous individualism . . . is that fundamental belief [that] I am my brother's keeper, I am my sister's keeper, that makes this country work." In Obama's thinking, the nation is one big family with all of the responsibilities that entails. What he does not make explicit, however, is that this belief revolves around government coercion rather than voluntary action. Families look out for one another because they want to. Taxes, on the other hand, are involuntary.

Obama delivered a commencement address in 2005 at the University of Chicago's Pritzker School of Medicine, arguing that "our individual salvation depends on collective salvation." For him, government is seen as a positive force that provides opportunity, rather than as the impediment to liberty that it really is. Government plays the central role in wealth creation, while labor unions play a central role in making sure that such wealth is distributed "fairly." And remember that inequality of outcomes is the great progressive scourge. Obama has called it "the defining challenge of our time," one that can only be solved, of course, by government intervention.

Obama is clear in *The Audacity of Hope* about his progressive view of the Constitution. After acknowledging the merits of Supreme Court Justice Antonin Scalia's originalism, he wrote: "I have to side with Justice Breyer's view of the Constitution—that it is not a static but rather a living document, and must be read in the context of an ever-changing world." This constitutional philosophy is consistent with the idea touched on earlier about Obama's Dewey-like "pragmatism" and is directly reflected in his appointments of Justices Sonia Sotomayor and Elena Kagan.

Several other themes come to the forefront throughout Obama's addresses: an emphasis on "shared prosperity" and the struggle for "social justice"; a belief in "global citizenship" and the idea that all nations, not just America, are "exceptional"; an acknowledgment of

America's past sins across the world and a belief that to rectify them requires apology, multilateralism, diplomacy, and treating even our mortal enemies with "mutual respect."

Most critical of all for Obama is the power of "change." Claremont-McKenna Professor Charles Kesler wrote that the president "believes that change is almost always synonymous with improvement, that history has a direction and destination, that it's crucial to be on the right side of history . . . and that it's the leader's job to discern which is the right side and to lead his people to that promised land of social equality and social justice."

Kesler continued:

> *Obama says, "Yes, we can" to slaves, abolitionists, immigrants, western pioneers, suffragettes, the space program, healing this nation, and repairing the world—and that's in one speech. . . . "Yes, we can" takes the place in his thought that "all men are created equal" held in Lincoln's thought. Insofar as it is America's national creed, it affirms that America is what we make it at any given time: America stands for the ability to change, openness to change, the willingness to constantly remake ourselves. . . . The country's saving principle, then, is openness to change.*

But Obama's obsession with change reflects a belief that America's fundamental principles of individual liberty, limited government, and peace through strength are rotten to the core. As a result, progress in his view can only be achieved by minimizing or, ideally, eliminating these principles from the American mind-set.

And that is exactly what Obama would seek to do as president.

OBAMA'S DOMESTIC POLICY: ROOSEVELTIAN BIG
GOVERNMENT FOR THE TWENTY-FIRST CENTURY

One political figure is mentioned more than any living Democrat in Obama's autobiography: Franklin Delano Roosevelt.

It should come as no surprise, then, that in many respects, Obama's domestic policy has paralleled that of the great progressive leader, beginning with his approach to the worst financial crisis since the Great Depression.

In Obama's first inaugural address, the newly minted president called for, what else, action. He declared:

> For everywhere we look, there is work to be done. The state of our economy calls for action, bold and swift. And we will act, not only to create new jobs, but to lay a new foundation for growth. We will build the roads and bridges, the electric grids and digital lines that feed our commerce and bind us together. We'll restore science to its rightful place, and wield technology's wonders to raise health care's quality and lower its cost. We will harness the sun and the winds and the soil to fuel our cars and run our factories.

Note the progressive implication here that jobs come from government rather than from private enterprise. Also note that everything the president advocates is about "we," that is, the collective, under the aegis of the state.

The president continued: "The question we ask today is not whether our government is too big or too small, but whether it works—whether it helps families find jobs at a decent wage, care they can afford, a retirement that is dignified."

Once in office, President Obama moved swiftly so as not to let this crisis go to waste. His first task was to address the financial sector, a

place where George W. Bush had set the tone and where, like Herbert
Hoover, Bush deserves scorn for abandoning "free market principles
to save the free market system."

The key piece of Bush's bank bailout was his Troubled Asset Relief
Program (TARP). The bailout of the private sector by the state was
a major coup for progressives. Obama expanded this initiative, ap-
propriating hundreds of billions of more dollars and overseeing the
bailout of the auto industry. TARP was supposed to be limited to
financial institutions, but the program provided an opportunity for
Obama to expand the government's tentacles into other industries
on behalf of "powerless" political allies. Specifically, Obama ran
roughshod over the bankruptcy code on behalf of the United Auto
Workers union that had bankrupted Chrysler and General Motors in
the first place, and he did so while abrogating the property rights of
creditors.

FDR had taken a similar view of state power during times of crisis
and, as Obama would, he had done so on behalf of his progressive
union allies. Labor's priorities are progressive priorities.

The sweeping Dodd-Frank financial regulation bill was purportedly created to help ensure that no financial institution would become
"too big to fail." But again, just like FDR's, the Obama administration's hyperregulation of the financial-services industry, purported
to protect Americans against needless risk-taking, instead ensures that
bailouts will become a regular part of the system.

Dodd-Frank's Title II allows federal regulators to "seize troubled
financial firms—with minimal judicial review—and close down their
affairs." Taxpayers will be on the hook for the most troubled assets
on financial institutions' books should the Federal Deposit Insurance
Corporation seize them. In other words, government's power to intervene rather than letting market forces work has only grown, and
moral hazard has grown right along with it.

Perhaps more insidiously, the Obama administration has used

its "crackdown" on the financial-services industry to pay off its community-organizing friends as part of settlements that several large banks have reached with the Department of Justice. So not only has punitive justice been brought against these firms, but the Obama administration has then gone on to redistribute their wealth to its friends. Remember, do as I say, not as I do. It's a hallmark of progressives everywhere.

On the other hand, the notion that implementing more onerous financial regulations would help make for a healthier banking system has, in reality, served to benefit the big banks, just as the regulatory framework that FDR implemented during the Great Depression helped turn the financial-services industry into a cartel. Small institutions have paid the price, with community banks seeing their total assets decline by forty percent since 1994, while big banks have only grown even bigger.

Obama's "stimulus" projects represented another Rooseveltian throwback, reflecting the progressive belief in the state as the employer of last resort. And just as with Roosevelt, the bang for the collective taxpayer buck was minimal, unless one was politically connected. According to George Mason University professor Veronique de Rugy, Democratic congressional districts received an average of $471.5 million in stimulus funds, while Republican congressional districts received an average of $260.6 million.

Billions more from the stimulus was doled out in the form of pork for Senate Democrats. Of the 594,754 jobs allegedly "created or saved," more than two-thirds were to be found in the Department of Education. One study even suggests that the stimulus destroyed or forestalled one million private-sector jobs.

Obama also took a page from the FDR playbook by using the IRS to chill political dissent, with the agency targeting Tea Party groups that were seeking tax-exempt status. The IRS's "slow-walking" of such groups' applications prevented many of them from being able to participate in the 2010 and 2012 federal elections. Progressives purport to believe in tolerance and diversity, but those things usually extend only to those who are progressive.

On the Second Amendment, Obama has tried repeatedly to take advantage of virtually every crisis and tragedy to work to limit Americans' gun rights, including taking executive action. Progressives argue that such restrictions will increase public safety. In reality, progressive enclaves such as Chicago, which have some of the most stringent gun laws in the nation, also have some of the highest rates of "gun violence." Harvard's John Lott, Jr., meanwhile has shown time and again that "more guns equal less crime." (See my book *Control* for every stat and study you've ever wanted to know about refuting the gun-grabber arguments that always appear after a tragedy.) And in another case of "do what I say," those in dangerous communities are left unarmed while "Operation Fast and Furious" authorized gun dealers to sell two thousand weapons to drug cartels, weapons that were used in the murders of hundreds of Mexicans, as well as U.S. Border Patrol agent Brian Terry.

Speaking of the Mexican border, Obama's unconstitutional executive amnesty reflects the progressive ethos that we are all citizens of the world, that there are no borders, and that the executive must be able to act in the face of an intransigent legislature. Amnesty is really about two things: multiculturalism, one of progressivism's highest values, and ensuring a permanent progressive majority in the country by adding millions of new likely Democratic voters to the rolls. (Not to mention the implications of the Cloward-Piven strategy of overloading the system to force a collapse.)

The Obama administration has also gone about purging individuals and documents describing the jihadist threat in the jihadists' own terms. Language has been removed, for example, from federal law-enforcement training materials because Muslim groups—including at least one with known ties to terror—told the FBI that they found it offensive. Among the "offensive" language? A mention of al Qaeda's connection to the 1993 World Trade Center bombing attempt.

Obama has repeatedly refused to acknowledge that jihadists have anything to do with Islam, calling their ideology "nihilistic." This view is consistent with the (contradictory) progressive idea that we should not judge another's religion but that Islam is a religion of peace and Muslim terrorists are merely perverting it. Worse, he put the very front groups that advanced the agenda of Islamic supremacists in America in charge of the "outreach" efforts created in order to "counter violent extremism."

Meanwhile, as jihadists have waged war on America's homeland, the Obama Justice Department has expressed its gravest concern over hostile speech toward Muslims by Americans, threatening that it could prosecute those who use such language. There is little more progressive than whitewashing a serious threat emanating from the Muslim community while then presenting the Muslim community as the victim and threatening the so-called aggressors by infringing on their constitutional rights.

Environmentalism is another key part of progressive ideology, dictating that ecological concerns trump economic ones. The Obama administration has argued that global warming is the greatest threat to the planet, requiring that Americans eschew economic progress by drastically curtailing their activities in order to prevent its acceleration. Ignored is that in order to achieve such goals, there are billions of public dollars, including $2.5 billion in annual "federal climate change expenditures" alone, being doled out (translation: redistributed) to advance this narrative.

Obama finally killed the job-creating Keystone Pipeline, after slow-walking it for years, citing environmental concerns. He did, however, use government funding to back "green jobs" initiatives that resulted in hundreds of millions of dollars and thousands of jobs being lost and/or outsourced, including those at Solyndra.

Meanwhile, economic costs of the policy aside, the president agreed to a deal with the Chinese in which America would reduce its emissions by between twenty-six percent and twenty-eight percent compared with 2005 levels by 2025. Who would pay for this drastic reduction? The coal industry, in theory, but ultimately, we all will pay. Obama's power-plant provisions associated with emissions reductions are expected to cost America 125,800 jobs and create a GDP loss of $650 billion over a ten-year period. This was consistent with Obama's 2008 statement that his cap-and-trade plan would bankrupt those who sought to build coal plants. Progressives are willing to destroy industries in the service of their ideological agenda.

And then there is perhaps the progressive movement's most important victory, the culmination of an obsession that began with FDR's Second Bill of Rights. It was Obama's analogue to Roosevelt's Social Security and Lyndon Johnson's Medicare and Medicaid, his great entitlement, now cast as a civil rights issue: Obamacare.

True to FDR's aim, Obamacare sought, at least superficially, to provide health care for all by way of government force, something those on the left had been pushing for more than a century. It treated health care as a right to be granted by the state. As Vice President Joe Biden clearly articulated it, it was a "big f*cking deal."

While not the vaunted "single-payer, universal health care" that Obama and his progressive allies relished, the deceptively named Affordable Care Act did fundamentally change not only market-based health insurance but the entire American health-care system itself. It laid the groundwork for a collapse (à la Cloward-Piven) that will inevitably shepherd in a more pure version of socialized medicine down the road. And most important, it made Americans begin to question those key principles of individual liberty and limited government and ask themselves, if the state can take control of health care, what can't it take control of?

Kesler makes the case that Obamacare is an echo of FDR's National Industrial Recovery Act, in that it gave the state power over "a huge swath of the economy through collusive price-fixing, restraints on production, aversion to competition, and corporatist partnerships between industry and government." Also in line with FDR's anticapitalist actions during the Great Depression, the multiple-thousand-page Obamacare bill created a staggering 159 new bureaucracies—programs, commissions, and boards. This massive expansion of the administrative state and the corresponding reduction in individual liberty grants unelected "enlightened technocrats" unprecedented power over Americans from pregnancy through old age. Woodrow Wilson could have only dreamed of such a system.

Obamacare, with its newly empowered and unaccountable bureaucrats, is what passes for law when you believe in a living constitution. At root, it turns the American system—where every man is supposed to be king—on its head by making us subjects of the state. All in the name of "progress" and change.

The undemocratic process by which Obamacare was rammed through, without any Republican votes in either house of Congress, was characteristic of progressives who shun the checks and balances enshrined in the Constitution. As revealed by MIT professor Jonathan Gruber—an architect of the legislation who traveled around the country shilling for it as a paid spokesman for the Obama administration—the promises of the law, namely lower health-care costs and the idea that "if you like your health plan, you can keep your health plan," were knowingly fraudulent claims. Just more evidence that, for progressives, the ends always justify the means.

Then-Speaker Nancy Pelosi made clear the Democrats' intent to ensure Obamacare's passage, no matter what: "We'll go through the gate. If the gate's closed, we'll go over the fence. If the fence is too high, we'll pole vault in. If that doesn't work, we'll parachute in but we're going to get health care reform passed for the American people." When questioned about the constitutionality of the legislation, Pelosi's response was only, "Are you serious?"

In granting government control over one-sixth of the economy (and, in particular, the one-sixth that affects every individual in the most personal way), Obamacare, in its passage, substance, and implementation, has proven to be the most progressive piece of legislation in U.S. history. It cost the Democrats the House of Representatives and ultimately the Senate, but those are just battles. The war itself was won.

In addition to this game-changing entitlement, there are numerous other progressive policies that Obama has pursued, echoing Depression-era governmental programs. Just like FDR, Obama purported to help struggling Americans with these policies, but what he primarily accomplished was growing government and executive power. Consider some of the other progressive wins Obama has racked up:

- Using recess appointment power when the Senate was not in recess—thwarting constitutional checks and balances.
- Seeking to force public schools to use racial quotas to determine how and when to punish students for misbehaving—thwarting the federalist structure in an attempt to socially engineer based on progressive notions of "fairness" and "justice."
- Forcing universities nationwide to strip protections from college students accused of sexual misconduct—violating due process rights.
- Ignoring the law requiring that the president give thirty days' notice to Congress before releasing jihadists from Guantanamo Bay, Cuba—thwarting the system of checks and balances.
- Attempting to impose an unconstitutional nationwide speech code on college campuses—thwarting the First Amendment.

PROGRESSIVE "HELP"
FOR THE NEEDIEST

What were the ultimate outcomes of policies designed to support society's underdogs? In 2009, 33.5 million Americans were on food stamps. By 2015, the average participation rate had risen to 45.8 million.

The unemployment rate, which was once as high as ten percent, has now fallen to five percent, but the numbers are misleading. The falling rate appears to have been driven by a mass increase in the number of people who have dropped out of the workforce altogether. In late 2009, as unemployment peaked, there were about 82.5 million people out of the workforce. That number has now grown to 95 million. Obama's "recovery" has been one of the slowest in American history. Blacks and Hispanics, constituencies that broadly supported the president's progressive agenda, have been hit particularly hard.

Those who have jobs aren't immune. Health-insurance costs have spiraled out of control since Obamacare's inception, with forty-nine states seeing premium hikes in 2016. There are also at least a thousand ongoing investigations into potential ISIS members in the United States. And last but not least, the national debt rose from $10.6 trillion when Obama took office in January 2009 to more than $19 trillion as of February 2016.

It is expected to reach $20 trillion by the end of his presidency.

- Arguing several property rights cases rejected unanimously by the Supreme Court, under which Obama's Environmental Protection Agency showed severe contempt for such rights through coercion—thwarting constitutionally protected private property rights.

The fact that these policies represent only a fraction of the progressive Obama priorities foisted on the public under the banner of "fairness, justice, and equality" indicates that the Obama administration has overloaded our system under one big Cloward–Piven crusade for privileges masquerading as "rights."

In 2008, Obama made an astute observation: "I think Ronald Reagan changed the trajectory of America in a way that Richard Nixon did not and in a way that Bill Clinton did not. He put us on a fundamentally different path because the country was ready for it."

It's clear that Obama fancied himself as the Democratic Reagan, the man who would lead the nation to the promised land of post-constitutional progressivism. Eight years later, there is no argument. Obama has achieved this fundamental transformation. He has changed the trajectory of the country in the way he prophesied. From unconstitutional executive orders to the abrogation of private property rights and his neglect of constitutional checks and balances, Obama has made a mockery of America's system in the service of his progressive agenda.

WILSON'S GHOST: FIGHTING GLOBAL SOCIAL INJUSTICE

Describing visions of foreign policy is a difficult business. On the left in particular, there is a divergent array of views, from interventionist Wilsonian internationalists to isolationist Code Pink "antimilitarists." The former believe that it is America's duty to spread democracy worldwide, arguing that all people share universal liberal principles and should coexist under international coalitions and norms. The antimilitarists echo the views of those during the Vietnam era who saw America's cause as a fundamentally negative one around the world and who wanted to end the "military-industrial complex" altogether.

During his first inaugural address, Obama unveiled an essential line with respect to how he would deal with America's adversaries: "To those who cling to power through corruption and deceit and the silencing of dissent, know that you are on the wrong side of history, but that we will extend a hand if you are willing to unclench your fist."

Only those on one side of that handshake wound up keeping their end of the bargain. America bent over backward repeatedly for its enemies. The Iran nuclear deal, for example, is the living embodiment of the core elements of progressive foreign policy, the culmination of Obama's most ambitious (and dangerous) project. The result is America's aiding, abetting, and enabling of Iran, the world's leading state sponsor of terror. Under a deal purportedly crafted to partially destroy and halt Iran's nuclear program (recall Obama's desire for a nuclear-free world), Obama not only agreed to allow Iran to maintain key parts of its nuclear infrastructure and protect it against attack but also released upward of $100 billion certain to be used for the mullahs' nefarious jihadist designs.

The Obama administration's easing of sanctions also opened up commerce with a regime that had been on life support. In the aftermath of the deal, Iran continued launching ballistic missiles, almost certainly violating the deal's terms. This sort of appeasement and, worse than appeasement, this active support of a terrorist regime is the kind of stance that could only make sense to a progressive who sees the world as he or she wishes it to be. Empowering your enemy does not make them a friend, it only makes them a stronger enemy. At the same time, caving to Iran only worked to undermine one of America's staunchest traditional allies, Israel, which Iran has repeatedly vowed to destroy.

While Iran was the worst and most egregious exercise in progressive naivety and willful blindness, there were many other Obama administration disasters born of the same ideology.

Another crucial element of the Obama doctrine was the long-held

progressive aim of self-determination for oppressed peoples. Ironically, like George W. Bush, Obama believed in spreading democracy
to the Middle East. However, his belief in this was based not on an
embrace of a pluralistic system grounded in individual liberty but
rather on majoritarianism. And if the majority party was the Muslim
Brotherhood, terrorists who formed the tip of the jihadist spear, so
be it. Secular authoritarians would have to either embrace reforms or
step aside.

As the so-called Arab Spring unfolded, Obama sought to get on
the right side of history, over and above the advice of his national
security team. He encouraged Egypt's President Hosni Mubarak, a
longtime U.S. partner and strategic ally of Israel, to implement reforms toward "fully representative democracy." Left unsaid was the
fact that the only organized political force beyond Mubarak's military
regime was the jihadist Muslim Brotherhood.

As protests swelled in Tahrir Square and the situation grew dangerous, the White House changed its tune and asked Mubarak to step
down. The Muslim Brotherhood filled the power vacuum, led by
notorious Islamic supremacist Mohamed Morsi. The Obama administration supported Morsi's radical regime by continuing to provide it
with monetary aid and heavy weaponry.

And then there was Libya, whose failures became real to all Americans on the night of September 11, 2012, when U.S. Ambassador
Chris Stevens, information officer Sean Smith, and CIA operatives
Glen Doherty and Tyrone Woods were murdered by jihadist terrorists. Libya's leader, Muammar Qaddafi, like Mubarak, had repressed
jihadist forces, jailing thousands of Islamist militants and largely disarming in response to America's invasion of Iraq. He had, in effect,
become an ally. But the Obama administration again sought the overthrow of an authoritarian leader in favor of "democracy." U.S. and
NATO air forces were responsible for aiding the "rebels" who over-
threw the Qaddafi regime, but what the United States really helped

accomplish was to turn Libya over to the worst of the jihadist forces. The United States, ousted from the country, was greeted in 2014 with images of jihadists diving into the swimming pool of its former embassy in Tripoli. There are now approximately sixty-five hundred ISIS fighters in the failed state.

Obama accomplished this feat while also subverting the Constitution. He never received congressional approval for military action, and then he violated the War Powers Resolution by claiming that bombing Libya did not constitute "hostilities" under the law. After all, the law can mean different things at different times to progressives; it depends on what they need to use it for. Also worth remembering is that as the situation on the ground in Libya deteriorated, Secretary of State Hillary Clinton, no doubt on behalf of the administration, held the line on keeping Ambassador Stevens in the country. The valuing of political correctness and progressive ideology even over life and limb proved to be fatal.

Volumes can and will be written on Obama's hostility toward Israel, the only liberal democracy in the Middle East. While his policies have helped empower those enemies posing an existential threat to the Jewish homeland, he has spent much of his presidency espousing moral equivalence between the Arabs of Palestine and the Israelis, in hopes of a peace deal that cannot be achieved when one side seeks the other's destruction.

Under Clinton's leadership at the State Department, it was revealed that the Obama administration went so far as to seek to literally undermine Israel's governmental position by strengthening the Palestinian Arabs. U.S. intelligence agencies spied on Israeli Prime Minister Benjamin Netanyahu, seeking to capture his communications. Following Clinton's tenure, Secretary of State John Kerry went so far as to threaten Israel over the so-called boycott, divestment, and sanctions (BDS) movement, warning that Israel could be subject to a crippling broad-based boycott. In effect, he legitimized the actions of its enemies. The United States eventually backed away from language in anti–BDS legislation that it deemed too controversial for "blurring the lines between Israel and the West Bank."

The Obama administration's stance toward Israel has been reflective of broadly held progressive views on the Jewish nation akin to those held in Arab studies departments across the United States, including the department led by Obama's friend Khalidi. Many progressives again believe that the "Zionist" entity is an illegitimate, repressive, apartheid state. It is treated as a colonialist Western occupier and oppressor. Obama's policies, while not overtly reflecting this mind-set, represent the maximum level of hostility that a sitting U.S. president can apply toward Israel. As a result, Israel is now in a perilous position, with threats from Arabs of Palestine, Hezbollah, ISIS, and the Iranian regime itself growing daily.

In Russia, Obama's "reset" and promises of "flexibility" have been met with the ascendancy of President Vladimir Putin as a world leader. What has been the effect of Obama's open hand to Putin's clenched fist? Russia walked into Ukraine and took it over. Obama, like so many other progressives who have underestimated dictators in the past, chose to ignore Putin's belief that "the demise of the Soviet Union was the greatest geopolitical catastrophe of the [twentieth] century." Obama has invited a new one.

China's saber-rattling in the South China Sea, including the continued expansion of man-made islands and its crippling and costly cyber-attacks on U.S. businesses, represents a further show of strength by America's adversaries in the face of Obama's "open hand" policy.

In Cuba, putting aside the fact that the Castros maintain a repressive Communist regime, Obama overturned decades of U.S. policy to open up diplomatic relations with the country, along with commercial ties that culminated in Obama and Raúl Castro sharing a hot dog at a Cuban baseball game. The end result will be a much-needed lifeline for Cuba in the form of foreign capital. This influx will not only sustain but also strengthen the Communist government, propping up an anti-American regime less than a hundred miles from our shores, a regime from which new threats can easily grow.

The sum of Obama's foreign policy has been the empowering of America's worst enemies, while its friends and America itself grow increasingly unsafe. Ideology has firmly trumped the national interest. Like those of progressives before him, Obama's actions reflect a man who sees the world as the utopian version he wishes it to be rather than what it actually is.

Obama set out to "change" and "transform" America, and he has done exactly that. He has pushed the country as close as it could stomach to socialized medicine. He has made a mockery of the Constitution. He has engaged in unprecedented diplomatic dealings with all manner of enemies, foreign and domestic. He has doubled the national debt to $20 million while growing the size and scope of the state and reducing individual liberties.

Some on the left have expressed disappointment with Obama, saying that he was, for example, a "counterfeit" progressive. I don't buy it. The nation looks radically different from how it looked at the start of his administration. And remember, waves all look different; some crash to the shore with ferocity, while others slowly roll in. But one wave always gives way to another. Wilson, Teddy Roosevelt, FDR, LBJ—they all paved the way for Obama, each pushing as far as their times would allow.

I have no doubt that the seeds planted during the last eight years will bloom in the years ahead, no matter who takes over the Oval Office next.

PROFILE IN FEAR:
FRANK MARSHALL DAVIS, OBAMA'S FATHER FIGURE

Frank Marshall Davis sat in the back of a patrol car and feared for his safety. Who knew what might happen to a young African-American in Kansas in the 1920s? The police car had pulled alongside him as he was walking down the street in his neighborhood, minding his own business.

"Git your black ass in the car with us," the chief of police had instructed. He told Davis that a white woman on a nearby street had complained of a prowler.

Frank was frightened, but he complied. Such was the life of a black man in America, he believed. He flashed back to a time when he was five years old. Two other kids had placed a noose around his neck, choking him. Freed with the assistance of a passing stranger, Frank had made it home and told his family what had happened. They, in turn, had complained to his school, which, in turn, had completely ignored them.

Now the police chief pulled the car up in front of an unfamiliar house. A white woman, the one who'd registered the prowler complaint, was brought forward to identify Frank.

It wasn't him, she told the policeman.

"You sure?" the police chief asked.

She said she was.

Frank was pretty sure the police chief was disappointed. *It's not every day they have a chance to whip a big black nigger,* he thought.

"Where do you live?" the chief asked him. Then he turned to

his buddies. "I didn't know any damn niggers lived in this part of town, did you?"

"There's a darky family livin' down here someplace," one of the others replied.

The conversation only fueled Frank's fear and enmity—and anger. *I'd give twenty years off my life to bind these three cops together, throw them motionless on the ground in front of me, and for a whole hour piss in their faces.*

It was easy to understand why he was filled with all-consuming hate. For the cops. For America. For anyone or anything that represented power and inequality. And eventually for the free-enterprise system that allowed such people to exist.

Davis had spent much of his life fixated on identity and race. After growing up in racially hostile Kansas in the early 1900s, he had eventually departed for the more inviting pastures of the leftist intellectual bastion of Chicago.

Prolific and creative, he moved in progressive circles in the 1930s and '40s, writing columns for various Communist-line publications and castigating America for its racism, colonialism, and imperialism. "The United States was the only slaveholding nation in the New World," he wrote, "that completely dehumanized Africans by considering them as chattel, placing them in the same category of horses, cattle, and furniture."

He mocked the notion of "the American way" as a slogan peddled by "flag-waving fascists and lukewarm liberals." He was angry, bitter, and seeking to change the world.

In 1948, at the urging of Stalin sympathizer Paul Robeson, Davis left Chicago for Honolulu, seeking a more inviting home for his interracial marriage. The legal barriers against interracial marriage in most American states only furthered his lifelong view of the United States as irreparably racist.

A literal card-carrying member of the Community Party USA, Davis was deemed a big enough threat that the FBI created a file on him that ran to six hundred pages. His Communist agitation culminated with testimony in front of the U.S. Senate in 1956 in which he pled the Fifth. From that point on, however, he lived out his days largely undisturbed in Hawaii, writing poetry and taking provocative photographs of nude women. He also took pictures of Hawaii's shorelines, which drew the interest of the FBI and others who suspected he was planning to send the photos to Soviet leaders should Hawaii ever need to be targeted.

Among his friends on the island was another Kansas transplant by the name of Stanley Dunham. The two friends would often play games like Scrabble and drink together. Mr. Dunham had a grandson who, as it happened, shared many things in common with Davis. His name was Barack Obama.

Young Obama also spent much of his adolescence in a profound identity crisis. The boy living in liberal Hawaii was suddenly conscious of the fact that he was at the intersection of very different worlds: black and white, African and American, foreign and near. His lack of identity, combined with the void created by the absence of his late father, accentuated the standard teenage angst of a sixteen-year-old.

Later in life, Obama described the context of his internal struggle during a library talk shortly after his book *Dreams from My Father* came out. "I end up coming into adolescence at a time when the tensions between the races even in a place like Hawaii are becoming more pronounced," Obama told the audience, "and sort of the identity politics that is so pronounced today was already starting to come to the fore." He went on:

> *I'm a very angry young man at the time . . . partly because my father is absent. Partly because I'm trying to struggle, "What*

does it mean exactly to be a black man in America?" Partly be-
cause I'm sufficiently isolated in Hawaii without a large African-
American community, without father figures around that might
guide me and steer my anger. What I end up relying upon are
the images and stereotypes that are coming through the media.
And I'm having to patch together and piece together exactly what
it means for me to be both African and an American.

It was in this frame of mind that Obama absorbed the lessons of his grandfather's drinking buddy, Frank Davis. After one instance in which Obama claims he felt particularly alienated about race, he sought out Davis for help and had "a discussion with him about the kind of frustrations I am having and he sort of schools me that I should get used to these frustrations."

This was one of many conversations the two would have. It was Davis who helped Obama sort out his feelings about race and who gave heed to his fears, hopes, and ambitions. Davis later explained that "black people have a reason to hate."

Davis remained a critical character at every turn of Obama's life journey. According to Davis biographer Paul Kengor, Obama memorialized his legacy in his first book:

In Dreams from My Father, *"Frank" is mentioned twenty-*
two times by name, and far more via pronouns and other forms
of reference. He is a consistent theme, appearing repeatedly
and meaningfully in all three parts of the book. He is part of
Obama's life and mind, by Obama's own extended recounting,
from Hawaii—the site of visits and late evenings together—to
Los Angeles to Chicago to Germany to Africa, from adolescence
to college to community organizing. "Frank" is always one of the
few (and first) names mentioned by Obama in each mile-marker
upon his historic path from Hawaii to Washington. When

Obama at last arrived in Chicago, where he would find himself politically, professionally, and ideologically—precisely as Frank Marshall Davis had 50 years earlier—the first thing he did was think of "Frank," literally visualizing him, picturing him there.

That a Communist Party member had any impact at all on the young, impressionable future president is disturbing in and of itself. But it is clear that Obama yearned for and needed direction. He was lacking a father figure to provide guidance, perspective, and wisdom—to help him find his identity. Davis was all too willing to play this role.

During a 2007 speech at the Communist Party USA archives at New York University, Professor Gerald Horne spoke about the parallels between these two men:

> *At some point in the future, a teacher will add to her syllabus Barack's memoir and instruct her students to read it alongside Frank Marshall Davis's equally affecting memoir,* Living the Blues, *and when that day comes, I'm sure a future student will not only examine critically the Frankenstein monsters that U.S. imperialism created . . . but will also be moved to come to this historic and wonderful archive in order to gain insight on what has befallen this complex and intriguing planet on which we reside.*

Perhaps anticipating this very comparison, Obama purged Davis's name from the abridged audio version of *Dreams from My Father.* The progressive president had learned well. He had "sacrificed the cheap satisfaction of the radical pose for the deep satisfaction of radical ends," as his environmental czar Van Jones would term it.

That, however, hasn't stopped Obama from carrying a torch

for communism wherever he can find it. In 2016, he headed to Castro's Cuba—the very same Castro and Cuba that John F. Kennedy had risked his entire presidency to confront—and offered the notorious Communist dictatorship his hand in friendship.

Days later, he told an audience of young leaders in Argentina, "So often in the past there's been a sharp division between left and right, between capitalist and communist or socialist. And especially in the Americas, that's been a big debate, right? Oh, you know, you're a capitalist Yankee dog, and oh, you know, you're some crazy communist that's going to take away everybody's property."

Then he told the students something astonishing. "I think for your generation, you should be practical and just choose from what works," he said. The clear implication is that communism can work—even though history has shown repeatedly that it can't.

Socialism, communism, capitalism—there's no real difference to Obama, and we can owe that view in large part to Frank Marshall Davis.

♠

QUIZ: ARE YOU A PROGRESSIVE?

1. How strongly do you agree/disagree with the following statement: "Economic inequality is a major problem in modern industrial societies"?

a. Strongly Agree
b. Somewhat Agree
c. Neither Agree nor Disagree
d. Somewhat Disagree
e. Strongly Disagree

2. One proper role of government is to ensure that nobody gets left behind due to circumstances beyond their control.

a. Strongly Agree
b. Somewhat Agree
c. Neither Agree nor Disagree
d. Somewhat Disagree
e. Strongly Disagree

3. Each of us bears responsibility for the safety, welfare, and happiness of our fellow men.

a. Strongly Agree
b. Somewhat Agree
c. Neither Agree nor Disagree
d. Somewhat Disagree
e. Strongly Disagree

4. When choosing between two possible laws, we should always choose the law that provides the greatest benefit to the largest number of people.

a. Strongly Agree
b. Somewhat Agree
c. Neither Agree nor Disagree
d. Somewhat Disagree
e. Strongly Disagree

5. Because individual people sometimes act selfishly, it's OK for a government to pass laws that limit choices to ensure that people don't get taken advantage of.

a. Strongly Agree
b. Somewhat Agree
c. Neither Agree nor Disagree
d. Somewhat Disagree
e. Strongly Disagree

6. It's acceptable for the government to provide public funding to private charitable organizations that provide useful services to the poor.

a. Strongly Agree
b. Somewhat Agree
c. Neither Agree nor Disagree
d. Somewhat Disagree
e. Strongly Disagree

7. The wealthiest people in society have the greatest responsibility to provide for services and basic needs for the poor.

a. Strongly Agree
b. Somewhat Agree
c. Neither Agree nor Disagree
d. Somewhat Disagree
e. Strongly Disagree

8. Because some people make unhealthy choices about what they put into their bodies, it's acceptable to pass laws that make certain things illegal or at least harder to acquire.

a. Strongly Agree
b. Somewhat Agree
c. Neither Agree nor Disagree
d. Somewhat Disagree
e. Strongly Disagree

9. Big companies who gain a monopoly over a given market pose a major threat to society and should be broken up or regulated to protect consumers.

a. Strongly Agree
b. Somewhat Agree
c. Neither Agree nor Disagree
d. Somewhat Disagree
e. Strongly Disagree

10. If we really wanted to, we could eliminate poverty through greater education, a safe environment, and fair workplaces.

a. Strongly Agree
b. Somewhat Agree
c. Neither Agree nor Disagree
d. Somewhat Disagree
e. Strongly Disagree

11. It's an unfortunate reality that many people are inherently greedy, selfish, and violent, causing most of the problems in society.

a.　Strongly Agree
b.　Somewhat Agree
c.　Neither Agree nor Disagree
d.　Somewhat Disagree
e.　Strongly Disagree

12. In any question of individual rights versus group rights, the rights of the group are greater because the individual is just one person, while the group is many people.

a.　Strongly Agree
b.　Somewhat Agree
c.　Neither Agree nor Disagree
d.　Somewhat Disagree
e.　Strongly Disagree

13. The idea of race is an old-fashioned social construct, and there really is no difference between various racial or ethnic groups.

a.　Strongly Agree
b.　Somewhat Agree
c.　Neither Agree nor Disagree
d.　Somewhat Disagree
e.　Strongly Disagree

14. The world would be a much better place if we treated males and females as completely equal in every way.

a.　Strongly Agree
b.　Somewhat Agree
c.　Neither Agree nor Disagree
d.　Somewhat Disagree
e.　Strongly Disagree

15. Because all cultures have something to offer, we should give every culture and social group an equal voice in making laws, policies, and setting standards.

a.　Strongly Agree
b.　Somewhat Agree
c.　Neither Agree nor Disagree
d.　Somewhat Disagree
e.　Strongly Disagree

16. The closer we get to a world where everybody has equal wealth and status, the more perfect the world will be.

a. Strongly Agree
b. Somewhat Agree
c. Neither Agree nor Disagree
d. Somewhat Disagree
e. Strongly Disagree

17. A true democracy where the majority vote rules is the only fair way for a government to operate.

a. Strongly Agree
b. Somewhat Agree
c. Neither Agree nor Disagree
d. Somewhat Disagree
e. Strongly Disagree

18. Individuals should have the right of free speech unless their speech can be shown to hurt or offend other people.

a. Strongly Agree
b. Somewhat Agree
c. Neither Agree nor Disagree
d. Somewhat Disagree
e. Strongly Disagree

19. If people aren't willing to contribute to charity when they can afford to, it's acceptable to pass laws to force them to give money to certain charities.

a. Strongly Agree
b. Somewhat Agree
c. Neither Agree nor Disagree
d. Somewhat Disagree
e. Strongly Disagree

20. Money (or the love of money) is the root of all evil in the world.

a. Strongly Agree
b. Somewhat Agree
c. Neither Agree nor Disagree
d. Somewhat Disagree
e. Strongly Disagree

21. People are better off when progress is driven by science and social discourse, rather than by religion or faith.

a. Strongly Agree
b. Somewhat Agree
c. Neither Agree nor Disagree
d. Somewhat Disagree
e. Strongly Disagree

See page 293 for Answer Key

PART II

THE LIES

Introduction:

The Great Lie

Hillary Clinton was doomed, and she knew it.

Trailing by double digits to a crazy-haired, wild-eyed, un-repentant socialist in every New Hampshire poll, she had little hope of turning things around. Time was too short. Bernie Sanders's crowds were too massive. The architect of the first effort to cram socialized medicine down America's collective throat was on the defensive, preposterously, as insufficiently radical.

With just days to go before the vote, this was no longer a fight for victory in the first primary state. This was a fight for her reputation. A fight for her political soul.

For most of the campaign, Senator Sanders had worked hard to define himself as the only true "progressive" in the Democratic hierarchy. That wasn't too hard for a radical who had been an apologist for Marxists around the globe for decades, cheering them to victory against the United States.

In the 2016 race, Sanders proudly dubbed himself the most "progressive" member of the U.S. Senate and suggested that his opponent, Clinton, was a "moderate" and a sellout. No charge could be more deadly in a primary dominated by modern-day hippies, race- and gender-obsessed victim groups, jobless millennials, union thugs, and the permanently aggrieved.

So on February 3, 2016, as Clinton climbed onto the stage in the tiny town of Keene, displaying her fiercest glare and donning her most formidable pantsuit, she expressed "disappointment" that Sanders would deny her the title of "progressive." Her record in such matters should be beyond question, she contended to a crowd of her supporters. As her spokesman later put it, "You would be hard pressed to find a more accomplished and passionate progressive."

Days later, standing only a few feet from her political nemesis in an MSNBC debate, she again laid claim to the progressive label. "I am a progressive who gets things done," she said, adding, "The root of that word—'progressive'—is progress." Secretary Clinton noted that in Sanders's view, even Barack Obama might not be a progressive.

As it happened, the president himself took umbrage with that suggestion only a few days later. At a speech in Springfield, Illinois, where eight years earlier he had all but claimed to be this century's Abraham Lincoln, Obama announced that he was a progressive, too: "I am a progressive Democrat. I am proud of that. I make no bones about it."

Which leads to the question, which of these three is the real progressive?

Easy. They are *all* progressives. The whole lot of them—Clinton, Sanders, Obama, and their allies in Washington, D.C. Progressives have hijacked the entire Democratic Party, which was once the proud political party that elected the tax-slashing and fiercely anticommunist John F. Kennedy as president. So, too, have they hijacked most members of the Republican Party, whose leaders are perfectly content to accede to the progressive status quo of a federal government that intrudes into our lives and confiscates our property daily. They deny this, of course, but that's because progressives are accomplished liars. The terms go hand in hand.

And that's what we're going to explore in this part of the book: the deceit that is used as a tool to stir and exploit fear. All of their lies prey on our most primal emotions: envy, jealousy, loneliness, and, above all else, the terror of death. Whether it's "rising oceans" that will swallow our coastal cities on account of melting ice caps, or "automatic assault rifles" that will be used to murder us all, or "income inequality" that will turn us into paupers, the Left has perfected the art of the Great Lie.

The Great Lie actually starts with word *progressive* itself. They constantly mislead about what it actually means. They want you to believe that progressives are basically forward-thinking liberals who believe in democracy, open debates, free thinking, and looking out for their fellow man. They are harmless leftists. You know, like the Swedes.

As Clinton herself noted, the root word of *progressive* is *progress*— and progress is a good thing, right? With each passing year, we have more miraculous innovations that extend our lives and make them more convenient. We have more scientific discoveries that reveal truths about subjects from the farthest reaches of the universe to the makeup of the smallest atomic particles. All of these are evidence of a species on the march. We move forward, not backward. Who could be against that? Who could stand in the way of that kind of "progress"? Why would anyone not call himself or herself a "progressive"?

This is one of the arguments that makes progressives so sinister. They harness the best marketing terms to mask the insidiousness of their ideology. To protect the Great Lie.

Progressives claim that they stand for the future. The truth is that progressives actually represent the oldest impulse known to mankind: the will to power, to dominate, and to exploit. At the heart of progressivism is a deeply regressive ideology, one that eliminates individual freedom and makes men serfs and slaves.

Progressives claim that they are basically warmed-over liberals. The truth, as you've seen in the history of the founding fathers of progressivism, beginning with Hegel through Marx and Wilson through LBJ and Obama, is that progressivism is the *opposite* of liberalism, at least as it was once properly understood. Liberals—philosophers such as John Locke, John Stuart Mill, and Adam Smith—invented the idea of individual freedom. This idea captured the imaginations of a generation of freedom fighters born in thirteen colonies some three centuries ago. They took those ideas and put them into practice with two radical documents: the Declaration of Independence and the Constitution. Theirs was a reaction against centralized government, a revolution of the individual against the collective.

But progressivism stands for the idea that freedom isn't enough, that voluntary cooperation and the free market and individual rights do not work. To improve the quality of life for everyone, government must intervene with rules and regulations. Progressivism is the salve for the struggle, pain, and anxiety of living in a difficult and unpredictable world.

Progressives claim to fight for the average man. The truth is that most of them have both pity and contempt for human beings. They see the rest of us as machines that can be tinkered with and perfected. They believe they know what's best for everyone. They think that if we submit to the government expert-determined progressive agenda—which included disenfranchisement of African-Americans in the Jim Crow South in the late nineteenth century, prohibition of alcohol in the 1920s, eugenics and eliminating supposedly defective races (which animated Hitler's campaign of extermination in the 1930s and '40s)—we can create utopia. They believe that under the banner of "social justice" we can, in effect, become God, that they can create heaven on earth. It may take centuries or even longer, but gradually, generation by generation, progressives can do it. If patience is a virtue, progressives are the most virtuous people on earth.

Progressives claim to believe in a compassionate, tolerant, live-and-let-live society. But in fact, the heart of progressivism lies in two core principles:

- Individual and human society is perfectible, and therefore all problems known to man have solutions.
- An enlightened few can impose these solutions on everyone else.

Both principles are obviously false. The first runs counter to everything most of us believe about human nature, selfishness, and sin—not to mention plenty of historical evidence that men living today are just as capable of depravity and evil as they were millennia ago. The second principle, a kind of tyranny of good intentions, is deeply antidemocratic. It rejects most Americans' fundamental belief in human equality.

Ideas have consequences. And no idea may be as catastrophic as progressivism. Progressivism spawned socialism, communism, and fascism. Many of the greatest evils of the twentieth century—Adolf Hitler, Benito Mussolini, Joseph Stalin—share their ideology, their belief systems, and their motivations with the progressive movement, the very same movement that Hillary Clinton and Barack Obama want to claim as their own.

In what follows, I'll go through some of the more common lies we hear from progressives or about the progressive ideology. I'll use their own words to show you the lies, and then I'll take each of them apart using facts, logic, and common sense.

▌ LIE 1 ▌

PROGRESSIVES WANT TO KEEP YOU SAFE FROM GUN VIOLENCE

I will use every single minute of every day, if I am so fortunate enough to be your president, looking for ways that we can save lives, that we can change the gun culture.

—HILLARY CLINTON, 2016 CAMPAIGN

This is our first task as a society, keeping our children safe. This is how we will be judged.

—BARACK OBAMA, UNVEILING NEW EXECUTIVE ACTIONS ON GUN CONTROL, 2013

THE LIE
....

In the spring of 1922, a group of men in sober dark suits met in a small hotel ballroom a few blocks from the U.S. Capitol. At the head of a square table sat the meeting's leader, a small-framed, unassuming man wearing wire-rimmed glasses that perched above a neatly trimmed mustache. He straightened his papers in front of him, cleared his throat, and read a short prepared statement to the group of assembled government officials of the Prohibition Bureau:

> We have made good progress in our efforts to forever stamp out the scourge of human inebriation, having won an Amendment to our beloved Constitution making the manufacture and ownership of

*liquor as illegal as the ownership of Slaves. However, as long as
any of our fellow citizens remains trapped by their inability to resist
the temptation to drink, there is still more we can do to protect our
citizenry, and their wives and children.*

He read on to the silent group and proposed a plan that would
help ensure that the government could both identify and "treat" those
citizens who still violated their hard-won temperance laws. It was
simple: they would add poisonous wood alcohol to bottles of whiskey
and then make sure those tainted bottles made their way into the
speakeasies and back-alley bars that had popped up across the country
in response to the Eighteenth Amendment. When people broke the
law by consuming the whiskey, they would get extremely sick or even
die, enabling the government to identify lawbreakers and also to discover exactly where alcohol was still being distributed.

The room of federal-government employees listened, nodded, and
then left to go dutifully about the business of poisoning and killing
thousands of their fellow citizens.*

Eighty-seven years later, government officials of the successor
agency to the Prohibition Bureau—the Bureau of Alcohol, To-
bacco and Firearms (ATF)—initiated a program to sell assault rifles
to known gunrunners and drug traffickers. The plan was simple, at
least in theory: by arming drug warlords with traceable firearms, they
could identify the chain of black-market firearms dealers who were
enabling drug dealers to be so heavily armed. The government agents
set about the work of stamping out the sale of deadly weapons to
known murderers . . . by selling deadly weapons to known murders.

Just more than a year after that, an officer of the U.S. Border Patrol
was killed in the Arizona desert by Mexican criminals. Assault rifles

....

* This scene is dramatized based on known facts. For more information, read Deborah Blum, "The
Chemist's War," *Slate*, February 19, 2010.

provided to the assailants by the U.S. government were found at the murder scene.

We've met the small-framed, unassuming man in glasses described in the first scene before. His name is Wayne Wheeler, the progressive "dry" zealot who, while not a government official himself, essentially functioned as the United States' Prohibition czar. In 1921, Wheeler handpicked a former ally in the Ohio temperance movement, Roy A. Haynes, to be the nation's official Prohibition commissioner.

"Through Haynes," according to historian John Kobler, "Wheeler controlled the Prohibition Bureau." Wheeler was a strong proponent of providing poisoned alcohol to America's illegal drinkers, reasoning that "the person who drinks this industrial alcohol is a deliberate suicide. . . . To root out a bad habit costs many lives and long years of effort." In the end, the government is estimated to have poisoned some ten thousand Americans.

The second scene above depicts the much more recent disaster of "Operation Fast and Furious," in which the ATF—which grew directly out of the liquor-poisoning Prohibition Bureau—let guns they were supposedly tracking fall into the hands of drug runners and then promptly lost them. Their strategy, in their own words, was "to allow the transfer of firearms to continue to take place in order to further the investigation." In reality, the only thing they furthered was murder.

Guns from the Fast and Furious program were linked to the killing of Border Patrol officer Brian Terry, as well as to the deaths of hundreds of Mexican citizens. After notorious drug lord (and apparent pal of Hollywood liberal Sean Penn) Joaquin "El Chapo" Guzmán was captured, authorities found that his arsenal included a .50-caliber rifle that had found its way to the kingpin through Fast and Furious.

Programs like Wheeler's deliberate liquor poisoning during Prohibition and Operation Fast and Furious under Barack Obama and Eric Holder's ATF show just how far progressives will go to further their control and limit your freedom, while telling you it's for your own good. This fight for control, driven by their fear of a free society, is on full display in the gun-control debate today.

The liberal public grief ritual following every attack by a deranged individual with a gun has become as sad a matter of routine as the shootings themselves. Quick to politicize senseless tragedies, progressives waste little time in using acts of gun violence to further their political agenda.

Barack Obama famously shed tears after the Sandy Hook shooting. "As a country, we have been through this too many times," he said. "We're going to have to come together and take meaningful action to prevent more tragedies like this, regardless of the politics."

About a month later, while taking the opportunity to unveil nearly two dozen executive orders on gun control (so much for "regardless of the politics"), Obama repeated a version of the standard justifications that progressives often use for these kinds of actions: "This is our first task as a society, keeping our children safe," he said. "This is how we will be judged."

Hillary Clinton's campaign takes the safety angle as well, vowing to "ensure that the safety of our communities is prioritized over the profits of the gun lobby." Clinton even held a campaign event with families of the Sandy Hook victims (again, what happened to "regardless of the politics"?) where she declared that "we just have too many guns in this country" and promised: "I will use every single minute of every day, if I am so fortunate enough to be your president, looking for ways that we can save lives, that we can change the gun culture."

Senator Dianne Feinstein of California, one of the most notorious progressive gun grabbers, used the Sandy Hook tragedy to push for an "assault weapons" ban in 2013. Her law seemed to choose the guns it wanted to ban simply based on how scary-looking they were or how much news coverage they got, prompting even the liberals at Slate.com to ask: "What's the real difference between an AR-15-style semi-automatic rifle (banned) and the fixed-stock Ruger Mini-14 semi-automatic carbine (allowed), for instance, besides the fact that the AR-15 has been in the news?" Feinstein's efforts ultimately failed, but in attempting to justify them on the Senate floor, she said, "The most important duty a government has is to protect its citizens' safety."

Progressives tell us, *Give us all of your guns, but trust us, it's for your own good.* Their promise: fewer guns, more safety.

But, as responsible gun owners know, that's a lie.

THE TRUTH

Let's consider the question of safety. How safe are we *really* in America, and what is the government doing to help?

The nonprofit National Safety Council has compiled data on causes of death. According to its analysis, 1 in 358 Americans will be killed by a firearm.

But:

- 1 in 144 Americans will be killed by a fall.
- 1 in 112 Americans will be killed in a car crash.
- 1 in 109 Americans will die of "unintentional poisoning" (as opposed to the "very much intentional poisoning" carried out by our government during Prohibition).
- 1 in 100 Americans will commit suicide.
- 1 in 7 Americans will die from heart disease or cancer.

The natural question, then, is, what is the government going to do about high surfaces? Or cars? Or poisoning? Or suicide? Or deadly diseases?

Do progressives scramble to hastily call press conferences and push for executive orders every time there is a massive car pileup on a freeway? Are hard-charging senators clamoring to call for a federally imposed height limit on all new structures in the United States so that falls from tall buildings can be eliminated? Not that I know of.

Progressives like Feinstein and Obama say they believe that government's top priority is "to protect its citizens' safety"—but what about the safety of American citizen Kimberly Corban? Corban survived a rape in college by a man who broke into her apartment. A decade later, she was still fighting the effects of post-traumatic stress disorder and depression after the assault. Now a mother of two, Corban feels it is her right to defend herself and her children as she sees fit, including with a firearm. She said as much to President Obama directly during a CNN town hall on gun control in January 2016, telling him that she believed her ability to purchase and carry a firearm was a "basic responsibility as a parent." She continued: "I have been unspeakably victimized once already, and I refuse to let that happen again to myself or my kids. So why can't your administration see that these restrictions . . . make it harder for me to own a gun, or harder for me to take that where I need to be, is actually just making my kids and I less safe?"

Obama struggled to come up with a response. He condescendingly told the rape survivor that she would "have to be pretty well trained" to use her gun effectively to prevent another assault, and even attempted to turn her concern for her children against her by ominously suggesting, "There's always the possibility that that firearm in a home leads to a tragic accident."

None of this fazed Corban. "I would say it was more of a nonresponse," she told reporters later. "He kind of dodged the question."

He dodged the question because this survivor exposed what progressives are desperately trying to hide: gun control isn't about safety at all, or even about guns. It's about control.

That's why progressive presidents do not launch dozens of executive orders aimed at curbing the use of cars in America, even though vehicles cause more deaths than guns. Even the fight against the most lethal killers—cancer and heart disease—does not generate as much sustained, passionate progressive fervor as guns.

The reason is simple: curing cancer does not lead to more power in D.C.; gun control does.

Progressives fear an armed citizenry that can stand up to defend itself once their tyranny becomes obvious. Progressives believe they can get away with their revolution as long as they carry it out behind the scenes, and, as we've already seen, that strategy has been working for them. But once they seize power outright, they will have to come out into the open.

Maybe there's even more to it than that. Some progressives want to grab guns because of personal trauma they've endured in their own lives. For example, one of the most strident gun-control advocates in Congress for nearly twenty years was New York Democratic Representative Carolyn McCarthy, known as the "Gun Lady." She first ran for office after her husband was shot and killed on a commuter train. Is it possible that her hatred for guns was driven by her fear of them, as well as her fear of the dark side of human nature?

Even progressives who have never had a personal encounter with a gun worry about what might happen if they had a firearm themselves. *Guns are scary.* Maybe they worry about their own ability to use guns safely. Maybe they're concerned that the next time they get angry, they'll grab their gun and start shooting. They are scared of guns, so they rail against them. They cannot fathom that plenty of responsible and sane citizens, like Kimberly Corban, exist in America, people who want a gun for nothing more than their constitutionally guaranteed right to have one.

Progressives cannot understand this because it undermines their fundamental faith in government. What people like Corban understand—and progressives never will—is that government cannot be trusted to keep us and our families safe. That's *our* job.

▌LIE 2 ▌

PROGRESSIVES CARE ABOUT
THE ENVIRONMENT

That is what is at stake, our ability to live on planet Earth, to have a future as
a civilization. I believe this is a moral issue, it is your time to seize this issue,
it is our time to rise again to secure our future.

—AL GORE, *AN INCONVENIENT TRUTH*, 2006

I am absolutely certain that generations from now, we will be able to look
back and tell our children that this was the moment . . . when the rise of the
oceans began to slow and our planet began to heal.

—BARACK OBAMA, NOMINATION ACCEPTANCE SPEECH, 2008

THE LIE
....

The fight over global warming, global cooling (yes, that was the
scientific Left's theory in the 1970s), "climate change," or whatever
they're choosing to call it at a given time might seem like the ultimate
cause of the modern progressive. It combines the pursuit of "justice"
(in this case, "climate justice"), calling for more regulation and bigger
government by elite, unaccountable bodies, with the imposition of
a secular orthodoxy based on supposedly "settled" climate science.
Never mind that by the progressives' own admission, the "science"
itself keeps changing.

Since the birth of the environmental movement in the 1960s, progressives have made sure everyone knows how much they care about the planet. And it hasn't just been progressive Democrats; Richard Nixon created a whole new government department of environmentalism, the EPA.

They are continuing the fight today. Hillary Clinton's campaign called climate change "a defining challenge of our time," and she promised not to "force our children to endure the catastrophe that would result from unchecked climate change." Bernie Sanders blamed the evil corporations, too: "While fossil fuel companies are raking in record profits, climate change ravages our planet and our people." And everyone probably remembers Barack Obama's messianic victory speech in 2008 in which he proclaimed that his election would be "the moment when the rise of the oceans began to slow and our planet began to heal."

It wasn't just campaign rhetoric for Obama, either. He made the global-warming obsession a matter of policy. His administration gave taxpayer money to "green" energy companies like Solyndra that then went belly-up. Disastrous "cap-and-trade" policies and all-out war on the coal industry cost American jobs, all for the sake of the environment.

Secretary of State John Kerry, who is supposed to be responsible for our foreign affairs, declared that climate change "ranks right up there" with "terrorism, epidemics, poverty [and] the proliferation of weapons of mass destruction." It is difficult to imagine a statement more insensitive to the real victims of terrorism, epidemics, poverty, or weapons of mass destruction—real problems that kill real people in the real world—but that is how far the progressive obsession with the environment (or at least the *exploitation* of the environment) really goes.

It also goes that far, in part, because it has the money to do so. Plants aren't the only green thing the environmentalists love; they love their cash, too. Despite all the liberal complaints about money in politics, "green billionaire" Tom Steyer—who made his hedge-fund money in fossil fuels before his miraculous conversion—was one of the top super-PAC donors in the 2016 elections. Of course, the patron saint of modern progressive environmentalism is none other than former Vice President Al Gore, and the movement's sacred text is his 2006 "documentary" *An Inconvenient Truth.*

But saving the planet is not the main goal of the progressive environmentalists. Their true aims are much more in character for people who practice an ideology that only the enlightened should lead.

At the end of *An Inconvenient Truth*, Gore admonishes his viewers: "Future generations may well have occasion to ask themselves, 'What were our parents thinking? Why didn't they wake up when they had a chance?' "

A better question might be what are the progressive environmentalists really thinking? That is what we need to answer so that one day, freedom-loving people crushed under a progressive agenda will not be forced to ask, *Why didn't we wake up when we had the chance?*

THE TRUTH

Progressives believe that the ends always justify the means. We explored plenty of examples of that in this book. At first glance, it would appear that the end in this case is saving the planet from supposed man-made destruction, and the environmental movement is the means for doing so. But what if that wasn't the case? What if the global warming "crisis" itself was, in fact, the means to a completely different end?

In 2014, Canadian author and activist Naomi Klein published a book, *This Changes Everything: Capitalism vs. the Climate.* Klein is an outspoken critic of capitalism; her previous book dealt with "disaster capitalism," and when it came out, the *New Yorker* called her "the most visible and influential figure on the American Left—what Howard Zinn and Noam Chomsky were thirty years ago." Klein has contributed to progressive organs such as the *Nation*, and her anti-capitalist views are well known.

In *This Changes Everything*, Klein is refreshingly honest, saying what few progressives are willing to admit. She argues, for example, for the use of a new weapon against the global capitalist system: the climate "crisis" itself. Klein writes that climate activism could actually bring down the capitalist system entirely.

"The really inconvenient truth is that it's not about carbon—it's about capitalism," the book explains. But there was good news, too: "The convenient truth is that we can seize this existential crisis to transform our failed economic system and build something radically better."

Building a better world has been the progressives' goal from the very beginning. And Klein says that climate alarmism is the "existential crisis" that gets us there. A documentary based on *This Changes Everything* came out a year after the book, and in the accompanying trailer, Klein asks what she calls "the big question": "What if global warming isn't only a crisis? What if it's the best chance we're ever gonna get to build a better world?" Then she delivers an ultimatum: "Change, or be changed." In other words, *help us build our better world willingly, or we will force you into it.*

But what can Klein force us to do after all? She's a prominent progressive theorist, yes, but she doesn't make policy. And the people who do make international climate policy really must care about the environment. Surely they can't share such a radical aim as the destruction of the world's economic system . . . can they?

As it turns out, yes, they can. Here is what Otto Edenhofer, a former official on the UN's Intergovernmental Panel on Climate Change (IPCC), told a Swiss newspaper while he was serving as a co-chair of one of the IPCC's working groups in 2010:

> [O]ne must say clearly that we redistribute de facto the world's
> wealth by climate policy. Obviously, the owners of coal and oil will
> not be enthusiastic about this. One has to free oneself from the illu-
> sion that international climate policy is environmental policy. This
> has almost nothing to do with environmental policy anymore, with
> problems such as deforestation or the ozone hole.

Edenhofer also said that an upcoming international conference, ostensibly about climate, was "actually an economy summit during which the distribution of the world's resources will be negotiated."

This was not just an isolated remark by one radical former offi-cial. The current top climate official at the UN has confirmed that the goal of bringing about economic change through climate policy remains in place. In February 2015, Christiana Figueres, head of the UN Framework Convention on Climate Change, told a press con-ference in Brussels that the goal was to "intentionally transform the economic development model." She went on: "This is the first time in the history of mankind that we are setting ourselves the task of in-tentionally, within a defined period of time, to change the economic development model that has been reigning for at least 150 years, since the industrial revolution."

The economic model that has been dominant since the industrial revolution is, of course, capitalism. And the UN has vowed to "inten-tionally transform" that model through climate policy—to dismantle capitalism.

Besides ignorance of basic economics and blinding ideology, what drives this cadre of scientists, CEOs, politicians, and bureaucrats to dismantle capitalism under the guise of saving the environment? It's fear. But not the kind you might think. They aren't afraid of actual harm to the planet. Yes, some passionate but ill-informed environ-mentalists might really believe that we will all die in a hail of fire and brimstone brought down by a vengeful Mother Earth, but those at the top who are pulling the strings of the movement are afraid of something much greater: the balance of power tilting back toward individual liberty and away from state control.

The free market has remained the dominant economic model for the last century and a half for a good reason: it works. Progressives have tried to fight it tooth and nail in any number of countries under any number of banners—from socialism to communism to progressivism—but they have never succeeded. Temporarily, perhaps, in some places, but never completely.

They fear the choice that the free market offers. There are too many possible paths for humanity to take, too many "wrong" roads to go down. Progressives don't like giving the masses too many options, because normal people cannot be trusted to make their own decisions.

That is the fundamental, though never stated, reason behind the embrace of the UN and its climate policies. It's the ultimate weapon in a last-ditch battle against the free-market system. Progressives have realized that they probably can't win the ideological battle—people will keep choosing freedom over authoritarianism any day—so instead they must use economics as a force. Millions of hardworking Indians and Chinese wouldn't choose to stay in poverty; they want electricity, cars, and all the perks of modern life that we are blessed to have. So, true to their nature, progressives opted for carrying out their revolution behind the scenes rather than in the open.

Climate policy has simply provided a convenient cover for an otherwise fairly standard progressive agenda item. The climate affects the entire world, so naturally, the UN should wield worldwide authority, they reasoned. And with that authority, progressives can build their "better world" by slowly regulating the free market out of existence, thereby eliminating the choice they fear—until their new world is the only choice left.

It's Cloward-Piven on a global scale.

▌LIE 3 ▌

PROGRESSIVES RESPECT THE CONSTITUTION

We believe in the wisdom of our founders and the Constitution.
—HILLARY CLINTON, NATIONAL CONSTITUTION CENTER, 2013

America has carried on not simply because of the skill or vision of those in high office, but because we, the people, have remained faithful to the ideals of our forebears and true to our founding documents.
—BARACK OBAMA, FIRST INAUGURAL ADDRESS, 2009

THE LIE

Progressives have been able to remain a force in American politics because they present themselves as "typical politicians." As we've seen, they can't show the true nature of their ideology because if they did, the vast majority of the American people would rise up and outright reject it. Unlike, say, self-declared socialists or communists, progressives don't call for open revolution to achieve their goals; they prefer "progression," gradual change over time. The progressive revolution will not be televised. In fact, if they do it the way they want to, most people won't even know it's going on. One day, we'll all wake up, and the "fundamental transformation" will be complete

Progressives need to blend in. They need to "talk the talk" and "walk the walk" so that they don't stand out from their more moderate colleagues. A big part of talking that talk is proclaiming their passion for the Constitution and the traditions on which America was founded.

But while progressives may pay lip service to the Constitution, their ideology actually calls for its subversion. In the progressive mind-set, the Constitution is—at best—flawed, outdated, and not up to the task of solving the problems of modern times, not helpful to the "progression" they are attempting to hasten along.

Woodrow Wilson talked a lot about a "living" constitution being "Darwinian in structure and in practice." Wilson believed that "Society is a living organism and must obey the laws of life, not of mechanics; it must develop. All the progressives ask or desire is permission—in an era when 'development,' 'evolution,' is the scientific word—to interpret the Constitution according to the Darwinian principle."

Franklin Roosevelt called the Constitution "the most marvelously elastic compilation of rules of government ever written." And now Barack Obama carries on the tradition.

When Obama stepped forward to give his inaugural address on January 20, 2009, throngs of admirers standing on the bitterly cold National Mall, along with millions more across the country and around the world, waited with bated breath to hear what he had to say. He was already a historic figure, the nation's first African-American president, but he was also the figurehead of a movement, someone who had vowed in his campaign to "fundamentally transform" the country.

With some of the first words he spoke as president of the United States—the sixth sentence of his inaugural address, to be precise—Obama paid tribute to the Constitution and our founding principles. In times of trouble, he said, "America has carried on not simply because of the skill or vision of those in high office, but because we, the people, have remained faithful to the ideals of our forebears and true to our founding documents."

It was all there. The purposeful appropriation of the phrase "we, the people" from the Constitution's preamble, the lofty language about "ideals of our forebears" and "our founding documents." It was exactly what the public would expect from someone who had just taken an oath to "preserve, protect, and defend" the Constitution. And in this case, the constitutional connection was even more appropriate: the incoming president was supposedly an expert who had even taught classes in constitutional law! Surely someone with that background would respect the primacy of the document on which all of our laws were based . . . right?

Obama's second inaugural address saw him reach another historic milestone: he was the first president in modern times to be reelected with fewer votes than in his first election. Considering the rancor of his first term and the controversies over Obamacare and other items of his policy agenda, that was hardly surprising. It's important to note that in 2013, Obama went right back to waxing poetic about the nation's founding principles, but he later pivoted to a more nuanced and perhaps more revealing view.

The president began with a reference to the "enduring strength of our Constitution." He spoke of the duty of every generation since 1776 "to keep safe our founding creed." Fair enough. But shortly thereafter, he presented a slightly different view, suggesting that our "founding principles" might be flexible after all: "[W]e have always understood that when times change, so must we; that fidelity to our founding principles requires new responses to new challenges; that preserving our individual freedoms ultimately requires collective action. When times change, so must we."

That was starting to sound awfully relativist, awfully progressive. And just in case there was any doubt, Obama later circled right around to the word itself: "Being true to our founding documents does not require us to agree on every contour of life. It does not mean we all define liberty in exactly the same way or follow the same precise path to happiness. Progress does not compel us to settle centuries-long debates about the role of government for all time, but it does require us to act in our time."

In his view, stale "debates about the role of government" (debates that help keep our republic vibrant and alive) were simply stumbling blocks to all-important progress. Who had time for debates when we had to "act in our time"? Who cared about what the Constitution actually said when action was more important? In fact, in Obama's logic, being "true to our founding documents" meant we should set aside our differences and just "act" in the name of progress.

THE TRUTH

In his second inaugural address—beginning a term in office when he would be free from the bother of having to persuade the American people to elect him ever again—Obama expressed a more flexible attitude toward our founding principles and their applicability to modern times. It would follow, then, that this same attitude was extended to the document in which these principles are enshrined: the U.S. Constitution.

Isn't that a bit of a leap? some of you may be asking. Fair question, but let's look back at a few comments Obama made long before his presidency for a glimpse into his real thinking on the usefulness of the Constitution.

In 2001, while serving in the Illinois State Senate and teaching constitutional law classes at the University of Chicago Law School, Obama gave several interviews to Chicago public radio station WBEZ. These first came to light and made some waves during the 2008 campaign, but they seem to have largely faded from public view since then. Though still early in his career, Obama had clearly formed sophisticated views on the Constitution by this point, no doubt one reason he was invited on the program in the first place.

In one interview, which got some attention because Obama decried our country's inability to achieve "major redistributive change through the courts," he also spoke about the Constitution in general, blaming it for blocking major judicial activism. He stated that the Supreme Court under Chief Justice Earl Warren, one of the most liberal phases in modern Supreme Court history, "didn't break free from the essential restraints that were placed by the Founding Fathers in the Constitution." In the context of the interview, it's clear that Obama wished Warren had. He continued: "[G]enerally the Constitution is a charter of negative liberties that says what the states can't do to you, what the federal government can't do to you, but it doesn't say what the state governments or the federal government must do on your behalf." Obama clearly believes it is inconvenient that the Founders set up the Constitution with a limited government in order to protect citizens from federal overreach, instead of laying out what government "must do" on behalf the people.

Another radio appearance that same year saw the future president participate in a panel discussion on the Constitution and slavery. Obama and the panelists discussed the debates and compromises over slavery in the Constitution's history, as well as the Thirteenth, Fourteenth, and Fifteenth Amendments added after the Civil War, which outlawed slavery and further expanded individual freedoms. After a fellow panelist, a history professor, noted the importance of judging the Founders' preservation of slavery in the Constitution in the context of their time, Obama offered his take, calling the Constitution "a remarkable document" but also "an imperfect document . . . that reflects some deep flaws in American culture, the Colonial culture nascent at that time."

Obama went on to talk about the Founders' lack of concern for

African-Americans, but it soon became clear that he was not confining his criticism to simply the historical, pre–Civil War Constitution:

> *I think we can say that the Constitution reflected an enormous blind spot in this culture that carries on until this day, and that the Framers had that same blind spot. I don't think the two views are contradictory, to say that it was a remarkable political document that paved the way for where we are now, and to say that it also reflected the fundamental flaw of this country that continues to this day.*

What is this "fundamental flaw"? Obama never clearly explained, but what *is* clear is that he thinks there are still problems with the Constitution today. For most of us, the amendments added to the Constitution in the wake of the Civil War represent a great triumph of how our constitutional system is supposed to work. The country rejected once and for all the brutality of slavery and enshrined that rejection forever in our founding document.

Yet Obama still sees the Constitution as fundamentally flawed more than 150 years later. Does that make it easier for him to subvert or ignore its constraints in the name of progress? Perhaps. Did his view of the "fundamental flaw of this country," reflected in its Constitution, lead him to run for president on a promise to "fundamentally transform" that flawed country? Perhaps. But in any case, the idea that the Constitution has outlived its usefulness is not new. If Obama does in fact believe that, then he is merely continuing in a long tradition of progressive scholarship.

Herbert Croly, an intellectual godfather of the progressive movement in the early twentieth century and founder of the *New Republic*, one of progressivism's main journals of record, was a friend and inspiration to progressive politicians such as Woodrow Wilson and Theodore Roosevelt. In fact, reading Croly's 1909 progressive tract *The Promise of American Life* was a direct factor in Roosevelt's decision to run as an independent "progressive Republican" candidate in the 1912 election. And Croly had some interesting views on the Constitution.

In *The Promise of American Life,* he argued that the Federalists who drafted the Constitution represented "chiefly the people of wealth and education," and as such they "demanded a government adequate to protect existing propertied rights." This resulted in a Constitution that, according to Croly, "did succeed in giving some effect to their distrust of the democratic principle." To Croly, the Founders were rich men looking out for their fortunes who were "distrustful" of democracy.

If Croly planted the seeds of the constitutional suspicion in 1909, he doubled down on them in 1914 in *Progressive Democracy.* In the introduction to that work, he complained: "Ever since the Constitution was established, a systematic and insidious attempt has been made to possess American public opinion with a feeling of its peculiarly sacred character."

Croly also approvingly cited the work of Charles Beard, another progressive scholar, who once wrote that the Constitution was created by "a small and active group of men immediately interested through their personal possessions in the outcome of their labors," because they were losing money under the earlier Articles of Confederation government. Croly found that "Professor Beard's investigations do indicate that the Constitution was . . . 'put over' by a small minority of able, vigorous and unscrupulous property owners" and concludes himself that "the American democracy rallied to an undemocratic Constitution."

This almost Marxist interpretation of the Constitution as a tool to advance the economic fortunes of the Framers would certainly render it a flawed document in the progressive calculus. But even before Croly and Beard, one of their progressive compatriots anticipated these ideas. Writing in *Congressional Government* in 1885, the book that was developed from his doctoral thesis, Woodrow Wilson criticized "blind worship" of the Constitution. He excitedly proclaimed that his generation was "the first Americans to hear our own countrymen ask whether the Constitution is still adapted to serve the purposes for which it was intended."

Obama echoed Wilson's sentiments in a slightly different way during his second inaugural address, saying, "When times change, so must we."

❚ LIE 4 ❚

PROGRESSIVES OPPOSE INCOME INEQUALITY

The dream of upward mobility that made this country a model for the world feels further and further out of reach and many Americans understandably feel frustrated, even angry. . . . Some are calling it a throwback to the Gilded Age of the robber barons.

—HILLARY CLINTON, NEW AMERICA FOUNDATION, 2014

To my mind, if you have seen a massive transfer of wealth from the middle class to the top one-tenth of one percent, you know what, we've got to transfer that back if we're going to have a vibrant middle class.

—BERNIE SANDERS, 2016 CAMPAIGN

THE LIE

Hillary Clinton says that "income inequality" is one of the "biggest issues we face." She wants to "reshuffle the deck" to address the issue. Bernie Sanders railed against both "income inequality" and "wealth inequality" during his campaign for president. Liberal outlets such as the *New York Times* routinely publish columns and editorials discussing the need to act urgently in the crisis.

Behind these sob stories is a pervasive fear. Some rich guy somewhere is taking more than his fair share. He's cheating you. He's using you. Only by giving power to progressives will these nefarious profit seekers be stopped. Only through progressivism will income distribution be balanced.

THE TRUTH

Rich liberals have no real interest in fixing "income inequality"—at least as it applies to their *own* income. Take Michael Moore, the socialist filmmaker who loves to rail against the evil millionaires in high-rises in New York who are looking down on the Everyman. While leading the Occupy Wall Street protests in 2011, Moore pretended to be a working-class hero, just like the demonstrators. When Piers Morgan asked Moore on national television about being part of the "one percent," Moore feigned shock and flat-out lied, responding, "Of course I'm not. How can I be in the one percent?" But independent analysts have estimated Moore's worth at around $50 million. In 2012, the cutoff for the "one percent" in America was a net worth of $20 million.

In other words, Moore lied. But why? Because even he recognizes the absurdity of a multimillionaire telling a working family that they aren't paying enough taxes. Because Moore is, in fact, the aloof millionaire looking down on poor people, just like the imaginary enemies he rails against.

Moore isn't the only millionaire entertainer who wants to make sure a wise progressive government makes decisions for us. Just look at some of the unbelievably wealthy celebrities who, along with Moore, supported Sanders in 2016:

- Singer Neil Young, with a net worth of $65 million, supported Sanders and let him use his music at rallies.
- Actors Tim Robbins and Susan Sarandon, while no longer a Hollywood power couple, threw their weight separately behind the democratic socialist and still have a combined net worth of more than $100 million.
- Dick Van Dyke, who has amassed a net worth of $30 million

during several decades on the stage and screen, specifically said he supported Sanders because he reminded him of a "New Deal Democrat" from the Franklin Roosevelt era. As we show in this book, Van Dyke is more right than even he probably knows.

You might further think it strange that Clinton, who made $3 million for giving three speeches in 2013, is telling the rest of us to fork over more money to the government. But it's not strange. It's predictable. Because none of this is really about helping the poor. It is about control.

What exactly does the phrase *income inequality* even mean? To take a literal definition, it's the fact that some people earn more money than others, something that obviously can't be prevented unless all salaries are set by the state. No modern-day progressives will go that far—at least not yet—so what they've said they really mean is that they want to narrow the gap between the rich and the poor in America. But that is a lie, too. Progressives don't have a realistic plan to make the poor richer. That would involve encouraging independence, entre-preneurship, ambition—all qualities the Left deplores. All they really do know is how to make everyone else poorer. Except, of course, themselves. *Do as I say, not as I do.*

Their preferred way to do that is through massive tax increases. Sanders, who is among the most extreme of the lot, advocated an astounding $19 trillion in new taxes. His supporters called it the "Robin Hood tax," because they claimed it would take from the rich and give to the poor.

Another tactic is a relentless increase in the minimum wage, which really benefits teenagers and punishes struggling workers. Wealthy liberals love this idea, pretending that it's an easy way to help the poor. Their logic says that if you set a minimum wage that's above the poverty level, then no one can be in poverty. That's another lie.

Since 1980, the federal minimum wage has been increased nine times. Yet according to the U.S. Census Bureau, the percentage of Americans who fall below the poverty level is now sixteen percent—a three percent *increase* since 1980, despite those nine minimum-wage hikes.

The truth is that raising the minimum wage actually has the opposite effect on poverty from what progressives would like everyone to believe. Rising minimum wages mean higher unemployment. A study conducted by the Federal Reserve Bank in San Francisco found that minimum-wage increases may have cost the economy as many as two hundred thousand jobs.

Those jobs are mostly entry-level. They are low-skill and do not usually require much experience. But they are important because they help new workers develop skills and climb up to the next rung on the ladder. These are the jobs the poor need the most—the alternative is welfare—but wealthy liberals want to make them more expensive for employers. So businesses, at least the ones interested in profits, eliminate positions, cut hours, outsource the jobs, or replace them with automation or computers.

If they can't do any of that and are instead forced to pay workers more, do you think they just eat the cost? Of course not. They simply charge more for their products. They pass the cost on to their customers, rich and poor alike. So the price of milk goes up sixty cents a gallon, the price of toothpaste goes up twenty-five cents, and so on. It adds up. And soon the cost overtakes the "raise" that a low-income worker received as part of the minimum-wage hike. Clinton, Sanders, and Moore can absorb that increased cost of living just fine. Do you know who gets hurt? Those who live paycheck to paycheck or have a kitchen-table budget. It's the poor and the middle class who suffer. And it's been proven time and time again.

A third favorite tactic to address "income disparity" is proposing a universal basic income, which, in reality, is money that working people pay to everyone else on an annual basis, regardless of what they contribute to society. Progressives say that if you replace all welfare programs with a fixed level of income, you will cure poverty (in Switzerland, they've proposed $2,700 a month). It's a somewhat new idea, and even some conservatives have gotten on board.

Simply handing out a couple of grand a month to every downtrodden citizen in America would be prohibitively expensive. The Swiss proposal would cost around $210 billion annually, or an astounding thirty percent of Switzerland's GDP. Some estimates show that a guaranteed basic income in the United States would cost Americans upward of $3 trillion a year. It would take Sanders' levels of taxation to pay for this massive redistribution. And it's not Clinton and Moore who would be paying for it. Millions of working Americans would pay for millions of nonworking Americans.

It's a direct transfer of wealth, so let's call it what it really is: socialism.

Socialism is the idea that the inherent unfairness of life can be regulated and altered by government to make everyone equal. There have been some historical examples of this succeeding—but not in the way it was promised. In places like the former Soviet Union, North Korea, or Cuba, socialism has instituted fairness by making everyone equally miserable and destitute.

It reminds me of a great line from P. J. O'Rourke. About traveling to the Soviet Union with a group of Communists, he wrote, "These were people who believed everything about the Soviet Union was perfect, but they were bringing their own toilet paper." You have to ask yourself, if liberals truly cared about income inequality, why do they want to make being poor more expensive?

There's also a social aspect to minimum wages and guaranteed incomes. Benjamin Franklin talked about it in 1766, and it's amazing how well the wisdom of the Founding Fathers holds up today. Franklin wrote:

I am for doing good to the poor, but . . . I think the best way of doing good to the poor, is not making them easy in poverty, but leading or driving them out of it. I observed . . . that the more public provisions were made for the poor, the less they provided for themselves, and of course became poorer. And, on the contrary, the less was done for them, the more they did for themselves, and became richer.

We value work in this country. What I find deplorable about the idea of a universal basic income is that it robs people of the pursuit of happiness. It makes them satisfied with mediocrity. It makes them comfortable with not aspiring to do great things or give back to the country.

Arthur Brooks, who runs the conservative American Enterprise Institute, suggests that policies like these are robbing people not only of their dreams but also of their happiness. According to Brooks, choosing to pursue the four key virtues of faith, family, community, and work is an important part of one's happiness. It takes, as you might imagine, a little bit of discipline.

The first three virtues are self-explanatory, not controversial. The last is work. I think it's the most important element, and I think it should be as uncontroversial as the others. Ronald Reagan said there is "dignity" in work. Is there anything more rotten than depriving someone of his or her dignity?

Not all jobs are fun. Not all work is enjoyable. But that's not why we toil. Happiness lies in the things that are hard. There is joy in accomplishment. There is passion and excitement in creativity. Hard work is a vehicle for those virtues.

Again, what lies at the root of the progressive obsession with wealth and attacking those who have it (even when they are wealthy themselves) is fear. The fear of one day being poor. The fear of failure and of being alone with no one to support them. These giant safety-net programs and guaranteed incomes and high minimum wages are *for them* in case they ever need it. They don't have confidence in themselves, and they don't have confidence in their communities and their families to help if illness strikes or they lose their fortunes. And so they turn to the government.

We should all reject redistributive philosophy, not only on economic and patriotic grounds but also on moral ones. People cannot be pulled out of poverty, they can only climb out of it themselves. We can all be there to lend a helping hand and a lot of encouragement, but the moment we try to eliminate the poor through federal policy, the whole system collapses.

And maybe that's exactly the way they want it.

▮ LIE 5 ▮

THE REPUBLICAN PARTY
OPPOSES PROGRESSIVISM

What is at stake is more than one small country; it is a big idea: a new world order, where diverse nations are drawn together in common cause to achieve the universal aspirations of mankind.

—GEORGE H. W. BUSH, 1991

I'm a George W. Bush conservative.

—GEORGE W. BUSH, 2008

THE LIE
....

We've seen how the Democratic Party has been hijacked by progressives. They've been very effective in enacting their agenda, but they couldn't have done it alone. They would never have been so successful if an opposition party was united and determined in its efforts to stop them, whatever the costs.

For decades now, we've heard from Republican leaders that we need to elect them to pursue conservative priorities. They are the ones who tell us they're the stalwart defenders of the Constitution against big-government Democrats. When Republicans were swept into the congressional majority by the Tea Party wave of 2010, the first thing new Speaker John Boehner did was to read the Constitution to the House Chamber. Mitch McConnell always talks about his "fidelity to the Constitution." Come election time, every Republican talks about his or her deep, abiding love for our nation's founding documents and his or her desire to thwart the progressive agenda.

I once believed that. I think most of us did. We knew the Left lied to us regularly. What we didn't know was that the Republicans were doing the same thing. They ask for our votes, promise to stand against the progressive agenda of Obama, Clinton, Reid, and Pelosi, and then they go to Washington only to enact it or, at best, make compromises on the margins. *We just didn't have the votes to stop it*, they tell us.

Almost all of these Republicans got into office because of our support. We believed in them. We campaigned for them and fought for them and voted for them. And yet we've ended up disappointed. The progressive agenda is more successful than it's ever been. Conservatives have lost ground in the culture war *and* the policy war.

How did it happen? Because Republicans—not all but many, and certainly the most influential—are advocates of progressivism, too.

THE TRUTH

The first president who actually enacted progressive policies and embraced the antidemocratic, antibusiness rhetoric of the progressive movement wasn't a Democrat. He was a Republican, one of the most popular in American history: Theodore Roosevelt. He is still lionized in certain Republican circles (like Bill Kristol's *Weekly Standard*) and other so-called neoconservative outposts that embrace TR's big-government philosophy.

Roosevelt was so zealous about creating a Washington, D.C.–based empire that he destroyed the Republican Party in 1912 to do it, running a mad, quixotic campaign against his former friend, William Howard Taft, that guaranteed the election of Woodrow Wilson.

But Teddy Roosevelt Republicanism—the kind that truly believes in a big government to solve all of our problems—never went away. Government continued to grow, and even so-called conservative politicians got used to the expansion of their own powers that grew along with it. After all, no matter what their party label, some people are just drawn to being career politicians because of the power and control that come with the position. Thus, the acceptance, and even furtherance, of big government remained the prevailing view of the GOP throughout the Eisenhower and Nixon eras and during the advent of the so-called Rockefeller Republicans of the 1970s.

Progressive Republicans hated the candidacy of Ronald Reagan in 1980. Reagan didn't just dislike their philosophy, he utterly repudiated it. That was why establishment Republicans at the time depicted Reagan as a senile fool or a dangerous loose cannon. As soon as he was out of office, the Republican Party was back at its big government tricks again.

George H. W. Bush implicitly criticized the guy who got him elected—Reagan—by calling for a "kinder, gentler" nation. We soon learned that this was actually code for being kinder and gentler to the nation's lobbyists. The first Bush raised taxes after promising not to, increased the size of the federal government, expanded burdensome environmental regulations on small businesses, and put one of the most liberal justices of the twentieth century, David Souter, on the Supreme Court.

Worrying about his reelection chances, Bush 41 delighted in supporting and helping to enact the Americans with Disabilities Act (ADA). This is another in a long line of those wonderful-sounding programs—who doesn't want to help the disabled?—that turned into a massive waste of taxpayer dollars and an excuse to greatly expand the federal government.

One problem with the ADA was that it broadly defined disability to mean basically, well, anything: "a physical or mental impairment that substantially limits one or more of the major life activities."

Within two decades, according to at least one report on the law, Congress expanded that definition to include diabetics, the depressed, and people having "significant" trouble "standing, sitting, reaching, lifting, bending, reading, concentrating, thinking, communicating and interacting with others." As a result, the ADA became known as "Attorneys' Dreams Answered" because it led to thousands, hundreds of thousands, of lawsuits against private industries. A few examples:

- In California, a P.F. Chang's restaurant was sued under the law because the coat hook on the door of a toilet stall was at an improper height.
- Using the ADA, the federal government sued United Parcel Service for its refusal to hire one-eyed drivers for its big trucks, even though UPS argued that such a hire would endanger "the health or safety of others to a greater extent that if an individual without a disability performed the job."
- One wheelchair-bound convicted child molester who lived in Arizona was said to take regular trips to California just to file nuisance lawsuits against businesses under the ADA.

Again, these suits, and thousands like them, occurred as a result of the actions of a *Republican* administration. Unfortunately, the next Bush administration didn't do any better.

With the full support of many Republicans in Congress, George W. Bush's administration passed Medicare Part D, a brand-new prescription-drug entitlement program that significantly expanded the federal government, not to mention the country's deficit. The administration also supported a taxpayer bailout of the bad decisions of Wall Street, under TARP, which was capped off by the bizarre, Orwellian pronouncement by the president that he had "abandoned free-market principles to save the free market."

I've heard from Republicans who were in the room during some of the debates over TARP. What they saw were Mafia tactics; people had to commit to the bill before they could leave the room. They were told they would be personally responsible for the downfall of civilization if the government didn't hand billions to Wall Street, without any real plan or accountability.

The Bush administration spent billions in Afghanistan and Iraq in a Wilsonian effort to remake two backward societies into perfectible democracies, to enact the progressive notion that we were gods who could create the perfect world. Both Bushes also talked about some variation of a "new world order."

Bush 43 signed into law a campaign-finance reform bill, a passion of *Republican* Senator John McCain, which was one of the most anti-free-speech laws passed by Congress since the Sedition Act under Wilson. As Senator Ted Cruz, among others, has pointed out, limiting the amount of contributions that an individual can make to a candidate of his or her choice is a racket designed to protect incumbents from being challenged by outsiders. Because incumbents already have good name recognition, they generally need far less money to win re-election than a challenger needs to get elected in the first place. (Not to mention that incumbents, because of their time in office, also usually have access to tons of money from lobbyists and special interests.)

Republicans are still at it. The Republican leadership in the House, led by men like John Boehner and Eric Cantor, pushed for amnesty for illegal immigrants. They were urged on and supported by corporate-welfare advocates, such as members of the U.S. Chamber of Commerce, who are prepared to flout all respect for the rule of law, as long as they can get cheap labor for their own businesses.

They also pushed for funding of the Export-Import Bank, a government entity created by Franklin Roosevelt that gives taxpayer-backed loans to the "right" corporations and supposedly helps them sell American products overseas. While it sells itself as a tool to help small businesses, the truth is that nearly ninety percent of the Export-

Import Bank's funding goes to big corporations such as Boeing, General Electric, and Caterpillar. These companies do a fine job of creating their products and providing American jobs all on their own. According to the classical liberal, free-market way of thinking, they do not need any extra handouts from the state. But that's not what progressives believe.

In case there's still any doubt, let's check in with Stuart Chase (discussed at more length in part III of this book), the key FDR adviser who coined the term *New Deal*. In his eighteen-point plan to move the United States from free enterprise to a new "Political System X"—which Chase also tentatively identified as "state capitalism"—he included this line at number nine: "The control of foreign trade by the government."

The Export–Import Bank, a product of Roosevelt and Chase's New Deal, is a major part of keeping the government's hand in foreign trade, clearly a progressive notion. But what does this have to do with Republicans?

In 2015, the Export–Import Bank faced its first real existential threat, as conservative lawmakers refused to renew its charter, actually putting it out of action for a matter of months. The fight over the Export–Import Bank that year led to many strident debates in both houses of Congress as Republicans found themselves drawing battle lines. In the Senate, Ted Cruz took to the floor to call out Majority Leader Mitch McConnell for refusing to disclose a secret deal McConnell had made to keep the Export–Import Bank open.

In the end, sixty-two Republicans in the House joined most Democrats on a measure to save the Export–Import Bank. In December 2015, final legislation that would preserve the bank until 2019 was tucked into a larger highway bill and passed both Houses. The Washington media called it "a paragon of Capitol Hill humming along as it was designed to."

Republicans voted for more government control of trade, a progressive principle straight out of the New Deal playbook. People like Cruz and Representative Jeb Hensarling tried to put a stop to it, but, as the media said, progressivism just kept "humming along" with bipartisan support. Why? Because too many politicians, including Republicans, were afraid of giving up even an inch of their own power and control. They feared the consequences if they failed to deliver for their corporate pals at the Chamber of Commerce and other big-money lobbyists. Given a chance to shut down a progressive New Deal program, Republicans instead decided to keep their heads down and keep their power, too afraid to give the real free market a chance.

▌ LIE 6 ▐

PROGRESSIVES BELIEVE IN
RACIAL EQUALITY (EUGENICS)

Hillary Clinton has spent her career fighting for equality for all Americans.
—PRIORITIES USA ACTION, PRO-CLINTON SUPER-PAC, 2016 CAMPAIGN

As president of the United States, nobody will fight harder to end institutional racism and to reform our broken criminal justice system.
—BERNIE SANDERS, 2016 CAMPAIGN

THE LIE
....

Progressives tell us over and over again how much they believe in
equality for everyone. They spend a lot of time talking about racial
equality—and definitely not because the African-American community is seen as a deep and critical reservoir for Democratic votes.

In the 2016 Democratic primary, Hillary Clinton and Bernie
Sanders tripped over each other in their attempts to shine as the greater
champion of black Americans. The Clinton campaign's line was that
"more than a half a century after Dr. King voiced his dream for a
more equal America, and civil rights activists marched and died for
the right to vote, America's struggle with racism remains far from
finished."

Clinton herself has declared: "We can't hide from any of these hard truths about race and justice in America. We have to name them, and own them, and then change them."

Sanders has also invoked Dr. Martin Luther King, Jr., pandering desperately for votes during the South Carolina primary with an ad highlighting his attendance at King's landmark "I Have a Dream" speech in 1963. "He was there when Dr. King marched on Washington," the ad says of Sanders, "unafraid to challenge the status quo to end racial profiling, take on police misconduct, and take down a system that profits from mass imprisonment." In the same spot, Sanders thunders, "There is no president who will fight harder to end institutional racism."

Even fellow authoritarian Donald Trump made his own ham-handed attempts to woo black voters—or, rather, to declare that he didn't have to: "I have a great relationship with African-Americans," he told CNN. "I just have great respect for them, and you know they like me. I like them." His outreach to Hispanic voters was best exemplified by his posting a picture of himself on Cinco de Mayo eating a taco salad. Flashing a grin and a thumbs-up, Trump declared in the photo's caption: "I love Hispanics!"

Another prominent minority community, Americans with disabilities, is less aggressively courted around election season, but progressives nevertheless take prominent stances on rights for the disabled. Clinton told us, "We should acknowledge how the disabilities community has played such an important role in changing things for the better in our country," and her campaign pointed out that "Hillary has spent her life fighting for the rights of Americans with disabilities."

According to "champion for the rights of people with disabilities" Sanders, "We as a nation have a moral responsibility to ensure that all Americans have access to the programs and the support needed to contribute to society, live with dignity, and achieve a high quality of life."

But what if all of this were a cruel lie? What if it were all a shallow and cynically rhetorical attempt to win votes and assume power? What if these minority communities were actually the object of progressive contempt rather than compassion?

THE TRUTH

Progressives actually do believe in equality for everyone—as long as everyone is equally strong, brilliant, and "Nordic." Progressives may talk a lot about fighting for the rights of African-Americans, disabled Americans, and other minorities now, but the movement from which they continue to claim inspiration fought for exactly the opposite: their lynching, their sterilization and abortion, and their political neutralization. In perhaps less offensive and less overt ways than a century ago, that fight continues today.

Here is one of the "hard truths about race and justice in America" that Clinton will never acknowledge: in traditional American progressivism, there is literally no place for those who don't fit into progressives' ideal society.

We learned about Margaret Sanger's obsession with eugenics in part I and her many unsavory quotes about culling the "intake and output on morons, mental defectives, epileptics . . . illiterates, paupers, unemployables, criminals, prostitutes, dope-fiends." Sanger recognized that eugenics' aim could be advanced by birth control, especially among the lower classes. Although there was some initial resistance to her methods—there were concerns that "desirable" people using birth control would be counterproductive—Thomas Leonard notes that Sanger "convinced skeptical eugenicists that birth control could be a valuable tool of eugenics."

The other valuable tool was forced sterilization, the removal of testicles and ovaries. Progressives across America in the 1910s and '20s championed "model laws" for sterilization. One early adopter was New Jersey, which passed an act "to authorize and provide for the sterilization of feeble-minded (including idiots, imbeciles and morons), epileptics, rapists and certain criminals and other defectives." The man who signed that law was Governor Woodrow Wilson.

Virginia passed its eugenics legislation in 1924. Three years later, it was challenged before the U.S. Supreme Court in the case of *Buck v. Bell*. The case involved Carrie Buck, a young woman who had given birth to an illegitimate child and who had been deemed "feeble-minded" and committed to a mental institution, which had then ordered her sterilized. Buck and her legal guardian protested, claiming that her right to due process as well as her rights under the Equal Protection Clause of the Fourteenth Amendment had been violated.

The Court ruled eight-to-one against Buck, and the majority opinion was written by progressive icon Oliver Wendell Holmes, Jr., in especially chilling language: "It is better for all the world, if instead of waiting to execute degenerate offspring for crime, or to let them starve for their imbecility, society can prevent those who are manifestly unfit from continuing their kind. The principle that sustains compulsory vaccination is broad enough to cover cutting the Fallopian tubes." Agreeing with the "evidence" presented that Buck's mother, Buck herself, and Buck's daughter were all "feeble-minded," Holmes declared: "Three generations of imbeciles are enough."

The state of Virginia cut Buck's Fallopian tubes. She was one of sixty thousand Americans forcibly sterilized under eugenics laws.

Decades later, when the world was sifting through the rubble of the World War II and the monstrosities of state-sponsored eugenics had been laid bare, Hitler's surviving eugenicists were put on trial at Nuremberg. From the dock, these men—whose leader had been inspired by Wilson's and Virginia's model sterilization laws—tried to argue their case. The presiding Allied judges were treated to a grim defense: the Nazis quoted Justice Holmes's opinion in *Buck v. Bell*.

State-sponsored eugenics has, by the grace of God, since been exposed for the horror show that it is. But one vestige of the progressive eugenicist heyday of the early 1900s remains: Planned Parenthood, Sanger's organization, whose explicit mission is to help women exterminate hundreds of thousands of human beings every year, with a disproportionate effect on children of color.

In 2009, Planned Parenthood conferred the Margaret Sanger Award on Hillary Clinton. Did Clinton refuse this award? Did she decline to associate herself with a vicious racist and eugenicist, a woman who explicitly wrote in a letter that "we do not want word to go out that we want to exterminate the Negro population"?

On the contrary. "I admire Margaret Sanger enormously, her courage, her tenacity, her vision," Clinton said, later adding that "there are a lot of lessons that we can learn from her life and from the cause she launched and fought for and sacrificed so bravely."

How could she admire a woman like this? Because at the very heart of the progressive movement is the belief that some people are better than others, that some people are more worthy, that some deserve to live, and others—so-called drains on society—deserve to die. They belittle conservatives for their "fetish" for life. What are they afflicted with, then, but a "fetish" for death?

Planned Parenthood carries out more than three hundred thousand abortions every year. And it continues to target minorities by disproportionately locating Planned Parenthood clinics in black and Hispanic neighborhoods (nearly eighty percent of its facilities are located in or near these areas). Black women, while making up only about 6.6 percent of the population, accounted for 35.7 percent of all abortions in 2010.

Could Sanger, a woman who once stood before an audience dressed in Ku Klux Klan robes in 1926, ever have imagined how her grand scheme would turn out?

If fear drives the progressives' quest for more power and more control, why do they fear those they seek to weed out through eugenics? What threat could possibly be posed by the "morons" and "mental defectives" Sanger railed against? It's simple: these people stood in the way of the progressive utopia. These "undesirables" could not overthrow a progressive state, but they could erode it from within with their imperfections. In order to create the perfect progressive society, mankind had to "progress" beyond mental illness and other impurities—by any means necessary.

Is it any wonder that progressive eugenicists made common cause with the Ku Klux Klan? Is it any wonder that American progressives' pioneering work in eugenics inspired Hitler? So many progressives threw themselves into the "scientific" work of figuring out whose genes deserved to live on and whose should be made to die out. But what drove them? What drove the zeal behind the eugenics movement and the creation of Planned Parenthood, which continues its work today?

Fear, of course. The same fear we've met on nearly every other page of this book. Yes, some eugenicists may have pitied the "undesirables" they sought to remove from the human gene pool, some certainly hated them, and some may have thought they were simply building a better society through science. But the common thread was fear, whether they knew it or not. They feared their world would be undermined by every "unfit" person allowed to continue to live in it. They looked at the population with mental, behavioral, or other issues, and they did not see their fellow men and women in need of help, they saw a menace to be feared. That, of course, was the ultimate irony: progressive eugenicists dismissed their targets as merely the "feeble-minded," yet they were apparently strong enough to constitute a threat to the whole progressive agenda.

This may all seem hard to take considering modern progressives' vow to fight for equality for all Americans. But the truth is, their ideological forebears fought for the exact opposite. And, like Clinton's continued veneration of eugenicist Sanger, modern progressives remain ignorant—most likely willfully ignorant—of the sordid history of their movement. Until they fully repudiate their past, however, their supposed commitment to "equality" for less fortunate Americans will continue to ring hollow.

▌ LIE 7 ▌

PROGRESSIVES OPPOSE NAZISM, FASCISM, AND COMMUNISM

The Nazis had destroyed the Left, but the Right remained. . . . For [Hitler], the Nazi socialist slogans had been merely propaganda, means of winning over the masses on his way to power.

—WILLIAM SHIRER, *THE RISE AND FALL OF THE THIRD REICH*

THE LIE
....

You recognize one of the Left's favorite parlor tricks, yes? They like to label any conservative they don't like (which is pretty much all of them) as the "next Hitler" and terrify the rest of us about a new Reich determined to strip away basic human rights.

Case in point: George W. Bush. (Although Bush was, as we've seen, hardly true to foundational conservative principles, he was nonetheless a favorite target of the leftist entertainment industry.)

Comedian and actress Janeane Garofalo was a constant critic of the former president, once referring to the Bush administration as the "forty-third Reich."

Following the 2004 elections, singer Linda Ronstadt attacked not only Bush but all newly elected Republicans, saying, "Now we've got a new bunch of Hitlers."

The left-wing hate group MoveOn.org celebrated a video sub-mitted as part of a contest in which Bush was compared to Hitler and proclaimed "what were war crimes in 1945 is foreign policy in 2003."

In 2008, Madonna used the song "Get Stupid" to display images of Senator John McCain alongside Hitler.

In 2012, there were a number of comparisons made by those on the left between Mitt Romney and the architect of the Holocaust. Liberal blogger Matthew Yglesias suggested that Hitler and Romney were somehow comparable because they both used Swiss bank ac-counts, and Obama adviser David Axelrod referred to Romney's campaign efforts in Illinois as a "Mittzkrieg," an obvious reference to the Nazis' Blitzkrieg military strategy in World War II.

And in 2016, TV's *The View*'s resident nutbar leftist, Joy Behar, called support for Ted Cruz akin to "Jews for Hitler."

There's a method to all of this madness. Progressives constantly terrify their followers by preaching that conservatives are would-be authoritarians who would return us to the years of Hitler, Mus-solini, and Stalin, a world of racists and political purges and eco-nomic punishment to those who don't rank among the privileged few. There's a reason the media loves to refer to supporters of Stalin, for example, as "conservatives." In 2014, the *Washington Post* pub-lished an article about neo-Stalinist Vladimir Putin entitled "Why U.S. Conservatives Love Russia's Vladimir Putin." (Spoiler alert: They don't.)

This tactic was perhaps most infamously employed back in 1987, when progressives like Senator Edward Kennedy railed against Ronald Reagan's nomination of Judge Robert Bork to the Supreme Court. This fearmongering was the beginning of a consistent pro-gressive attack against nearly all conservatives by likening them to authoritarians of yesteryear.

Kennedy ranted on the floor of the U.S. Senate:

Robert Bork's America is a land in which women would be forced into back-alley abortions, blacks would sit at segregated lunch counters, rogue police could break down citizens' doors in midnight raids, schoolchildren could not be taught about evolution, writers and artists could be censored at the whim of the government, and the doors of the Federal courts would be shut on the fingers of millions of citizens.

THE TRUTH
....

The reality is that it's progressives, not conservatives, who have been backers of authoritarians throughout history, from Hitler to Mussolini to Stalin. But they've realized that playing defense is not a fun place to be, so they go on offense, leveling these ridiculous charges against conservatives as though a love of individual liberty and constitutional principles were somehow related to the Third Reich.

Let's take Hitler for starters. Progressives didn't oppose Hitler in the 1930s; they mostly embraced him as a visionary.

Writer H. G. Wells, who was one of the most influential progressives of the twentieth century, said in 1932 that progressives must become "liberal fascists" and "enlightened Nazis." Regarding totalitarianism, he stated, "I have never been able to escape altogether from its relentless logic."

W. E. B. Du Bois, cofounder of the NAACP, called the establishment of the Nazi dictatorship in Germany "absolutely necessary to get the state in order."

Joseph P. Kennedy, father of Jack, Bobby, and Teddy, was a legendary apologist for the Nazis, a truth that the mainstream media glossed over for years. Kennedy had supported the disastrous Munich appeasement treaty with Hitler negotiated by British prime minister Neville Chamberlain, and he shared a Hitler-like animus toward the Jews that led him to argue that they should be shipped to Africa. Kennedy also doubted the success of democracy as a long-term enterprise. "Democracy is finished in England," the ambassador told the *Boston Globe*. "It may be here." His views, for a time, even affected his young son, the future president. "Fascism?" the youthful president-to-be once wrote. "The right thing for Germany."

Contrary to progressive revisionism and acclaimed Nazi chroniclers such as William Shirer, Hitler was not a man of the right who paid lip service to socialist causes. He was, in fact, as author Jonah Goldberg and others have pointed out, a "man of the left." This wasn't something Hitler tried to hide, given that the word *Nazi* is short for the National Socialist Party.

In 1998, historian George Watson wrote, "It is now clear beyond all reasonable doubt that Hitler and his associates believed they were socialists, and that others, including democratic socialists, thought so too." Hitler privately acknowledged to acquaintances his "profound debt" to Marxism. "I have learned a great deal from Marxism," he remarked, "as I do not hesitate to admit."

Hitler's Nazi platform sounded a lot like Obama's or Clinton's does today: a planned centralized economy with strict gun control, separation of church and state, a ban on private schools, universal health care, and a demand that "the state be charged first with providing the opportunity for a livelihood." That's not to mention sharing the eugenics vision of progressives such as Margaret Sanger, by attempting to exterminate an entire race of people in the most monstrous crime in history. Small wonder that today's progressives like to overlook their support for the Nazi dream.

The Left's love affair with Nazism was no random flight of fancy. Leftists had a similar ardor for another great visionary and noted humanitarian: Benito Mussolini. Historian Charles Beard was among those who praised Il Duce, a venomous thug and Hitler ally: "Beyond question, an amazing experiment is being made [in Italy], an experiment in reconciling individualism and socialism."

Muckraking journalists almost universally admired Mussolini. Lincoln Steffens—a progressive writer who also hailed the Soviet Union as "the future"—said that Italian fascism made Western democracy, by comparison, look like a system run by "petty persons with petty purposes." Mussolini, Steffens proclaimed reverently, had been "formed" by God "out of the rib of Italy."

Edward M. House, a leading adviser to Woodrow Wilson, touted Mussolini as a "beneficent dictator," proclaiming, "Italy has such a government now functioning under the able and courageous Mussolini." And one of Franklin Roosevelt's prized advisers, Rexford Guy Tugwell, praised Italian fascism as "the cleanest, neatest, most efficiently operating piece of social machinery I've ever seen."

Perhaps no vicious authoritarian received more elite progressive praise than "Uncle Joe" Stalin, the iron-fisted thug and accomplished con artist who charmed dim-witted Westerners while murdering his opponents in the Soviet Union and otherwise running the Russian economy into the ground.

Franklin Roosevelt's own vice president, Henry Wallace, who would have moved into the Oval Office had he not been replaced on a whim by Harry S. Truman in 1944, was one of the most notorious Soviet apologists in American history. "Even at his most murderous, as with the purge trials of the 1930s," one Wallace chronicler reported, "Stalin was defended by Wallace, who swallowed the party line that the dictator's execution of hundreds of people was a necessary anti-fascist action against a Hitler-backed fifth column."

There was also the infamous Walter Duranty, Moscow bureau chief for the *New York Times*, who won a Pulitzer Prize for parroting Stalinist propaganda. In one of his (many) notorious "reports" from the Soviet Union, Duranty denied the deaths of thousands of Soviet citizens resulting from Stalin-imposed starvations: "There is no famine or actual starvation nor is there likely to be," he wrote in the *Times* on November 15, 1931. When other reporters began spreading the news of the famine, Duranty was asked what he'd write. He responded: "Nothing. What are a few million dead Russians in a situation like this? Quite unimportant. This is just an incident in the sweeping historical changes here. I think the entire matter is exaggerated." Meanwhile, peasants in Ukraine, the *Weekly Standard* reported, "were dying at a rate of 25,000 a day."

Malcolm Muggeridge, a correspondent and contemporary of Duranty's, labeled him "the greatest liar of any journalist I have met in fifty years of journalism." Muggeridge went on to summarize the thinking of progressives of the day—the fools who were intent on romanticizing communism and ignoring obvious signs of its evil:

> *"Wise old [George Bernard] Shaw, high-minded old [Henri] Barbusse, the venerable [Sidney and Beatrice] Webbs, [André] Gide the pure in heart and [Pablo] Picasso the impure, down to poor little teachers, crazed clergymen and millionaires, driveling dons and very special correspondents like Duranty, all resolved, come what might, to believe anything, however preposterous, to overlook nothing, however villainous, to approve anything, however obscurantist and brutally authoritarian, in order to be able to preserve intact the confident expectation that one of the most thorough-going, ruthless and bloody tyrannies ever to exist on earth could be relied on to champion human freedom, the brotherhood of man, and all the other good liberal causes to which they had dedicated their lives.*

In 2003, the *New York Times* decided to "investigate" whether Duranty's Pulitzer Prize should be revoked. Did it rescind the award and apologize to the country? Of course not. The *Times* did what progressives always do: let the lies stand.

PART III
FEAR THE FUTURE

STUART CHASE, THE PROGRESSIVE PROPHET

At the time of this writing, more than a hundred years since the progressive movement first took root in America (though, as we've seen, its roots elsewhere go far deeper), Barack Obama—the progressive heir to men such as Woodrow and Teddy and Franklin and Lyndon—is preparing to leave office, having successfully presided over the "fundamental" transformation of America that he had long promised.

Fighting to replace Obama is Hillary Clinton, a self-proclaimed progressive, and the Republicans determined to stop her.

Or are they?

Ah, yes, the Republicans. The party that once stood for self-reliance and independence has been invaded and perverted by faux-conservatives—and even some legitimate progressives—who don't mind expanding government as long as their own power and perks are preserved. It's getting harder and harder (and, in some cases, impossible) to tell the political parties apart.

The Republican Party is, however, still home to a few staunch constitutionalists, such as Senator Ted Cruz, who understand that our founding documents serve as a road map. Throughout history, these documents have allowed us to course-correct ourselves and to be sure that despite the inevitable gyrations, we ultimately stand on the side of freedom.

It's also home to a few staunch authoritarians, such as Donald Trump, who has used fear and anger to transfix legions of otherwise good and faithful conservatives. He has evinced this in the bullying tone of his rhetoric, the bullying nature of his "policies" (if they can be called that), and the bullying tactics employed by his campaign.

Trump's goal is not to shrink government back to a more constitutionally appropriate size; he would much prefer to preside over a massive government as though he were an all-powerful CEO of a massive corporation. He doesn't want to reduce government, he just wants to run it more efficiently.

Trump, a defender of the human-extinction platform of Planned Parenthood, a contributor to the Clintons, Jimmy Carter, and even Walter Mondale, is a Trojan horse from the progressive movement being rolled into the GOP.

How did it come to this? Who could have seen the day coming when America would be on the precipice of a complete progressive revolution?

At least one man did. He was a Harvard-educated economist who was active in progressive politics from the Wilson administration all the way to Johnson's Great Society. He was one of the most important political thinkers most people have probably never heard of.

You've already heard his name earlier in this book: Stuart Chase.

Boston
Autumn 1911
A gust of wind sent a chill through the already-crisp fall air, rustling the almost barren trees in Copley Square. The piles of leaves that had already fallen were gathered up by the sharp winds and swirled

around the feet of those who found themselves walking through this busy Boston hub—including one wiry young man who was striding across the Square toward the Boston Public Library.

Stuart Chase walked with his shoulders hunched, not only against the cold but seemingly weighed down by the problems that plagued his mind. On the surface, everything appeared to be going well for him. He was twenty-two, almost twenty-three, and had already achieved a lot for himself.

Chase had been educated at fine schools, including MIT (his father's alma matter) and Harvard, from which he had graduated just a year before. He had a decent job working at his father's accounting firm, but something inside Chase hungered for more than debits, credits, and dusty old ledgers.

Here was a man who was coming of age at a heady time. And he knew it. He felt a similar enthusiasm for this new era among his contemporaries at Harvard, such as progressive journalist Walter Lippmann and Communist writer John Reed.* The three schoolmates were all active in socialist groups at Harvard, such as the Intercollegiate Socialist Society (ISS), which was founded in New York City in 1905 with the "influence and guidance" of Fabian socialists.

There was a movement growing that sought not just to solve the social problems of the age but also to advance society to ensure that these problems would never reoccur. Young Chase imbibed books like *Progress and Poverty* that had predicted a revolution. He worried deeply that the world would go down the wrong path during the coming change in the new twentieth century and that humanity would need a strong hand to push it onto the right path. Stirring in Chase was the feeling that he had to do something about it.

The winds of change, as much as the cold Boston breeze, pro-

---

* Reed would become a useful propaganda tool for the Bolshevik regime in subsequent years. He was lionized by Hollywood in Warren Beatty's 1981 film, *Reds*.

pelled him as he crossed Dartmouth Street and scurried up the library steps. He paused before entering the library and looked at the inscription above the entrance: BUILT BY THE PEOPLE AND DEDICATED TO THE ADVANCEMENT OF LEARNING.

Built by the people.

Chase remembered from Boston lore that architect Charles McKim had called his Renaissance Revival masterpiece a "palace of the people." Did "the people" appreciate it? he wondered. Moreover, could "the people" to whom this great edifice was dedicated ever be trusted to take their society down the right path?

He entered the library and breathed a little easier. This was where he felt most at home, a place he went to get away from the drudgery of accounting work and to educate himself about the great problems of the age.

Chase's footsteps echoed off the rounded ceiling of Bates Hall, whose high windows let in generous, bright sunlight for the readers at the long tables below, as he made his way to his inner sanctum: the economics section. There, among the tomes by men who sought to define the massive system of capital in which his father's accounting business was a mere cog, Chase sat down at a secluded table, pulled out a pen and some paper, and began to write.

So many are the roads and lanes and byways that branch from this open portal. I look back and see the straight, calm thoroughfare that has led me here. I look forward and stand dazed and blinded before the myriad ways that lead to ultimate darkness or light. Now I must choose my own path . . . from among the many and follow it in all faith and trust until experience bids me seek another. The world always turns aside to let one pass who knows where they are going.

Chase knew exactly where he was going—and how the world would turn aside to let progressives like him lead it.

The passage by Chase may read at first as if written by a young man who felt he was destined for great things, but upon closer inspection, it's easy to see evidence of something deeper: fear, specifically fear of the unknown. Chase seemed positively overwhelmed by all "the roads and lanes and byways" before him, especially in contrast to the "straight, calm thoroughfare" that was his relatively privileged upbringing. Far from confident about the path he would take, he was "dazed and blinded" and feared making the wrong choice between the "ultimate darkness or light." Chase realized that not only did *he* have to make the right choice between "ultimate darkness or light," but all of mankind would have to make that choice as well.

This was a choice that could not be left up to chance. He realized that in order to conquer this fear of the unknown, to make sure that everyone was not "dazed and blinded," he had to get involved. He had to help *make* the world turn aside.

As a result, Chase threw himself into progressive causes. By 1917, a profile in the journal of the Co-operative League of America noted that he was "active in various progressive movements," including the Fabian Club of Boston and the Massachusetts Single Tax League. The profile also revealed that he was "connected as an officer with the Massachusetts Birth Control League." ("Birth control" at that time was, of course, a thin veneer for eugenics.)

With the help of his father, Chase joined the administration of progressive hero Woodrow Wilson, serving as an investigator with the Federal Trade Commission. His beat was the Chicago meatpacking industry, a favorite target of progressives ever since Upton Sinclair's *The Jungle* had been published beginning in 1905. Chase was subsequently fired after members of the U.S. Senate discovered he had organized socialist activities while on government business investigating meatpackers in Chicago. They denounced him as a "Red accountant" who had "inflated" government data to make the industry look bad.

Chase was already learning that the ends justified the means, even when those means were illegal.

After losing his position in the Wilson administration, Chase dabbled in progressive circles and wrote books on economics, but he was mostly adrift until the summer of 1927, when he took a trip along with other economists as part of the "First American Trade Union Delegation" to the Soviet Union. Chase, with his lifelong socialist sympathies, must have jumped at the chance to see the grand socialist experiment up close. By that time, Lenin and Trotsky were both gone and Stalin was in charge, but that hardly mattered.

Apparently, Stalin did not disappoint. Historian Amity Shlaes recounts that despite only meeting with the Soviet dictator for six hours, the American delegation was "bowled over." It was part of a general fascination with totalitarian regimes among American progressive thinkers at the time. Shlaes explains that these scholars would travel abroad, and then "they come back and you see them . . . implementing things they learned from fascist Italy or from the world of Stalin." Shlaes notes: "The influence of these European entities from Russia to Italy was not parenthetical." As they advanced in their careers, "these people were not working for Moscow, but they were influenced by Moscow."

In 1931, Chase made the acquaintance of a man whose destiny would intertwine with his own: Franklin D. Roosevelt. At the time they met, Roosevelt was serving as governor of New York, while Chase had yet another book coming out that argued for greater government intervention in the private sector and more central economic planning (to be supported, of course, by increased federal spending). It was a look toward the future, and the book ended with Chase putting a question to his readers: "Why should Russians have all the fun remaking a world?"

The book's title? *A New Deal.*

Roosevelt was known for having, in the words of Oliver Wendell Holmes, "a second-class intellect, but a first-class temperament." The latter helped him to be an effective politician, and he made up for his deficiencies in the former by cherry-picking ideas from others. One such idea clearly came from Chase. As FDR accepted the Democratic presidential nomination in 1932, he declared: "I pledge you, I pledge myself, to a new deal for the American people."

Chase became a member of FDR's "Brain Trust," advising the president as he directed the unprecedented expansion of government that became a hallmark of the Roosevelt administration. After his brief and unfortunate experience in government nearly two decades earlier, Chase had finally found a progressive hero who shared and appreciated his social sentiments. While not a philosopher-king in the mold of Woodrow Wilson, FDR was at least a king who valued his philosophers.

Philosophers like Stuart Chase.

As he continued to produce popular books and articles, Chase became an important evangelist for New Deal policies, one of the administration's "foremost public analysts and interpreters." Throughout the 1930s, every year saw a new Chase book published, most continuing to preach "the inevitability of a planned economy." In 1937, FDR remarked that Chase was "teaching the American people more about economics than all the others combined." It certainly helped that it was the same brand of economics that FDR himself adhered to.

Chase didn't always see eye to eye with Roosevelt, especially when it came to foreign policy. Chase was a pacifist who supported the isolationist view that the United States should keep out of World War II. He wrote an entire book making exactly that argument, 1939's *The New Western Front.*

When the United States entered the war after the attack on Pearl

Harbor, Chase must once again have found himself confronting his fear of the unknown. Everything had been going so well. He was one of the most popular economics writers in America and a trusted adviser to the president. Government was expanding and spending money all in the name of helping the people. Chase and the United States were firmly on the right path toward the ultimate light.

And then came the war. Chase knew it could ruin everything and undo all of his work. The progression of mankind that he had taken a direct hand in guiding could be set back dramatically. The "ultimate darkness" that he feared in 1911 could easily be brought on by war. Chase knew he could not sit back and let that happen. He had to control his country's destiny as best he could.

During the war years, a progressive think tank called the Twentieth Century Fund—which had grown out of the Co-operative League and is still in operation today as the Century Foundation—commissioned Chase to write "a series of exploratory reports on postwar problems." The first of these was published in 1942 as *The Road We Are Traveling: 1914–1942*, with the subtitle "Guide lines for America's future as reported to the Twentieth Century Fund."

Despite the boring and scholarly title, this is an extremely important book. Today it remains obscure, and complete original copies, with all pages intact, are difficult to find. But if you locate one, you'll quickly see that Chase does indeed offer guidelines for America's future, just as the title suggests. A very chilling future.

In *The Road We Are Traveling*, Chase described his vision for the American and world economy after the end of World War II, but it was not a simple economic treatise. It was the journey into the mind of a man who feared that his life's work may be coming to ruin and who feared the unknown after a world-changing war. It was the fevered effort of a Fabian socialist, an admirer of Stalinist Russia, and an architect of central planning in the American economy to preserve his progressive vision for the future.

Chase, the onetime isolationist, opened *The Road We Are Traveling* with this statement: "America is at war. The objective of all of us must be to win." Why the shift? Once again, it was a classic progressive maneuver; he was justifying the war as a means to achieve his end goal of more government control. He learned to make the war work for him. He learned not to let a crisis go to waste.

Chase argued from the outset that a "retreat to free enterprise" would be impossible after the end of the war. The American economic system had been drifting away from free enterprise, he claimed, since before World War I. "In war and peace, boom and depression, the march toward centralized, collective controls has continued," he wrote.

This was not entirely inaccurate, considering that the time period between the world wars encompassed much of the first progressive era and FDR's New Deal. But by calling it a "retreat," Chase not so subtly framed the reembrace of free enterprise as regressive, a step backward for the country. "Many people, especially older people," he wrote, "will be weary to death of taxes, priorities, armaments, government decrees, forced savings, lease-lending around the globe." Imagine, Americans "weary to death of taxes" and "government decrees"? Fortunately for Chase, he believed that these people would not be able to stop the march of progress.

He feared that America would abandon FDR's planned economy after the war, so he attempted to convince Americans that *that* was their natural future, not a return to free enterprise or "business as usual." Never mind that "business as usual" also means a limited, sensible government. Never mind that "business as usual" means following the constitutional road map back to America's founding principles and values.

Chase's America had progressed beyond that system. And as Chase continually and manically drove home to his readers, "we can't go back."

THE ROAD MAP FOR POLITICAL SYSTEM X

So where *can* we go? What sort of government and economic system *should* we adopt if constitutionalism and the free market are passé? Good news: Chase sketched that out for us, too. There was just one problem: he couldn't come up with a name for it.

Chase tossed around terms such as *socialism*, *fascism*, and *state capitalism*, but those didn't seem to fit the bill. And it's not hard to figure out why. The United States was at war with fascists, of course, and like any good Fabian, he shied away from calling socialism by its name. State capitalism seemed closer to the mark, but it still wasn't quite right.

Instead, he labeled America's future system "something called X." This Political System X, according to Chase, was already "displacing the system of free enterprise, all over the world."

He offered a list of the "major characteristics" of this new system:

- "A strong, centralized government."
- "An executive arm growing at the expense of the legislative and judicial arms. In some countries, power is consolidated in a dictator, issuing decrees."
- "The control of banking, credit and security exchanges by the government."
- "The underwriting of employment by the government, either through armaments or public works."
- "The underwriting of social security by the government— old-age pensions, mothers' pensions, unemployment insurance, and the like."
- "The underwriting of food, housing and medical care, by the government. The United States is already experimenting with providing these essentials. Other nations are far along the road."

- "The use of the deficit spending technique to finance these underwritings. The annually balanced budget has lost its old-time sanctity."
- "The abandonment of gold in favor of managed currencies."
- "The control of foreign trade by the government, with increasing emphasis on bilateral agreements and barter deals."
- "The control of natural resources, with increasing emphasis on self-sufficiency."
- "The control of energy sources—hydroelectric power, coal, petroleum, natural gas."
- "The control of transportation—railway, highway, airway, waterway."
- "The control of agricultural production."
- "The control of labor organizations, often to the point of prohibiting strikes."
- "The enlistment of young men and women in youth corps devoted to health, discipline, community service and ideologies consistent with those of the authorities. The CCC camps have just inaugurated military drill."
- "Heavy taxation, with special emphasis on the estates and incomes of the rich."
- "Not much 'taking over' of property or industries in the old socialistic sense. The formula appears to be *control without ownership*. It is interesting to recall that the same formula is used by the great corporations in depriving stockholders of power."
- "The state control of communications and propaganda."

The characteristics of Political System X, Chase wrote, are "clearly contrary to the liberal democratic ideal," and "most of them are anathema to the doctrines of Adam Smith." (I guess it's good that he was at least aware about how far afield this system was from our founding.)

"Study this list and think hard about it," Chase challenged readers.

"[T]here is not an item on this list, which is not applicable in some degree to the United States."

What's perhaps most striking about Chase's utopian vision is how much of it seems to have already come to pass in the United States. Let's take them one by one:

- We obviously have a "strong, centralized government" that politicians of both parties have no compunction about expanding.
- The executive branch of government is "growing at the expense of the legislative and judicial arms"; this should be plainly obvious after the Obama administration's singular legacy of executive overreach.
- Government continues to exert "control of banking, credit and security exchanges," and the recent Dodd–Frank legislation has only further cemented that.
- The "underwriting of social security" and other social programs was realized as part of Johnson's Great Society, which Chase supported enthusiastically in his later life.
- "The underwriting of food, housing and medical care" is evident in First Lady Michelle Obama's signature issue: federal intervention into what local school districts feed their children.
- The prediction of government underwriting medical care has come true with a vengeance in the age of Obamacare.
- How about "use of the deficit spending technique to finance these underwritings"? Not even Chase could have conceived of a federal deficit of more than $500 billion, as is predicted for fiscal year 2017. Democratic *and* Republican politicians seem to agree with Chase's assessment that the quaint notion of a balanced budget has "lost its old-time sanctity."
- We achieved "the abandonment of gold in favor of managed currencies" under a Republican president when Richard Nixon took us off the gold standard in 1971.

- Government continues to have a hand in "the control of foreign trade." Starting under FDR, Congress began regularly ceding its own authority on trade by granting the president authority to "fast-track" trade negotiations.
- As for the "control of natural resources" and "energy sources," look no further than the environmental policies of the Obama administration. It propped up disastrous energy companies that fit its own agenda (Solyndra, for example) and fought to systematically shut down entire projects (the Keystone Pipeline) and industries (coal, for example) that didn't.
- "Railway, highway, airway [and] waterway" transportation have absolutely become more heavily regulated since Chase's writing. The 1950s saw both the establishment of the FAA and the federalization of highways (under Republican Dwight Eisenhower). And 1971 saw the creation of the National Railroad Passenger Corporation, or Amtrak, which is partially owned and subsidized by the government. Amtrak today holds a monopoly on passenger rail transportation in the United States.
- Chase mentioned government's "control without ownership" of industries instead of "'taking over' . . . in the old socialistic sense." This would be accomplished, of course, by government gradually inserting itself into the private sector through increased regulation. It's the "new" form of socialistic control. Chase's attempt to compare that to corporations "depriving stockholders of power" was flawed socialist logic.
- When discussing "state control of communications and propaganda," Chase himself mentioned the FCC, which still exists. But rather than control the media outright, the Obama administration prefers to circumvent or stymie it. In 2015, the Associated Press reported that "the Obama administration more often than ever censored government files or outright denied access to them under the U.S. Freedom of Information Act." Former *Washington*

Post editor Leonard Downie, Jr., wrote in a report for the Committee to Protect Journalists that Obama's "efforts to control information are the most aggressive I've seen since the Nixon administration." Meanwhile, the administration uses its own social-media platform to break its own news directly from the White House without the filter of the press, which some might characterize as propaganda.

- Does the government completely "control" agriculture? No, but it does exercise some ridiculous regulatory controls over it. For instance, the Cherry Industry Administrative Board is a real-life government office funded by real-life tax dollars. In 2009, its machinations to control the U.S. cherry market forced farmers to dump 30 million pounds of fruit onto the ground to keep it out of the marketplace.

- The government does not totally control the labor movement, either, but it's worth nothing that Richard Trumka, head of the AFL-CIO, visited the White House 104 times between 2009 and 2014. Instead of "control," it's likely more of a partnership.

- Today's government does not underwrite employment to the degree that Chase suggested, but the Obama administration's stimulus package could be regarded as a failed attempt to do just that.

- One of the most specific items is the establishment of "youth corps" to instill government ideology. Chase specifically mentioned the Civilian Conservation Corps (CCC), which ceased to exist in 1942. It's hard to find a direct analogue today, but some alert Americans may have noticed similarities in 2012, when the administration created the FEMA Corps. Americans ages eighteen to twenty-four could sign up for training in "disaster preparedness, response, and recovery." That is a benign enough goal, but the imagery of their graduation ceremony—photos showing rows of American youths wearing identical uniforms emblazoned with "FEMA Corps" seated before a giant government logo as they listened with rapt attention to a "deputy administrator"—conjured up some unpleasant associations.

As it happened, Chase's own influence in government waned after World War II. His service in the Roosevelt administration wound up being the apex of his career. In 1956, he found himself with enough spare time to join the planning commission of his hometown of Redding, Connecticut. In 1961, he traveled with other "American intellectual leaders" to Russia—more than thirty years after the visit when his group had been "bowled over" by Stalin in order to help "seek better understanding" with the Cold War foe. And he surfaced again to lend his support to Johnson's Great Society agenda.

When Chase died in 1985 at age ninety-seven, he was, according to the *New York Times*, "one of the last surviving members of the small group of advisers who helped President Roosevelt shape the New Deal." The *Times* further memorialized him as "an outspoken advocate of Government planning and intervention in the economy."

It's pretty remarkable how well someone writing in 1942 predicted the current state of the American government and economy. But it's less remarkable when you think about the gradualism that is so essential to the Fabian socialism Chase embraced first and the progressivism he adopted later. The ends justify the means. He knew the revolution would not be achieved with any one shock to the system or international crisis. It had to take place over time. Year after year. Wave after wave. It had to seem organic, as if it was something that the American people themselves desired. He knew that if the progressives stuck around long enough, they would eventually triumph.

While Chase was certainly a visionary, his vision—at least, that which he published—was incomplete. With Political System X, he captured a central part of the grand progressive plan. But we need to widen the lens a bit and look further out to see what America might look like once we get there.

The Three Phases of the Progressive Plan

I have studied progressivism extensively; this book represents just a fraction of my research. One thing I've learned is that progressives hold their playbooks close, and they've done so from the beginning. It takes digging to uncover nuggets like Stuart Chase's road map. But after taking in the whole picture, I believe I've pieced together the grand progressive strategy.

But remember, progressives are not only strategic but also persistent. You probably noticed that we organized part I of this book into "waves." As Charles Kesler, a Claremont professor and scholar of progressivism, notes, progressivism is best understood as a metaphor of waves, "interrupted by wars and by rather haphazard reactions to modern liberalism's excesses."

For Wilson, there was Coolidge. For FDR, there were Eisenhower and JFK. For Johnson, there was Reagan. The good news for us is that this means that good leaders can stop, or at least slow down, progressivism.

The question remains whether there will be someone or some movement to push back the fourth wave of progressivism of Obama and whoever follows him. As we'll see, this wave threatens to inundate America, creating the political turmoil that Chase predicted as an interim stage before America becomes a socialist utopia unrecognizable from its founding.

There are three main phases to the progressive plan: organization and infiltration, sowing political turmoil, and Political System X.

PHASE I: INFILTRATION

Phase I was the genesis of the modern progressive movement in the late nineteenth and early twentieth centuries. It was launched by the cast of characters we covered at the beginning of this book, people such as Teddy Roosevelt, William Jennings Bryan, Margaret Sanger, Wayne Wheeler, John Dewey, and others. It got especially heated during the 1912 presidential election, when Teddy Roosevelt and Woodrow Wilson tried to out-progressive each other. Wilson won out, and his administration was the first wave of the progressive movement. It would be followed by three more waves, each of which shared the following goals of the infiltration phase:

- **Goal 1: Organize groups for control.** The collectivization of society began. Instead of focusing on individual rights and freedoms, progressives focused on organizing people into groups that set them apart. Sanger organized around "birth control" (i.e., eugenics), Wheeler organized around temperance, labor groups organized workers, and so on. This was the genesis of "community organizing," and it has changed little from then to the days of Obama—herding people into groups, motivating them with fear.

- **Goal 2: Infiltrate.** Slowly but deliberately, progressives inserted themselves into key American institutions, including the government, the labor movement, academia, the media, the military, and the courts. Progressives not only ran for high office, but they also made a point of inserting their operatives into a permanent government bureaucracy. They took control of the labor movement and of academia, which became a hotbed for progressivism at all levels. The leading "race-theory" eugenicists came from America's top universities such as Princeton and Johns Hopkins, the latter of which was designed specifically to bring the "German university" model to the United States. Progressives such as Dewey influenced the education of the youngest Americans.

- **Goal 3: Weaken the social fabric.** For the collectivization of society to succeed, the natural, organic fibers of our social fabric—faith, tradition, family, heritage—needed to be ripped apart. Progressives systematically drew wedges between different segments of society by collectivizing and organizing them against one another. And all with an unceasing agenda of political correctness to revise history and remove all traces of faith from public life.

- **Goal 4: Confuse the concept of right and wrong.** Sometimes it feels as if we're living in a moral house of mirrors—up means down, down means up, and everything is distorted. That is exactly how progressives want it. By preaching moral relativism and shaming us into thinking our traditions are wrong and outdated, by convincing us that our moral compass needs to "progress," they can lead us ever closer to the final step of phase I . . .

- **Goal 5: Bring society to a state of near crisis.** At some point, the confusion becomes too great, and those who could stand up to bring some sanity to the public sphere are successfully shamed into silence. The nation is brought to the edge of collapse so that progressives can step in and take power, all in a false-prophet effort to relieve people's fears and anxieties.

PHASE II: SOWING POLITICAL TURMOIL

I believe this is where we are right now. This is the phase of turmoil that was accelerated by Obama and precedes the introduction of
Chase's Political System X. Look at the characteristics of this phase,
and see if anything sounds familiar:

- **Allow chaos.** Chaos is an essential ingredient for the eventual
  rise of a new order. Progressives and authoritarians of all stripes
  understand this. It's why the Occupy movement was allowed to
  disrupt American cities for so long. It's why leftist commentators
  such as Al Sharpton encourage protest movements that lead to
  rioting, looting, and communities in flames. It's why violence
  breaks out at Trump rallies and the supposed leader offers to personally pay the perpetrators' legal fees. Chaos is becoming part of
  our society, and their hope is that very soon we will call out for
  order.
- **Enforce negative stereotypes.** This is an ongoing part of progressives'
  efforts to divide our society. Efforts in the media, academia,
  and elsewhere—even in government—to shame certain segments of Americans are simply accepted. Concerned (peaceful)
  Americans in Tea Party groups are dismissed as radicals, while
  disenfranchised (and often violent) youths in Occupy Wall Street
  and Black Lives Matter groups are held up as heroes. White
  people are automatically assumed to be racist, and the wealthy
  are assumed to be covetous and out to screw over everyone else.
  People of faith are seen to be hateful and closed-minded. Another stereotype frequently reinforced is that "white people are
  hate mongers" and racists, or faith-seekers are "backward" and
  closed-minded. We stop seeing each other as individual countrymen and simply as stereotypes.

- **Isolate, destroy, and discourage "truth."** Progressives have a narrative, and they've been sticking with it for more than a hundred years. If you attempt to question them, you must be stopped. That's why those who attempt to explain their strategy are mocked, ridiculed, and condemned—as I'm sure this book will be by those who'd rather its message never got out.

- **Encourage reckless habits.** Progressives want us to become ever more reliant on the government. In order to make that happen, they degrade our ability to rely on ourselves, even when we want to. Even something as rational as preparing for a natural disaster is mocked. Meanwhile, Americans are running themselves into debt—just like their government—and we are told that destructive personal habits should be accepted, or even embraced, as some states have legalized marijuana. Once these individual reckless behaviors get out of control, where are we all supposed to turn for help? To the government, of course.

- **Remain in shadows.** It is important in phase II that progressives stay out of the spotlight or at least that they define themselves as basically conventional liberals, offering no real damage to the country. They will have an important hand in controlling events, as they always have, but they are not yet ready to reveal themselves. The revolution is still in a gradualist phase at this point.

It is difficult to say with certainty how long we will remain in phase II. We saw that phase I took more than a century, although phase II is by definition more fast-moving and likely will not last quite as long. Its end point is phase III, the total shift of our free-market, republican system of government into Political System X.

PHASE III: POLITICAL SYSTEM X

We've discussed what X itself will look like in detail, but phase III also contains some additional steps to stop the chaos of phase II and solidify X as the system of the future:

- **Grab control for "protection."** This is the moment when progressives make their move in the open. When the reckless behavior that progressives have encouraged and the chaos that they have sown become overwhelming, they will arrive like the cavalry at the end of a western movie to save the day. But their help will come at a price: they will propose System X as the only way out of the mess.

- **"Liquidate" those who oppose or allies who have served their purpose.** During phase II, we saw condemnation or marginalization of those who did not agree with the government line. Silencing of opponents is a hallmark of autocratic systems, from Nazi Germany to Soviet Russia (which Chase so admired) to fascist Italy (which Wilson's adviser Colonel Edward House so admired). Wilson himself threw political opponents into jail when they spoke out against World War I, and FDR imprisoned Americans in camps just for sharing heritage with the Japanese enemies in World War II. Remember these lessons of history the next time someone tells you it can't happen here.

- **Activate shadow system.** This is the unveiling of the progressives who have been infiltrating government since the beginning. While it obviously won't be the same individuals, inculcating a progressive culture in national institutions has produced ideological descendants of the Sangers and Wilsons and Roosevelts and Chases of the world, people like Barack Obama and Hillary

Clinton. Now, in their moment of triumph, they'll be able to
show their true colors.

- **Remain in crisis mode**. The crisis that began in phase II will never
  end, despite the promises made by the white knights coming in
  during phase III to rescue us. It can't. After all, if the crisis goes
  away, people might forget how much they need their government to take care of them.

This is a lot to take in. But it is our duty as active, thinking citizens
of our republic to look at these issues with open eyes and clear minds.
We shouldn't refuse to see something simply because we have been
conditioned to believe it is not there.

Fight, Flight, or Surrender

You're sitting at your desk at work. You hear something, a loud thud. An explosion, maybe? Or more likely, just a car backfiring. It seemed too distant to be something to worry about. And then you hear the *tap-tap*, a rapid-fire succession of popping noises. A gun? Not likely. Not here. Not in the office.

The decisions made in these moments make the difference between survival and death.

Do we ignore the commotion because the idea of someone going on a shooting rampage in our workplace is too ridiculous to take seriously? Those are things that happen on the news. Things that happen to other people. The difference between what we expect to be normal and what is actually happening delays our reaction time.

There are the different reactions to the unknown that we all exhibit. The most common of these is fear. Fear can be paralyzing. It can be all-consuming. It can delay our reaction time. But fear—along with the flood of neurochemicals associated with it—is also what drives us to make decisions. We can choose fight or flight. Or we can surrender altogether.

When progressives use fear, they expect us to surrender. They want to drive us right into the arms of those who promise to save us. They want us to surrender our rights to an omniscient and omnipotent big government that can save us from the unknown and the dangers that lurk at home and abroad.

But we can do something else entirely. Our surrender isn't foreordained. We can fight back. We can recognize that something is amiss and take action. We can train our brains to see the threat for what it is, and instead of surrendering like lemmings, we can choose a different path.

It appears that the progressive moment of crisis is now at hand. Thanks mainly to the efforts of Wilson, the Roosevelts, Johnson, and Obama, the structures are in place, ready for the next person to push things even further. We don't know how long it will take to get to phase III, but thanks to Stuart Chase, we do have an idea of what that phase will look like: direct government control over nearly every aspect of our lives.

Progressives have been motivated by fear for so long, the fear that if given too much freedom, mankind will go down a dark path. They are convinced that they can save us from ourselves with more control. But this is the great lie and the great tragedy of progressivism.

We have a remarkable and unique gift: the U.S. Constitution. This document, the triumph of Enlightenment thought merged with Judeo-Christian values, protects our natural rights and freedoms while laying out the groundwork for a society that keeps everyone safe and free—including progressives. If only they could let go of their fear and see that we might have a chance of progressing toward *more* freedom, liberty, and, ultimately, happiness.

We need to show the progressives that there is a better way, that they don't need to be "dazed and blinded" as Chase was. There is a better path to the ultimate light: the full embracing of our founding documents as a compass that always points us back toward liberty.

It starts with you, in your homes, your families, your schools, your communities. You must be on the lookout for creeping progressivism and, when you find it, fight it with ideas. Be firm in your commitment to your rights, and show others that true freedom comes from respect for the individual, not mindless collectivism. Be true to the ideas that have sustained us since our founding and remain enshrined in our Constitution.

They have saved us before, and they can save us again.

Epilogue:

Defeating the Fear Factory

It's midday, downtown in a major American city.

You're walking along at your typical brisk pace, almost striding, and before you know it, you're quickly encroaching on the three people walking ahead of you on the sidewalk.

They hear your footsteps coming toward them, and they peer back to catch a glimpse of you. Your eyes meet theirs, and you can't help but notice a look of fear that you've rarely witnessed on city streets. Real terror.

It's not because of you. You're pretty unassuming. It's not even because of them.

No, it's because of where you are: Detroit, where nightmares of violence and decay long ago replaced the American dream. Motown has become the poster child for the failure of progressivism's good intentions.

It wasn't always like that in Detroit.

The city wasn't perfect, of course. It always had its faults. In the early 1920s, Henry Ford spewed forth anti-Semitic venom in his *Dearborn Independent* newspaper. In the 1930s, the "Radio Priest,"

Father Charles Coughlin, broadcast from his headquarters in suburban Royal Oak. Communists infiltrated Ford Motor Company's massive River Rouge plant, fomenting labor strife. In 1943, an ugly three-day race riot rocked the city. Franklin Roosevelt dispatched federal troops to maintain order, and tanks, which should have been rolling toward Berlin, instead rolled down the city's main drag, Woodward Avenue.

But for all its shortcomings, Detroit was the model for modern American industrial growth—*world* industrial growth, really. In terms of major northeast-quadrant urban areas, though, Detroit was a real latecomer. In 1900, the city had only 285,704 people (fewer than Anchorage, Alaska, has today). But once Ford and his newfangled auto industry arrived, the city took off like a rocket—or, rather, like a Model T.

Most major Eastern cities owed their population growth to European immigrants. But Detroit was different. Sure, it had its share of Irish and Polish and Italian immigrants, but a large chunk of Detroit's newer citizens migrated not from Europe but from elsewhere in America. White Americans from Appalachia and blacks from farther South came in droves. They came to Detroit for the same reasons Jews and Italians sailed in steerage class for Ellis Island: opportunity, freedom, and a better life for themselves and their children.

Back then, Detroit's economy, like that of America as a whole, was unfettered by regulations and bureaucrats. When America wanted better mousetraps—but mainly better cars—it counted on Detroiters to figure out not only how to make them but how to make them *cheaper* and *better* than anyone else.

They had a name for the way things worked back then. They quaintly called it capitalism.

The city boomed, and Ford wasn't the only game in town for long. Newcomers Chrysler and General Motors muscled their way into his markets. But because capitalism isn't a zero-sum game, people didn't get poorer. Competition was good—for everyone. The Motor City grew from 285,704 people in 1900 to 1,568,662 in 1930 and then to 1,849,568 in 1950. From 1920 through 1950, it was the nation's fourth-largest city. In 1960, it enjoyed the nation's highest per-capita income.

Pearl Harbor caused Detroit to retool, moving from making autos and trucks to churning out tanks and jeeps and planes. FDR had vowed that America would become the Arsenal of Democracy. A lot of folks think that Detroit earned that same title. FDR tapped Ford's once right-hand man Bill Knudsen to mobilize the country for war— and to do it within a matter of weeks. The six-foot-three former boxer and Danish immigrant had worked his way from the factory floor in his youth to the executive suites of Ford, eventually becoming the head of Chevrolet. With four military stars on his shoulder and the title of chairman of the Office of Production Management, Knudsen worked with CEOs and businesses across America to retool their factories to produce war machines—all for the exorbitant salary of one dollar a year.

Knudsen was, in many ways, Henry Ford's opposite. Where Ford believed in centralized, top-down mandates, managed efficiency ("Any customer can have a car painted any colour that he wants so long as it is black"), and artificially inflated minimum wages (his five-dollar-a-day wage, which nearly doubled wages at the time, shocked his fellow businessmen), Knudsen was a fervent believer in the spontaneous and voluntary actions of the free market. He persuaded FDR to scrap many of the New Deal's burdensome regulations and onerous taxes and instead to implement incentives for private business to retool for war products. And he took away power from Washington, which earned him hatred from Eleanor Roosevelt and the more extreme progressives in FDR's Cabinet, and gave that power to executives who knew better how to mobilize their businesses than bureaucrats who operated by fiat.

And it worked. America had virtually no war industry in 1940. But by the close of 1943, America's industrial might surpassed that of Germany, Britain, and the Soviet Union combined. National GDP doubled, and unemployment was one percent.

This was capitalism, and its living, beating heart for half a century was Detroit.

A couple of years ago, Pulitzer Prize–winning author David Maraniss, a native Detroiter, wrote a book called *Once in a Great City: A Detroit Story*. He set his story in 1963, when, even that late into the game, Detroit was still a great city, boasting 296,000 manufacturing jobs. Yes, its population had slipped to 1,514,063, but just about every American city was in decline back then. Many recuperated. Detroit, instead, committed urban suicide.

Motown went on to lose jobs and population as no other major American city had done—ever. Today, fewer than 700,000 residents remain, and no one's quite sure that the city has even hit rock bottom yet. Remember that figure of 296,000 manufacturing jobs in 1963? Well, that dropped to just 54,000 in 2000, and now it's down to a mere 27,000.

Detroit can't provide public services or pay its bills. There are more than one hundred thousand different city creditors owed a staggering $20 billion (that's $25,000 per resident). The city has long held the unenviable title of Murder Capital of America, although it has recently lagged behind such other progressive bastions as Chicago, St. Louis, Baltimore, and New Orleans.

In May 2015, Detroit's unemployment rate was 13.1 percent, mercifully down from 18.6 percent in May 2013, but it remained twice the national average. Pamela Moore, president and CEO of Detroit Employment Solutions Corporation, said:

We know that the unemployment rate is at least double, perhaps triple the 13.1 percent reported for Detroit. The rate does not include those who are no longer seeking employment or receiving unemployment benefits. Recent research . . . indicated that there were 175,000 Detroiters in the labor pool who were not working and are not actively seeking a job. The number of jobs available is growing, but businesses are looking for employees who are ready to work and skilled.

Ready to work and skilled? Unfortunately, that does not exactly describe every Detroiter. In 2011, the National Institute for Literacy reported that a shocking forty-seven percent of adult Motor City residents were functional illiterates. But it gets even worse. The Detroit Regional Workforce Fund reports that half of that forty-seven percent who are illiterate hold high school degrees. Too bad they can't read them.

What's Detroit like beyond the depressing statistics? What are the little details of life within the city limits of America's progressive poster child? Here are a few examples, from a friend's personal experiences.

It's a beautiful sunny day outside a major league ballpark. You pull into a nearby parking lot for an afternoon of peanuts, popcorn, and Cracker Jack with your family. But before you get any further, you see an object glistening in the gravel below. You bend down and retrieve something. A live round of ammunition. That's a ball game in Detroit.

On a trip to church, you drive past block after block of nothingness. No houses. Nothing. Once people lived here, businesses functioned, neighborhoods thrived. Now there's nothing. And when you get there, before you are greeted by an usher or a clergyman, a guard—a very necessary guard—patrolling the parking lot salutes you. That's Easter Sunday morning in Detroit.

You visit the Detroit Public Library. A staffer retrieves a roll of microfilm for you, and you head for the reader. The machine's turning mechanism is broken and held together by tiny bars of scrap metal that are in turn held together by wire. You look at it and think this looks like nothing you've seen in a normal American library. *Is this America?* you silently ask yourself. And then the horrible thought: *This is how they hold things together in Cuba. This is Cuba.* That's academic research in Detroit.

So how did Detroit go from being the Arsenal of Democracy to one step above "Soylent Green"? Somehow progressives always blame Republicans—or the Koch brothers or climate change or something else completely irrelevant—for the disasters they've created. Republicans rarely run big cities, and when they do, they sometimes even help turn them around (see what Rudy Giuliani did with what was left of New York). But from Baltimore to St. Louis to Philadelphia to Detroit, progressives have run America's major cities for decades—usually right into the ground.

Back in the "Progressive Era," it was fashionable to say that the states were the "laboratories of democracy." States like Wisconsin or Oregon passed initiatives and referendums that other states might emulate. Well, for quite a while now, big cities have been Frankensteinesque "laboratories of progressivism."

It didn't start with Detroit. The most famous pioneer progressive mayor was actually New York City's Fiorello "the Little Flower" LaGuardia. He might have been a little flower, but he was a big RINO (Republican in name only). He supported Franklin Roosevelt, pushed for rent control, increased welfare programs, and built public housing. He ran for reelection with the support of the Communist-dominated American Labor Party. His great protégé was the renowned fellow-traveling (pro-Communist) congressman Vito Marcantino. Mainstream historians still rank LaGuardia as one of America's great mayors, but he helped set the world's greatest city on a decades-long path of decline. (Helping to keep it on that dreadful path was another media-darling RINO, 1960s mayor John V. Lindsey.)

LaGuardia was from the left wing, and many left-wing mayors, in city after city, have been following in his path. They all use the same basic playbook, the one first articulated by FDR's top aide, Harry Hopkins, in 1938: "We will spend and spend, and tax and tax, and elect and elect."

In between spending, taxing, and electing, progressives also did a lot of regulating the hell out of business, coddling public employee unions, handcuffing the police, and eviscerating the remains of a once-functioning public school system. Even the dumbest tenured professor should be able to figure out that the road to urban hell is paved with progressive intentions. But progressives never, never, never learn. Rather than honestly asking themselves what went wrong, they paraphrase 1920s New York governor Al Smith's saying that "The cure for the ills of democracy is more democracy" and scream "The cure for the ills of progressivism is *more* progressivism."

Think it's impossible to be more progressive than FDR's buddy LaGuardia? Think again. The most progressive, left-leaning mayor in American history was not the Little Flower. It's not even New York's current chief executive, Bill de Blasio (a former Sandinista supporter and Hillary Clinton campaign manager). It was actually Detroit's longtime mayor Coleman A. Young. He is the key to understanding how Motown spun so badly out of control for so long.

Young was Detroit's first black mayor, elected in 1973, when the majority of the city remained narrowly white. He might have been a bridge to racial harmony and have reversed, or at least stabilized, the city's slow slide.

He wasn't, and he didn't.

Young was radical through and through. Like many radicals—from Lenin to Jane Fonda to Obama—he didn't grow up in proletarian circumstances. He was reasonably comfortable. Not wealthy but not broke, either. His father ran a dry-cleaning business. Young attended white schools, even a Catholic parochial school, and soon landed a decent job on the assembly line at the Ford plant and quickly became involved in United Auto Workers politics. During World War II, he served with distinction with the famed Tuskegee Airmen and battled segregation in Franklin Roosevelt's segregated armed services.

But early encounters with racism embittered Young, and he wasn't satisfied to be a mere garden-variety liberal. Walter Reuther, head of the UAW, wasn't exactly Milton Friedman in his economic beliefs, but even he soon found Young too radical for comfort (as Young boasted, Detroit was "the center of the radical universe in those days").

In April 1948, Reuther narrowly escaped a mysterious assassination attempt that permanently crippled his right arm. Young was reportedly heard to say, "Too bad they didn't kill that [expletive]." Later that year, Young backed Henry Wallace's Communist-dominated Progressive Party and even ran for state senator as a progressive. In 1950, he helped found the National Negro Labor Council, an organization that was soon officially labeled a Communist front. A year later, when the House Un-American Activities Committee summoned Young to ask him if he was a member of the Communist Party, he took the Fifth Amendment.

That should have ended Young's political career. But time heals all wounds (except Reuther's arm, that is), and the Democratic Party is incredibly forgiving of progressive indiscretions. Young eventually got himself elected as a state senator, was named the Democrats' senate floor leader, and then, in November 1973, won a narrow election to become Detroit's first black mayor.

He wasn't, however, Detroit's first *progressive* mayor. Jerome Cavanagh was just thirty-three years old when he was elected in

1963, the youngest chief executive in the city's history. He did everything a progressive was supposed to do. He brought in a progressive police chief, marched with Martin Luther King, implemented Lyndon Johnson's Great Society urban-renewal pipe dreams, and supported affirmative-action programs.

Liberal observers thought Cavanagh was doing a magnificent job. "Retail sales are up dramatically [in Detroit]," gushed the *National Observer* in 1965. "Earnings are higher. Unemployment is lower. . . . Physically Detroit has acquired freshness and vitality. Acres of slums have been razed, and steel and glass apartments . . . have sprung up in their place." People seemed to think that Cavanagh was the next Jack Kennedy.

But Cavanagh's progressive visions—and his political ambitions—exploded on a Saturday night in July 1967, when his city was overtaken with deadly race riots ignited by a police raid on an African-American nightclub. Twenty-three civilians and sixteen national guardsmen died; 696 civilians and 493 guardsmen were wounded.

Cavanagh's progressive policies hadn't done much for Detroit. And neither would Young's. He might have chosen to be a healer—like Virginia's first black governor, Doug Wilder, or Los Angeles's first black mayor, Tom Bradley. But Young never outgrew his early progressive roots. He remained angry, bitter, confrontational, and often profane. Sociologist James Q. Wilson summed him up like this: "Young rejected the integrationist goal in favor of a flamboyant, black-power style that won him loyal followers, but he left the city a fiscal and social wreck." Even the *New York Times* had to admit that Young seemed "to revel in the sort of polarization that other politicians dread."

Young pursued the same sort of big-government projects Cavanagh had loved. He built the most expensive public mass-transit project in American history, a 2.94-mile "People Mover," as well as a grandiose $350 million "Renaissance Center" in Detroit's fading

1860 BALMORAL DRIVE

By now, you know what a mess Detroit is. Abandoned neighborhoods. Derelict houses. High crime and unemployment. Hundreds of murders every year. Ruin on an unimaginable scale.

They say that if you look at pictures of Hiroshima and Detroit taken in 1945 and then of both cities taken in 2016, and you weren't told which were which, you'd match up the photos of 1945 Detroit with those of 2016 Hiroshima and—much, much, much more disturbingly—vice versa. Progressive policies can lay ruin to a greater area for a greater period of time than even a nuclear warhead.

In 2010, however, Detroit mayor Dave Bing (a basketball hall-of-famer) was a man with a plan: if you couldn't build or rebuild Detroit, then at least remove some of the rot. He aimed to demolish ten thousand of the city's ninety thousand abandoned homes, three thousand in the first year alone. What would he do with the land involved? Well, he'd turn it into parks, maybe even farms.

Yes, farms. That's what Detroit, the Motor City, the Arsenal of Democracy, had come to. Fantasies about farms.

Now, you might think these properties would all be in Detroit's slum areas. Not so. Detroit's blight is essentially citywide. Even historically "better" neighborhoods slid downhill. "The city has never done this before," admitted Detroit Building Department director Karla Henderson. "We had to make a culture change."

"Culture change," by the way, is progressive speak for *Bring in the bulldozers to bury our mistakes.*

Which takes us up the driveway to a 5,412-square-foot home at 1860 Balmoral Drive in the city's once grand (and actually still pretty good) Palmer Woods neighborhood.

Or at least it used to be a home.

As late as 2002, 1860 Balmoral Drive sold for $645,000. But that was then. Its value plummeted to just $150,000 by February 2007. And by 2010, it was abandoned and heading for outright demolition. "This is an eyesore, and it makes no economic sense to fix it," said neighbor Joel Pitcoff. "Who wants to spend $1 million on a house so it will be worth $400,000?"

What was newsworthy about this property? After all, it was just one of many thousands of eyesores, even if it was in a good neighborhood. Well . . . it just so happened to be the boyhood home of Mitt Romney. As he geared up to run for the presidency in 2012, that childhood abode (not exactly Abe Lincoln's log cabin) lay forlorn, abandoned, and ready for a very public wrecking ball in dystopian Detroit—a testament to failed progressivism.

downtown. Few citizens ever used the People Mover and the Renaissance Center also flopped. Young later sold it to General Motors for $80 million. Scandals on the Water Board and in the Police Department marred his later terms, and federal investigators probed his efforts to guide contracts to black-owned companies.

Young left office in January 1994, but Detroit's die had already been cast. The city was too far gone along the path of progressive politics to reform itself. Young's worst successor was a fellow who took Cavanagh's title of Detroit's youngest mayor. Elected at just thirty-one years old in 2001, Kwame Kilpatrick eventually found himself convicted on a staggering multiplicity of corruption charges.

His Honor is scheduled to be released in 2041.

♣

CRONY PROGRESSIVISM

They say that if you move far enough left or right on the political circle, eventually you'll meet up with the other side.

Exhibit A: The Progressive Nonworkers Paradise of Detroit.

You see, Donald Trump isn't the only guy who believes in pushing little people around to hand over their homes to big corporations.

Coleman Young did the same thing.

Back when Detroit was in its prime, it not only featured substantial populations of Southern whites and blacks, but it also boasted numerous ethnic neighborhoods. There was a Jewish area, a "Greektown," an Irish "Corktown," and, once upon a time, a "Poletown."

When General Motors wanted to build a new plant in Poletown, residents said: *No, thank you. We don't want to move.* But Mayor Young thought he could use the tax revenue and the supposed economic benefits from the plant to prop up the rest of his decomposing city. So even though Poletown's homes and its business property would be used not for a true public purpose but rather for a purely private one (think "crony capitalism" or, rather, "crony progressivism"), residents found themselves squarely in progressive eminent-domain crosshairs.

Here's an account from one Poletown homeowner, Harold Kaczynski, who tried—and failed—to stop GM's land grab:

We filed [our objections]. We were told to sign the first one of these with a lot number. This would take care of what we were after. And then we appeared at [Detroit's] Cobo Hall. . . . And [the judge] never said one word. All the city did was read off all the lists of parcels they wanted. He granted them [1,366] parcels, and that was the end of it. Plus, they searched us coming in like we were a bunch of criminals.

Forty-two hundred people lost their homes. One hundred forty businesses closed. A thriving neighborhood disappeared. That was bad enough. But there was more.

Harold and Bernice Kaczynski had to move out of Detroit. Harold died in November 1987, and on the very day he was buried, the headline on the front page of the *Detroit Free Press* announced that GM's "Poletown Plant" was closing, costing twenty-five hundred workers their jobs.

When progressives pick winners and losers, everybody loses.

A lot of people have written Detroit off. It's been forever ruined by the Left, they say. It has no hope.

But that's not true.

Detroit has a chance at rebirth, just as America does. If we allowed the city to be truly free (creating incentives to bring in private enterprise and create jobs, lifting red tape and regulations that make it more cost-effective for industries to locate elsewhere), then Detroit could rise again. There is nothing in the DNA of the people of Detroit that keeps them from succeeding.

But we need to do more than just provide job opportunities and ease regulations. We need to cure the citizens of Detroit—and increasingly many citizens across America—of a debilitating and, in some cases, lifelong addiction. Addiction to broken promises. Addiction to the same leaders offering the same failed ideas. Addiction to dependency and learned helplessness. Addiction to fear. Addiction to lies.

I know something about addiction. I'm an alcoholic. Which means that I am an addict. I know how hard it is to quit something that can do you great damage. The first step to recovery is to recognize what you are addicted to. And to find ways to substitute something else for that drug, whatever it may be.

For those who have become addicted to fear because of their progressive dealers, we must offer the counter to fear. That is hope.

History has always been about a choice between fear and hope. World War II pitted an ideology based on fear of Jews, of gays, of "outsiders," of Germany's loss of prestige and power, against the free-enterprise system, an ideology based on the hope that people can transcend and rise about their circumstances, can strive, can achieve, can fail and try again.

Or consider the Cold War, which pitted America against Communists whose ideology thrived on the fear of inequality and the evils of the "capitalist system" that supposedly enriched only the few.

Progressives, as we've seen, promote the state—more regulations, more taxes, more rules, more restraints—as the answer to these fears. That is always their mantra, always their default. Give your power to us. We'll take care of you.

Like the saber-toothed cat, fear stalks us all. The question is, what do you do about it? Was Steve Jobs, who was once fired from Apple before returning to the company, afraid of failing again? Of course he was. Was Walt Disney afraid that his movies wouldn't sell or that his theme parks—which were thought impractical and too expensive by almost everyone—would become duds? Of course.

The greatest people in America—the most successful pioneers in all walks of life—experience fear, uncertainty, and doubt. Even those who are working in their own communities and neighborhoods—fighting for the lives of the unborn, opposing new laws and rules that restrict freedom—are often afraid. Speaking out, being criticized, being ignored—they are all scary things. But the successful don't let fear control them. They acknowledge it and say, *Yes, I'm afraid, so what?* That's the secret.

What separates most of those who are able to use fear motivationally from those who succumb to it is usually a higher sense of purpose, a greater meaning to their life. For me—and this isn't the answer for everybody—that greater meaning is service to God. For others, maybe their purpose is as simple as being a good parent, leaving an important legacy to their children, or just being a responsible citizen. But the key is that you need to find something that is bigger than you. Something that will outlast you.

I remember reading a book a few years back called *The Survivor's Club: The Secrets and Science That Could Save Your Life*, by Ben Sherwood. Ben went out and interviewed survivors of various incidents, tragedies, and illnesses, as well as experts, to analyze what qualities helped these people survive. What makes an effective survivor? Why do some people beat the odds and others don't? What he found was a mentality, an outlook, inherent in survivors: honesty about the situation they faced.

But honesty alone was not enough to survive; action was also required. When we are confronted with danger, our minds don't always recognize it at first. If we see something out of the ordinary that could be a threat, we don't immediately see the danger, because we're not *used* to seeing it and because we don't *want* to see it. It's called the normalcy bias. Our minds are programmed to find the normalcy in every situation in an effort to comfort and give us hope. That is usually a good thing—your brain rationalizes that turbulence on an airplane happens all the time, that bumps are part of flying, and that thousands of flights a day have turbulence with no consequences. But every so often, the normalcy bias gets in the way of seeing the reality of a situation: the noise in the night that's not just the house settling, the person acting strangely on the plane who isn't just afraid to fly, the backpack on the street corner that wasn't just forgotten by a kid.

What differentiates survivors from victims is that survivors act.

Armed with situational awareness, they overcome their normalcy bias and see danger coming well before anyone else.

I hope this book has given you that situational awareness. After this journey through the sordid, even bloody history of progressivism, you will see this danger where it lurks in modern political and cultural life. You will see the truth about what progressivism stands for and what it will do to America if we can't get our friends and neighbors to wake up.

Seeing the truth is brave. Seeing the truth is consoling. Seeing the truth gives people resolve. And seeing the truth gives us all the strength to face it with action.

God, hope, reason, action. These are the keys to fighting the fear factor.

Which is why, perhaps, progressivism these days seems to work so much better in the major metropolises of America. When I first moved to New York City and had an apartment somewhere up in the clouds, I would stand every night at the windows, looking at the sprawling city beneath me. Towering buildings, buses, taxis, parks—it was incredible. And it was all made by man.

When I left New York, I once again started looking up. The sky, the clouds, the stars at night. All made by God.

In New York, I didn't even know the people who lived on the same floor as I did. In rural America, you'd be hard pressed to find a family who doesn't know everyone in town. It's a big deal because it speaks to why progressivism does so well in cities. People don't feel that they need one another—let alone God—because they've got the city of New York, the MTA, the state of New York, and, of course, the federal government all looking out for them.

Sure they do.

Americans didn't use to believe, as progressives do, that individuals couldn't progress and become better without help from government and elites who know better than us. Americans didn't use to believe, as progressives do, that we must surrender to others in order to improve our lives.

We can progress and improve ourselves. But only as individuals.

We recognize the danger. We've been able to put aside our normalcy biases and realize that this is not OK, that we are in clear and present danger.

Now it's time to act.

Notes

PART I: THE ROAD WE'VE TRAVELED

CHAPTER 1: ROOTS: HEGEL, MARX,
AND THE MAKING OF HEAVEN ON EARTH
PAGE 14: "frantically waving red bandanas" Richard Franklin Bensel, *Passion and Preferences: William Jennings Bryan and the 1896 Democratic National Convention* (New York: Cambridge University Press, 2008), p. 224. • PAGE 15: "'hopes of their own inmost souls'" Richard Franklin Bensel, *Passion and Preferences: William Jennings Bryan and the 1896 Democratic National Convention* (New York: Cambridge University Press, 2008), p. 231. • PAGE 16: "leader Europe had been waiting for" Terry Pinkard, *Hegel: A Biography* (New York: Cambridge University Press, 2000). • PAGE 19: "he dubbed the 'general will'" David Wootton, "Introduction," in Jean-Jacques Rousseau, *Basic Political Writings*, trans. Donald A. Cress, 2nd ed., (Indianapolis: Hackett Publishing, 2011), p. xxiv. • PAGE 20: "'were the first to attain the consciousness'" Georg Wilhelm Friedrich Hegel, *The Philosophy of History*, trans. J. Sibree, (Kitchner: Batoche Books, 2001), p. 32. http://www.hegel.net/en/pdf/history.pdf. • PAGE 21: "trying to build their individual fortunes" Georg Wilhelm Friedrich Hegel, *The Philosophy of History*, trans. J. Sibree, (New York: Colonial Press, 1900). • PAGE 23: "'conveyed across the border'" Karl Marx, "Suppression of the Neue Rheinische Zeitung," *Neue Rheinische Zeitung*, No. 301, May 18, 1849. • "'the Young Hegelians'" Francis Wheen, *Karl Marx: A Life* (New York: W. W. Norton & Company, 2001). • PAGE 25: "'interested in their welfare'" Elmer Roberts, *Monarchical Socialism in Germany* (New York: Charles Scribner's Sons, 1913), p. 119. • "'to the government'" Richard M. Ebeling, "Marching to Bismarck's Drummer: The Origins of the Modern Welfare State," Foundation of Economic Education, December 1, 2007, https://fee.org/articles/marching-to-bismarcks-drummer-the-origins-of-the-modern-welfare-state/. • "'a certain degree of circumspection and distrust'" James Madison, "The Total Number of the House of Representatives," *Federalist* No. 55, in *The Federalist Papers*, February 15, 1788, https://www.congress.gov/resources/display/content

/The+Federalist+Papers - TheFederalistPapers-55. • **PAGE 26: "a national stan-dardized time system"** Thomas C. Leonard, *Illiberal Reformers: Race, Eugenics, and American Economics in the Progressive Era* (Princeton: Princeton University Press, 2016), p. 3. • **PAGE 27: "guided by disinterested, expert social scientists"** Steven Mueller et al., *A Spirit of Reason*, ed. Jackson Janes (Washington, D.C.: The American Institute for Contemporary German Studies, 2004), http://www.aicgs.org/site/wp -content/uploads/2011/11/muller.pdf. • **"had influenced the American Found-ers"** Thomas C. Leonard, *Illiberal Reformers: Race, Eugenics, and American Economics in the Progressive Era* (Princeton: Princeton University Press, 2016), p. 17. • **"'than through any other institution'"** David Henderson, "Richard Ely, Racist and State Worshipper," Library of Economics and Liberty, May 14, 2011, http://econlog .econlib.org/archives/2011/05/richard_ely_rac.html. • **PAGE 29: "'the advance-ment of common interests'"** Richard M. Ebeling, "American Progressives Are Bismarck's Grandchildren," The Future of Freedom Foundation, June 17, 2015, http://fff.org/explore-freedom/article/american-progressives-bismarcks -grandchildren/. • **"'an industrial civilization demands'"** David Henderson, "Richard Ely, Racist and State Worshipper," Library of Economics and Liberty, May 14, 2011, http://econlog.econlib.org/archives/2011/05/richard_ely_rac.html. • **"He campaigned to bar immigrants"** Thomas C. Leonard, *Illiberal Reformers: Race, Eugenics, and American Economics in the Progressive Era* (Princeton: Princeton University Press, 2016), p. 8. • **PAGE 30: "'replace laissez-faire from within men's hearts'"** Jonah Goldberg, *Liberal Fascism: The Secret History of the American Left, From Mussolini to the Politics of Change* (New York: Crown Forum, 2009), p. 95. • **"a new generation of social scientists"** Clifford F. Thines and Gary M. Pecquet, "The Shaping of a Future President's Economic Thought: Richard T. Ely and Wood-row Wilson and 'The Hopkins'," *The Independent Review* 15, no. 2 (Fall 2010), https:// www.independent.org/pdf/tir/tir_15_02_06_thies.pdf. • **"*Everything* could be improved"** Thomas C. Leonard, *Illiberal Reformers: Race, Eugenics, and American Eco-nomics in the Progressive Era* (Princeton: Princeton University Press, 2016), p. 9. • **"'pay to educate the Negro'"** W. Barksdale Maynard, "More Than a Mere Student," *Johns Hopkins Magazine*, September 2007, http://pages.jh.edu/jhumag /0907web/wilson.html. • **PAGE 31: "the best being allowed to reproduce"** Nathaniel Comfort, "Better Babies," AEON, November 17, 2015, https://aeon.co /essays/the-dream-of-designing-humans-has-a-long-and-peculiar-history. • **"'gal-axy of genius might we not create'"** Nathaniel Comfort, "Better Babies," AEON, November 17, 2015, https://aeon.co/essays/the-dream-of-designing-humans -has-a-long-and-peculiar-history. • **"American Breeders Magazine"** Thomas C. Leonard, *Illiberal Reformers: Race, Eugenics, and American Economics in the Progressive Era* (Princeton: Princeton University Press, 2016). • **"Major Leonard Darwin, Charles Darwin's son"** Stefani Engelstein, "Controlling Heredity: The American Eugenics Crusade: 1870–1940" (exhibition, University of Missouri, Columbia, MO, 2011). • **PAGE 32: "'remaining least valuable types'"** Larry Stern, "Perspec-tives: What Is a Human Being," (internet lecture, Collin College, McKinney, TX, 2013), http://ftp.collin.edu/lstern/INTRO-WEB-UNIT1B-LECTURE.html. • **"'to carry on the race'"** Larry Stern, "Perspectives: What Is a Human Being," (internet lecture, Collin College, McKinney, TX, 2013), http://ftp.collin.edu/lstern /INTRO-WEB-UNIT1B-LECTURE.html. • **"'grateful to you for writing it'"** Larry Stern, "Perspectives: What Is a Human Being," (internet lecture, Collin College, McKinney, TX, 2013), http://ftp.collin.edu/lstern/INTRO-WEB-UNIT

1B-LECTURE.html. • **"would come to know Adolf Hitler's name"** Edwin Black, "Hitler's Debt to America," *The Guardian*, February 5, 2004, http://www .theguardian.com/uk/2004/feb/06/race.usa. • **"'something to be achieved'"** Ronald J. Pestritto and Thomas G. West, eds., *Modern America and the Legacy of the Founding* (Lanham, MD: Lexington Books, 2007). • **PAGE 33: "build a kingdom of heaven on earth"** Thomas C. Leonard, *Illiberal Reformers: Race, Eugenics, and American Economics in the Progressive Era* (Princeton: Princeton University Press, 2016), p. 12. • **"create a "sober and pure world'"** Ian Tyrrell, *Woman's World/Woman's Empire* (Chapel Hill: The University of North Carolina Press, 2010). • **PAGE 34: "give debt relief by coining silver"** Michael Kazin, *A Godly Hero: The Life of William Jennings Bryan* (New York: Knopf Doubleday Publishing Group, 2006), p. 26. • **PAGE 35: "Dubbed 'hayseeds' and 'anarchists'"** Richard Franklin Bensel, *Passion and Preferences: William Jennings Bryan and the 1896 Democratic National Convention* (New York: Cambridge University Press, 2008), p. 14. • **PAGE 36: "voice their concerns when he addressed the delegates"** Richard Franklin Bensel, *Passion and Preferences: William Jennings Bryan and the 1896 Democratic National Convention* (New York: Cambridge University Press, 2008), p. 183. • **PAGE 37: "the ice trade, a booming business on the eastern seaboard"** Robert C. Kennedy, "Hunting the Octopus," *On This Day* (blog), *The New York Times*, October 6, 2001, https://www.nytimes.com/learning/general/onthisday/harp/1006 .html. • **PAGE 38: "'We want something to eat'"** Margaret Sanger, *Margaret Sanger; An Autobiography* (New York: W.W. Norton & Company, 1938), p. 32, https:// archive.org/details/margaretsangerau1938sang. • **PAGE 39: "'Toss! Beauty!'"** Margaret Sanger, *Margaret Sanger; An Autobiography* (New York: W.W. Norton & Company, 1938), p. 32, https://archive.org/details/margaretsangerau1938sang. • **PAGE 43: "'under government medical protection and segregate . . .'"** Margaret Sanger, "My Way to Peace," *The Margaret Sanger Papers*, Library of Congress., Library of Congress Microfilm 130:198, 1931, http://www.nyu.edu/projects /sanger/webedition/app/documents/show.php?sangerDoc=129036.xml. • **"a policy of 'race improvement'"** Paul Kengor, "Race and Margaret Sanger," *The American Spectator*, September 14, 2015, http://spectator.org/articles/64049/race -and-margaret-sanger. • **"is to kill it"** Margaret Sanger, *Margaret Sanger; An Autobiography* (New York: W.W. Norton & Company, 1938), p. 32, https://archive.org/de tails/margaretsangerau1938sang. • **PAGE 44: "'those who should never have been born'"** Kevin Vance, "Sec. Clinton Stands by Her Praise of Eugenicist Margaret Sanger," *The Weekly Standard*, April 15, 2009, http://www.weeklystandard .com/sec.-clinton-stands-by-her-praise-of-eugenicist-margaret-sanger/article /28444. • **"'her courage, her tenacity, her vision'"** Kevin Vance, "Sec. Clinton Stands by Her Praise of Eugenicist Margaret Sanger," *The Weekly Standard*, April 15, 2009, http://www.weeklystandard.com/sec.-clinton-stands-by-her-praise-of-eugen icist-margaret-sanger/article/28444.

CHAPTER 2: FIRST WAVE: WILSON, THE PHILOSOPHER PRESIDENT
PAGE 47: "*Titanic* was built and marketed as 'unsinkable'" Mary Karmelek, "2 Ships Passing in the Fog: 35 Years before the Titanic, Uneasy Sailing on the White Star Line," *Anecdotes from the Archive* (blog), *The Scientific American*, May 31, 2013, http://blogs.scientificamerican.com/anecdotes-from-the-archive/2-ships-passing -in-the-fog-35-years-before-the-titanic-uneasy-sailing-on-the-white-star-line/. • **PAGE 48: "'the furthest-reaching disaster'"** Wyn Craig Wade, *The Titanic:*

End of a Dream (New York: Penguin Books, 1992), p. 98. • **PAGE 49: "'the gaining represents benefit to the community'"** "The New Nationalism," Theodore Roosevelt, Osawatomie, KS, August 31, 1910. http://www.heritage.org/initiatives /first-principles/primary-sources/teddy-roosevelts-new-nationalism. • **"'general right of the community to regulate its use'"** "The New Nationalism," Theodore Roosevelt, Osawatomie, KS, August 31, 1910, http://www.heritage.org/initia tives/first-principles/primary-sources/teddy-roosevelts-new-nationalism. • **"'as the steward of the public welfare'"** "The New Nationalism," Theodore Roosevelt, Osawatomie, KS. August 31, 1910, http://www.heritage.org/initiatives/first-princi ples/primary-sources/teddy-roosevelts-new-nationalism. • **PAGE 50: "'the foundation of every other relationship'"** Ray Stannard Baker, ed., *The Public Papers of Woodrow Wilson: Life and Letters, Volume 1* (New York: Harper & Bros., 1925), p. 432. • **"Yes, even Jimmy Carter"** "Washington, Lincoln Most Popular Presidents: Nixon, Bush Least Popular," Rasmussen Reports, July 4, 2007, http://www.ras mussenreports.com/public_content/politics/people2/2007/washington_lincoln _most_popular_presidents_nixon_bush_least_popular. • **"routinely rank Wilson among the top ten"** "List of Presidential Rankings," NBC News, February 16, 2009, http://www.nbcnews.com/id/29216774/ns/politics-white_house/t/list-presi dential-rankings/#.V0Sb0OcrIy6. Brandon Rottinghaus and Justin Vaughn, "New Ranking of U.S. Presidents Puts Lincoln at No. 1, Obama at 18; Kennedy Judged Most Overrated," *Monkey Cage* (blog), *Washington Post*, February 16, 2015, https:// www.washingtonpost.com/blogs/monkey-cage/wp/2015/02/16/new-ranking-of -u-s-presidents-puts-lincoln-1-obama-18-kennedy-judged-most-over-rated/. • **"rated Wilson behind only Lincoln, Washington"** "A Comparison of Polls of Presidential Greatness," Syracuse University, accessed May 24, 2016, http://classes.max well.syr.edu/hst341/presgreatness.htm. • **"'Today's concerns shape our views of the past'"** Kenneth T. Walsh, "Historians Rank George W. Bush Among Worst Presidents," *U.S. News and World Report*, February 7, 2009, http://www.us news.com/news/history/articles/2009/02/17/historians-rank-george-w-bush -among-worst-presidents. • **PAGE 51: "'Woodrow Wilson was one of America's greatest Presidents'"** "Woodrow Wilson: Life in Brief," Miller Center, accessed May 24, 2016, http://millercenter.org/president/biography/wilson-life-in-brief. • **PAGE 52: "one of America's greatest presidents"** "American Experience: Woodrow Wilson," PBS, accessed May 24, 2016, http://www.pbs.org/wgbh/amex /wilson/index.html. • **"even likened him to Jesus Christ"** "David Lloyd George," New World Encyclopedia, accessed May 24, 2016, http://www.newworldencyclo pedia.org/entry/David_Lloyd_George. • **"'than an institution devoted to the highest ideals'"** Lyndon B. Johnson, "Statement by President Upon Signing Bill to Establish a National Memorial to Woodrow Wilson, October 25, 1968," in *Lyndon B. Johnson: 1968–1969 (in two books) containing the public messages, speeches, and statements of the president [book 2]* (Ann Arbor, MI: University of Michigan Library, 2005), p. 1070, accessed May 24, 2016, http://quod.lib.umich.edu/p/ppotpus /4731573.1968.002/376?rgn=full+text;view=image. • **"'but He Deserves Our Understanding'"** Richard Cohen, "Woodrow Wilson Was Racist, but He Deserves Our Understanding," *Washington Post*, November 23, 2015, https://www .washingtonpost.com/opinions/taking-woodrow-wilson-out-of-context/2015/11 /23/5eb509ee-920c-11e5-8aa0-5d0946560a97_story.html. • **PAGE 53: "he grew up mostly in Georgia and South Carolina"** "Biography," The Woodrow Wilson Presidential Library and Museum, accessed May 24, 2016, http://www.woodrow

wilson.org/about/biography. • **"Confederates like the Wilsons"** "Woodrow Wilson: Life Before the Presidency." Miller Center of Public Affairs, University of Virginia, accessed June 8, 2016, http://millercenter.org/president/biography/wilson -life-before-the-presidency. • **"through the streets in chains"** Josephus Daniels, *The Life of Woodrow Wilson*, (Chicago: The John C. Winston Company, 1924), p. 37. • **"Wilson did not learn to read or write until he was nearly ten"** "American Experience: Woodrow Wilson," PBS, accessed May 24, 2016, http://www.pbs.org /wgbh/amex/wilson/index.html. • **PAGE 54: "he received his doctorate in political science and history"** "Biography," The Woodrow Wilson Presidential Library and Museum, accessed May 24, 2016, http://www.woodrowwilson.org/about /biography. • **"'Woodrow Wilson, United States Senator'"** E.S., "The President," *The Atlantic Monthly*, March 1913, p. 289, accessed May 24, 2016, http://www .unz.org/Pub/AtlanticMonthly-1913mar-00289?View=PDF. Josephus Daniels, *The Life of Woodrow Wilson* (Chicago: The John C. Winston Company, 1924), p. 38. • **"early progressive economist Richard Ely"** Jonah Goldberg, *Liberal Fascism: The Secret History of the American Left, From Mussolini to the Politics of Change* (New York: Doubleday, 2007), p. 95. • **PAGE 55: "'critical to society's evolution'"** Jonah Goldberg, *Liberal Fascism: The Secret History of the American Left, From Mussolini to the Politics of Change* (New York: Crown, 2009), p. 84. Note: Goldberg also reminds us of Wilson's admiration for Lincoln, which may seem odd, considering Wilson's Confederate sympathies. "[W]hat appealed to Wilson about the Great Emancipator," Goldberg notes, "was Lincoln's ability to impose his will on the country. Lincoln was a centralizer, a modernizer who used his power to forge a new, united nation. In other words, Wilson admired Lincoln's means—suspension of habeas corpus, the draft, and the campaigns of the radical Republicans after the war— far more than he liked his ends." • **"'glorified power'"** Jonah Goldberg, *Liberal Fascism: The Secret History of the American Left, From Mussolini to the Politics of Change* (New York: Crown, 2009), p. 104. • **"'sincere body of thought in politics'"** Josephus Daniels, *Life of Woodrow Wilson* (New York: Greenwood Press, 1971). • **"'enlisting them in our purposes'"** Charles R. Kesler, *I Am the Change: Barack Obama and the Future of Liberalism* (New York: Broadside Books, 2012), ch. 2, accessed May 24, 2016, http://bi.hcpdts.com/reflowable/scrollableiframe/9780062325204. • **"'a new theory of the presidency'"** Charles R. Kesler, *I Am the Change: Barack Obama and the Future of Liberalism* (New York: Broadside Books, 2012), ch. 2, accessed May 24, 2016, http://bi.hcpdts.com/reflowable/scrollableiframe/9780062325204. • **PAGE 56: "'then start your business'"** Geoffrey Perrett, *America in the Twenties: A History* (New York: Simon & Schuster, 1982), p. 22. • **"'threatened his own prestige'"** William Allen White, *Masks in a Pageant* (New York: Macmillan, 1928), p. 357. • **PAGE 57: "'could have prevented that'"** William C. Spragens, *Popular Images of American Presidents* (New York: Greenwood Press, 1988), p. 247. Marvin Olasky, *The American Leadership Tradition: The Inevitable Impact of a Leader's Faith on a Nation's Destiny* (New York: Free Press, 1999), p. 197. • **"a one-term limit on the presidency"** Josephus Daniels, *The Wilson Era: Years of Peace—1910–1917* (Chapel Hill: The University of North Carolina Press, 1944), p. 102. Kirk H. Porter and Donald Bruce Johnson, *National Party Platforms: 1840–1960* (Urbana, IL: The University of Illinois Press, 1961), p. 170. Michael J. Korzi, *Presidential Term Limits in American History: Power, Principles, and Politics* (College Station: Texas A&M Press, 2011), p. 71. Woodrow Wilson: Life Before the Presidency," The Miller Center, accessed May 24, 2016, http://millercenter.org/president/biography/wilson-life-be

fore-the-presidency. • "'**State' is 'Family' writ large'**" Ronald J. Pestritto, ed., *Woodrow Wilson: The Essential Political Writings* (Lanham, MD: Lexington Books, 2005), p. 33. • **PAGE 58:** "'**press onward to something new'**" "Woodrow Wilson Asks 'What Is Progress?'" The Heritage Foundation, accessed May 24, 2016, https://support.office.com/en-us/article/Word-keyboard-shortcuts-c0ca851f-3d58 -4ce0-9867-799df73666a7. • "'**Darwinian in structure and in practice'**" Woodrow Wilson, *Constitutional Government in the United States* (New York: Columbia University Press, 1908), p. 57. "The Constitution: Anchor or Rudder," *The Outlook*, September 26, 1908, p. 148, http://www.unz.org/Pub/Outlook-1908sep26-00147. • "'**as checks, and live'**" Woodrow Wilson, *Constitutional Government in the United States* (New York: Columbia University Press, 1908), p. 57. "The Constitution Anchor or Rudder," *The Outlook*, September 26, 1908, p. 148, http://www.unz.org /Pub/Outlook-1908sep26-00147. • **PAGE 59:** "'**the document in which they are embodied'**" Ellis Washington, "Mark Levin on President Woodrow Wilson," WND.com, January 11, 2013, http://www.wnd.com/2013/01/mark-levin-on-pres ident-woodrow-wilson/#.V0q4ekeBULDHzg0w.99. • "'**and not a machine'**" Woodrow Wilson, *The New Freedom: Call for the Emancipation of the Generous Energies of a People* (New York: Doubleday, Page & Co., 1918), p. 48. • "'**do not repeat the preface'**" Woodrow Wilson, "Address to the Jefferson Club of Los Angeles," (speech, Los Angeles, May 12, 1911), Hillsdale College, http://cdn.constitution reader.com/files/pdf/coursereadings/Con201_Readings_Week2_JeffersonClub .pdf. • "'**know they are not'**" Woodrow Wilson, "Address to the Jefferson Club of Los Angeles," (speech, Los Angeles, May 12, 1911), Hillsdale College, http://cdn .constitutionreader.com/files/pdf/coursereadings/Con201_Readings_Week2_Jef fersonClub.pdf. • "'**make and unmake governments'**" Ronald J. Pestritto, ed., *Woodrow Wilson: The Essential Political Writings* (Lanham, MD: Lexington Books, 2005), p. 4. • **PAGE 60:** "'**of all just political theory'**" George F. Will, "The Simple Arithmetic That Could Jump-Start America's Economic Growth," *The Washington Post*, January 29, 2016, https://www.washingtonpost.com/opinions /smart-tax-reform-would-ignite-growth/2016/01/29/3f03bac2-c5e8-11e5-8965 -0607e0e265ce_story.html. • "'**upon strict analysis, none'**" George F. Will, "The Simple Arithmetic That Could Jump-Start America's Economic Growth," *The Washington Post*, January 29, 2016, https://www.washingtonpost.com/opinions /smart-tax-reform-would-ignite-growth/2016/01/29/3f03bac2-c5e8-11e5-8965 -0607e0e265ce_story.html. • "'**not a difference of primary motive'**" Ronald J. Pestritto, ed., *Woodrow Wilson: The Essential Political Writings* (Lanham, MD: Lexington Books, 2005), p. 78. • **PAGE 61:** "'**glorious privilege'**" George F. Will, "The Simple Arithmetic That Could Jump-Start America's Economic Growth," *The Washington Post*, January 29, 2016, https://www.washingtonpost.com/opinions /smart-tax-reform-would-ignite-growth/2016/01/29/3f03bac2-c5e8-11e5-8965 -0607e0e265ce_story.html. • **"from seven percent to thirteen percent"** "Tax History Museum: 1901–1932: The Income Tax Arrives," Tax Analysts, accessed May 24, 2016, http://www.taxhistory.org/www/website.nsf/Web/THM1901 ?OpenDocument. • **"marginal income tax of seventy-three percent"** Meg Fowler, "From Eisenhower to Obama: What the Wealthiest Americans Pay in Taxes," *ABC News*, January 24, 2011. http://abcnews.go.com/Politics/eisenhower -obama-wealthy-americans-mitt-romney-pay-taxes/story?id=15387862. • **PAGE 63:** **"remained above seventy percent"** "Historical Individual Income Tax Parameters," Tax Policy Center, accessed May 25, 2016, http://www.taxpolicycenter.org

/statistics/historical-individual-income-tax-parameters. • **"the Sixteenth Amendment"** Dr. Thomas G. West and William A. Schambra. "The Progressive Movement and the Transformation of American Politics," The Heritage Foundation, July 18, 2007, http://www.heritage.org/research/reports/2007/07/the-progressive-movement-and-the-transformation-of-american-politics. • **"tainted his decisions"** "Editorial," *The Crisis* 4, no. 4, August 1912, p. 181, https://www.marxists.org/history/usa/workers/civil-rights/crisis/0800-crisis-v04n04-w022.pdf. • **"'the question will ever assume practical form'"** Shan Wang, "Sorry, Ben Stein, These Presidents Were Way More Racist Than Obama," Boston.com, November 4, 2014, http://www.boston.com/news/national-news/2014/11/04/sorry-ben-stein-these-presidents-were-way-more-racist-than-obama. • **"'unwarranted'"** A. Scott Berg, *Wilson* (New York: G. P. Putnam's Sons, 2013), pp. 155-56. • **"was governor of New Jersey"** Nathaniel Weyl & William Marina, *American Statesmen on Slavery and the Negro* (New Rochelle, NY: Arlington House, 1971), p. 329. • **PAGE 64: "'brought Jim Crow to the North'"** Paul Rahe, "Progressive Racism," *The National Review,* April 11, 2013, http://www.nationalreview.com/article/345274/progressive-racism-paul-rahe. • **"resegregated parts of the federal workforce"** Paul Rahe, "Progressive Racism," *The National Review,* April 11, 2013, http://www.nationalreview.com/article/345274/progressive-racism-paul-rahe. • **"serving as undersecretary"** Nathaniel Weyl & William Marina, *American Statesmen on Slavery and the Negro* (New Rochelle, NY: Arlington House, 1971), p. 329. • **"'except to do them justice'"** Nathaniel Weyl & William Marina, *American Statesmen on Slavery and the Negro* (New Rochelle, NY: Arlington House, 1971), p. 329. • **"'humiliating but a benefit . . .'"** "Commentary: Conversation, January, 1915: Mr. Trotter and Mr. Wilson," *The New Crisis,* July/August 2000, p. 60. • **"banning interracial marriage"** Larry Schwarts, "Who Was the Most Racist Modern President? 5 Surprising Candidates Who Fit the Bill," AlterNet.org, December 28, 2014, http://www.alternet.org/civil-liberties/who-was-most-racist-modern-president-5-surprising-candidates-who-fit-bill. • **"the opportunity to fight for their country"** Larry Schwarts, "Who Was the Most Racist Modern President? 5 Surprising Candidates Who Fit the Bill," AlterNet.org, December 28, 2014, http://www.alternet.org/civil-liberties/who-was-most-racist-modern-president-5-surprising-candidates-who-fit-bill. • **"'the ugliest hazards of a time of revolution'"** Woodrow Wilson, *A History of the American People,* vol. 5 (New York: Harper & Bros., 1903), pp. 58, 60. See also: Melvyn Stokes, *D.W. Griffith's The Birth of a Nation: A History of the Most Controversial Motion Picture of All Time* (New York: Oxford University Press, 2007), p. 119. Note: Another version of this quote—taken from a title card of *Birth of a Nation* is often cited—but this is the more account version of what Wilson really wrote. • **PAGE 65: "based on Thomas J. Dixon Sr.'s 1905 novel *The Clansman*"** Charles Paul Freund, "Dixiecrats Triumphant: The Menacing Mr. Wilson," Reason.com, December 18, 2002, http://reason.com/archives/2002/12/18/dixiecrats-triumphant. • **"white actors in blackface"** Charles Paul Freund, "Dixiecrats Triumphant: The Menacing Mr. Wilson," Reason.com, December 18, 2002, http://reason.com/archives/2002/12/18/dixiecrats-triumphant. • **"'it is all so terribly true'"** Melvyn Stokes, *D.W. Griffith's The Birth of a Nation: A History of the Most Controversial Motion Picture of All Time* (New York: Oxford University Press, 2007), p. 111. • **"The details are too horrific to repeat here"** *The Crisis* 12, no. 3, July 1916, pp. 6–13. • **"Wilson took no action"** "The Chicago Race Riot of 1919," History.com, accessed May 25, 2016, http://www.history.com/topics/black-history/chicago-race

-riot-of-1919. • "'**Kikes, Koons, and Katholics**'" David Kennedy and Lizabeth Cohen, *The American Pageant, Volume 2: Since 1865* (Boston: Wadsworth, Cengage Learning, 2014), p. 665. • **PAGE 66: "then not delivering"** William Keyor. "The Long-Forgotten Racial Attitudes and Policies of Woodrow Wilson," *Professor Voices,* Boston University, March 4, 2013, http://www.bu.edu/professorvoices /2013/03/04/the-long-forgotten-racial-attitudes-and-policies-of-woodrow-wil son/. • "'**American workmen had never dreamed of hitherto**'" Woodrow Wilson, *A History of the American People* (New York: Harper & Bros., 1902), pp. 212– 13. • **PAGE 67: "most disgusting notions of his time: eugenics"** *Merriam-Webster Online,* "Simple Definition of Eugenics," accessed May 25, 2016, http:// www.merriam-webster.com/dictionary/eugenics. • **"the nation's first eugenics law"** Dean A. Kowalski and S. Evan Kreider (eds.), *The Philosophy of Joss Whedon* (Lexington: The University of Kentucky Press, 2011), p. 23. Paul Rahe, "Progressive Racism," *The National Review,* April 11, 2013, http://www.nationalreview.com/arti cle/345274/progressive-racism-paul-rahe. • "'**other defectives**'" Harry Hamilton Laughlin, *Eugenical Sterilization in the United States* (Chicago: Psychopathic Labora-tory of the Municipal Court of Chicago, 1922), pp. 23–24. Jonah Goldberg, *Liberal Fascism: The Secret History of the American Left, From Mussolini to the Politics of Change* (New York: Crown, 2009), p. 255. • **"overturned by the New Jersey Supreme Court"** Eugenics Record Office, *II. The Legal, Legislative and Administrative Aspects of Sterilization,* Harry H. Laughlin, Long Island, NY, February 1914 (Eugenics Record Office, Bulletin no. 10B), pp. 54–61, https://repository.library.georgetown. edu/bitstream/handle/10822/556986/Bulletin10B.pdf?sequence=1&isAllowed=y. The "Eugenics Record Office" described itself as the "Committee to Study and to Report on the Best Practical Means of Cutting Off the Defective Germ-Plasm in the American Population." You can't make this stuff up. • **"minimum wage"** Meghan, "The Real History Behind the Minimum Wage (HINT: It Involves Progressives and Eugenics)," GlennBeck.com, February 14, 2014, http://www.glennbeck.com/2014 /02/14/the-real-history-behind-the-minimum-wage-hint-it-involves-progressives -and-eugenics/. • "'**bring forth more of their kind**'" Royal Meeker, review of *Cours d'Economie* Politique, by Georges Blanchard, *Political Science Quarterly* 25, no. 3, September 1910, p. 544. Qtd. in Jonah Goldberg, *Liberal Fascism: The Secret History of the American Left, From Mussolini to the Politics of Change* (New York: Doubleday, 2007), p. 264. See also: Meghan, "The Real History Behind the Minimum Wage (HINT: It Involves Progressives and Eugenics)," GlennBeck.com, February 14, 2014, http://www.glennbeck.com/2014/02/14/the-real-history-behind-the-minimum -wage-hint-it-involves-progressives-and-eugenics/. • **"those students never chal-lenged him"** Robert M. Saunders, *In Search of Woodrow Wilson: Beliefs and Behavior* (West Port, CT: Greenwood Press, 1998), p. 16. • "'**the intellectual equal of men**'" Robert M. Saunders, *In Search of Woodrow Wilson: Beliefs and Behavior* (West-port, CT: Greenwood Press, 1998), p. 16. • **PAGE 68: "'insulting, unfeminine, and unpatriotic'"** "Woodrow Wilson—A Portrait" Women's Suffrage, PBS, ac-cessed May 25, 2016, http://www.pbs.org/wgbh/amex/wilson/portrait/wp_suf frage.html. • **"were force-fed"** "President Woodrow Wilson Picketed by Women Suffragists," *This Day in History* (blog), History.com, August 28, 2009, http://www .history.com/this-day-in-history/president-woodrow-wilson-picketed-by-women -suffragists. • **"an 'unconstitutional governor'"** Ronald J. Pestritto, *Woodrow Wilson and the Roots of Modern Liberalism* (Lanham, MD: Rowman & Littlefield Pub-lishers, 2005), p. 170. • **PAGE 69: "'seditious' materials through the U.S.**

Mail" T. Jefferson, "Glenn Beck: Propaganda in America," GlennBeck.com, May 28 2010, http://www.glennbeck.com/content/articles/article/198/41221/. • **"the Boy Spies of America"** T. Jefferson, "Glenn Beck: Propaganda in America," Glenn Beck.com, May 28 2010, http://www.glennbeck.com/content/articles/article/198 /41221/. • **"threat to the U.S republic"** T. Jefferson, "Glenn Beck: Propaganda in America," GlennBeck.com, May 28 2010, http://www.glennbeck.com/content/ar ticles/article/198/41221/. • **" 'He kept us out of war' "** Herbert Eaton, *Presidential Timber: A History of Nominating Conventions, 1868–1960* (New York: The Free Press of Glencoe, 1964), p. 258. • **PAGE 70: " 'in armed neutrality' "** Woodrow Wilson, "Second Inaugural Address," (speech, Washington, D.C., March 5, 1917) Bartleby.com, http://www.bartleby.com/124/pres45.html. • **"More than three hundred thousand were killed or injured"** "WWI Casualty and Death Tables," PBS, accessed May 25, 2016, https://www.pbs.org/greatwar/resources/casdeath _pop.html. • **" 'I could not bear him' "** Thomas Fleming, *The Illusion of Victory: Americans in World War I* (New York: Basic Books, 2004), p. 324. • **PAGE 71: " 'hanged on gibbets as high as heaven' "** "Sherman Makes 'Em Laugh," *The Indianapolis News,* March 4, 1919. p. 26., https://newspapers.library.in.gov/cgi-bin/in diana?a=d&d=INN19190304-01.1.26 • **" 'separated from his human kind forever' "** *The New York Times Current History: The European War* (New York: The New York Times Company, 1919), p. 88. • **PAGE 72: "the sordid chauvinism, elitism, and bigotry"** Patrick Howley, "Flashback: Hillary Clinton Receives Woodrow Wilson Award," Breitbart, November 20, 2015, http://www.breitbart.com /big-government/2015/11/20/flashback-hillary-clinton-receives-woodrow-wilson -award/. • **PAGE 79: "banned 'the manufacture, sale, or transportation of intoxicating liquors' "** U.S. Const. amend. XVIII (repealed 1933), http://www .archives.gov/exhibits/charters/constitution_amendments_11-27.html#18.

CHAPTER 3: SECOND WAVE: FDR, WARTIME PROGRESSIVE
PAGE 83: "our Commander-in-Chief, Woodrow Wilson" Franklin D. Roosevelt, "Address Accepting the Presidential Nomination at the Democratic National Convention in Chicago," (speech, Chicago, July 2, 1932), The American Presidency Project at the University of California, Santa Barbara, http://www.presidency.ucsb .edu/ws/?pid=75174. • **"his rightful office"** Jonathan Alter, *The Defining Moment: FDR's Hundred-Day Triumph of Hope* (New York: Simon & Schuster, 2007). • **PAGE 84: "any new problem of democracy"** Frank Freidel, *Franklin D. Roosevelt: A Rendezvous with Destiny* (New York: Back Bay Books, 1991). • **"there is no vision the people perish"** Frank Freidel, *Franklin D. Roosevelt: A Rendezvous with Destiny* (New York: Back Bay Books, 1991). • **PAGE 85: "it required action"** Frank Freidel, *Franklin D. Roosevelt: A Rendezvous with Destiny* (New York: Back Bay Books, 1991). • **"tilted in his favor"** Frank Freidel, *Franklin D. Roosevelt: A Rendezvous with Destiny* (New York: Back Bay Books, 1991). • **"invaded by a foreign foe"** Frank Freidel, *Franklin D. Roosevelt: A Rendezvous with Destiny* (New York: Back Bay Books, 1991). • **"the crowd's raucous reaction a bit terrifying"** Michael Waldman, *My Fellow Americans* (Naperville, IL: Sourcebooks Mediafusion, 2010), p. 96. • **"to assume dictatorial power"** Michael Waldman, *My Fellow Americans* (Naperville, IL Sourcebooks Mediafusion, 2010), p. 96. • **" 'Never let a serious crisis go to waste' "** "Rahm Emanuel 'Never Let a Good Crisis Go to Waste,' " YouTube video, 0.12, from an appearance on *The Wall Street Journal*'s 2008 Shaping the New Agenda, posted by Ron Grant, Oct 30, 2012, https://www.youtube.com/watch?v=Pb-Yuh

FWCr4. • **PAGE 86: "'changing and growing social order'"** Franklin D. Roosevelt, "Commonwealth Club Address," (speech, San Francisco, September 23, 1932), The Heritage Foundation, http://www.heritage.org/initiatives/first-principles/primary-sources/fdrs-commonwealth-club-address. • **"'side by side with economic plutocracy'"** David M. Kennedy, *The American People in the Great Depression: Freedom from Fear, Part One* (New York: Oxford University Press, 2003). • **"who's who of other progressives"** Raymond Moley, *After Seven Years* (New York: Harper & Brothers, 2006), p. 14. • **PAGE 87: "'the greatest number of our citizens'"** Franklin D. Roosevelt, "Address Accepting the Presidential Nomination at the Democratic National Convention in Chicago," (speech, Chicago, July 2, 1932), The American Presidency Project at the University of California, Santa Barbara, http://www.presidency.ucsb.edu/ws/?pid=75174. • **"Before the 1930s, *liberalism* hadn't been a term"** Charles R. Kesler, *I Am the Change: Barack Obama and the Future of Liberalism* (New York: Broadside Books, 2012), p. 111. • **"a new word for Republicans: *conservatives*"** Charles R. Kesler, *I Am the Change: Barack Obama and the Future of Liberalism* (New York: Broadside Books, 2012). • **"*Tory*, vaguely monarchical and fascist"** Charles R. Kesler, *I Am the Change: Barack Obama and the Future of Liberalism* (New York: Broadside Books, 2012), p. 113. • **PAGE 88: "'be the theory of the Democratic Party'"** Franklin D. Roosevelt, "Address Accepting the Presidential Nomination at the Democratic National Convention in Chicago," (speech, Chicago, July 2, 1932), The American Presidency Project at the University of California, Santa Barbara, http://www.presidency.ucsb.edu/ws/?pid=75174. • **"'the individual and freedom change with time'"** John Dewey, *The Later Works of John Dewey, Volume 11, 1925–1953,* ed. Jo Ann Boydston (Carbondale, IL: Southern Illinois University Press, 2008), pp. 291–92. • **"would require enlightened experimentation"** John Dewey, "The Future of Liberalism," (speech to the America Philosophical Association, Chicago, December 28, 1934), The Heritage Foundation, http://www.heritage.org/initiatives/first-principles/primary-sources/john-dewey-on-liberalisms-future. • **"'persistent experimentation'"** Franklin D. Roosevelt, "Address at Oglethorpe University," (speech, Brookhaven, GA, May 22, 1932), The American Presidency Project at the University of California, Santa Barbara, http://www.presidency.ucsb.edu/ws/?pid=88410. • **PAGE 91: "'the Age of the Professors'"** John T. Flynn, *The Roosevelt Myth*, (Greenwich, CT: The Devin-Adair Publishing Company, 1948), p. 34, https://mises.org/library/roosevelt-myth. • **"risen to a peak of more than twenty-eight percent"** Robert P. Murphy, *The Politically Incorrect Guide to the Great Depression and the New Deal* (Washington, D.C.: Regnery Publishing, 2009), p. 42. • **"the lowest it would ever get during the Great Depression"** Andrew Glass, "Dow Jones falls to its lowest point, July 8, 1932," *Politico*, July 8, 2013, http://www.politico.com/story/2013/07/this-day-in-politics-july-8-1932-093787. • **"the economy healed on its own"** Benjamin Weingarten, "The story of America's last 'governmentally unmedicated' depression that they never taught you in school," TheBlaze, November 11, 2014, http://www.theblaze.com/blog/2014/11/11/the-story-of-americas-last-governmentally-unmedicated-depression-that-they-never-taught-you-in-school/. • **PAGE 92: "'enlightened administration . . . has come'"** Franklin D. Roosevelt, "Commonwealth Club Address," (speech, San Francisco, September 23, 1932), The Heritage Foundation, http://www.heritage.org/initiatives/first-principles/primary-sources/fdrs-commonwealth-club-address. • **"role of repressive central government"** Franklin D. Roosevelt, "Commonwealth Club Address," (speech, San Francisco,

September 23, 1932), The Heritage Foundation, http://www.heritage.org/initia tives/first-principles/primary-sources/fdrs-commonwealth-club-address. • **"under seven hundred competition-killing industrial codes"** Jim Powell, *FDR's Folly: How Roosevelt and His New Deal Prolonged the Great Depression* (New York: Crown, 2003), p. 77. • **"fixed wages and controlled prices"** Jim Powell, "Government Jobs Don't Cure Depression," *National Review*, March 23, 2009, http://www.national review.com/article/227121/government-jobs-dont-cure-depression-jim-powell. • **"NRA released 2,998 administrative orders"** Jim Powell, *FDR's Folly: How Roosevelt and His New Deal Prolonged the Great Depression* (New York: Crown, 2003), pp. 77, 162. • **" 'is the Blue Eagle' "** John T. Flynn, *The Roosevelt Myth*, (Green- wich, CT: The Devin-Adair Publishing Company, 1948), p. 43, https://mises.org /library/roosevelt-myth. • **PAGE 93: "more than two thousand strikes during FDR's first term"** John T. Flynn, *The Roosevelt Myth*, (Greenwich, CT: The Devin- Adair Publishing Company, 1948), p. 86, https://mises.org/library/roosevelt-myth. • **"dared so much as sew pants after dark"** John T. Flynn, *The Roosevelt Myth*, (Greenwich, CT: The Devin-Adair Publishing Company, 1948), p. 45, https://mises .org/library/roosevelt-myth. • **"five hundred thousand black workers lost their jobs"** Jim Powell, *FDR's Folly: How Roosevelt and His New Deal Prolonged the Great Depression* (New York: Crown, 2003), pp. 117–19. • **"took their case to the Su- preme Court"** David Leonhardt, "No Free Lunch," review of *The Forgotten Man: A New History of the Great Depression*, by Amity Shlaes, *The New York Times Book Review*, August 26, 2007, http://www.nytimes.com/2007/08/26/books/review /Leonhardt-t.html?_r=1. • **PAGE 94: "the president could not legislate from the Oval Office"** Jim Powell, *FDR's Folly: How Roosevelt and His New Deal Prolonged the Great Depression* (New York: Crown, 2003), p. 164. • **"burying jars of money"** Paul Krugman, "Time for Bottles in Coal Mines," *The New York Times*, April 14, 2009, http://krugman.blogs.nytimes.com/2009/04/14/time-for-bottles-in-coal-mines /?_r=0. • **"increased WPA expenditures more than three thousand percent"** Robert P. Murphy, *The Politically Incorrect Guide to the Great Depression and the New Deal* (Washington, D.C.: Regnery Publishing, 2009), pp. 142–43. • **PAGE 95: " 'a mere subsistence diet' "** John T. Flynn, *The Roosevelt Myth*, (Greenwich, CT: The Devin-Adair Publishing Company, 1948), p. 49. • **" 'the depression would be cured' "** Jim Powell, *FDR's Folly: How Roosevelt and His New Deal Prolonged the Great Depression* (New York: Crown, 2003), p. 117. • **"FDR be given control over the currency"** Robert P. Murphy, *The Politically Incorrect Guide to the Great Depression and the New Deal* (Washington, D.C.: Regnery Publishing, 2009), p. 115. • **"FDR could set the price himself"** Jim Powell, *FDR's Folly: How Roosevelt and His New Deal Prolonged the Great Depression* (New York: Crown, 2003), pp. 71–72. • **PAGE 96: "the 'court-packing' scheme"** "Roosevelt Announces 'Court Packing' Plan," *This Day in History* (blog), History.com, February 5, 2010, http://www.history.com /this-day-in-history/roosevelt-announces-court-packing-plan. • **"modern condi- tions demanded action"** Franklin D. Roosevelt, "Fireside Chat 9: On 'Court Packing' (March 9, 1937)," The Miller Center, accessed May 26, 2016, http://miller center.org/president/speeches/speech-3309. • **"shift in public opinion against FDR"** Larry DeWitt, The United States Social Security Agency, "The 1937 Su- preme Court Rulings on the Social Security Act," ssa.gov, accessed May 26, 2016, https://www.ssa.gov/history/court.html. • **"shaping decisions for decades to come"** John G. Roberts, Jr., "Remarks of the Chief Justice: Symposium on Judicial Independence," (remarks, University of Richmond T.C. Williams School of Law,

March 21, 2003), SupremeCourt.gov, http://www.supremecourt.gov/publicinfo
/speeches/sp_03-21-03.html. • **PAGE 97: "restricted all 'partisan' broadcasts"**
Thomas West, "The Liberal Assault on Freedom of Speech," *Imprimis* 33, no. 1 (January 2004), http://imprimis.hillsdale.edu/the-liberal-assault-on-freedom-of-speech/.
• **"dramatically increased unemployment"** Thomas J. DiLorenzo, "The New
Deal Debunked (Again)," Mises Institute, September 27, 2004, https://mises.org/li
brary/new-deal-debunked-again. • **"to fourteen million from less than three
million"** "Franklin D. Roosevelt: The American Franchise," The Miller Center,
University of Virginia, accessed May 26, 2016, http://millercenter.org/president/bi
ography/fdroosevelt-the-american-franchise. • **"most of them loyal FDR Democrats"** "Franklin D. Roosevelt: Campaigns and Elections," The Miller Center,
University of Virginia, accessed May 26, 2016, http://millercenter.org/president/bi
ography/fdroosevelt-campaigns-and-elections. • **"to expand and create new
jobs"** Jim Powell, *FDR's Folly: How Roosevelt and His New Deal Prolonged the Great
Depression* (New York: Crown, 2003), pp. 106–7. • **"actually to prevent frauds"**
Jim Powell, *FDR's Folly: How Roosevelt and His New Deal Prolonged the Great Depression*
(New York: Crown, 2003), pp. 109–10. • **"but paid more for them"** Jim Powell,
FDR's Folly: How Roosevelt and His New Deal Prolonged the Great Depression (New
York: Crown, 2003), pp. 110–11. • **PAGE 98: "during the 1932 presidential
race"** William J. Bennett, *America: The Last Best Hope (Volume 2)*, (Nashville:
Thomas Nelson, Inc., 2006), https://ronloneysbooks.files.wordpress.com/2013/03
/america-the-last-best-hope-volume-2-by-william-j-bennett.pdf. • **"eighty-two
hundred pages by the end of it"** Jason Russell, "Look at How Many Pages Are
in the Federal Tax Code," *The Washington Examiner*, April 5, 2015, http://www.wash
ingtonexaminer.com/look-at-how-many-pages-are-in-the-federal-tax-code/arti
cle/2563032. • **"annual unemployment rate averaged 18.6 percent"** Robert P.
Murphy, *The Politically Incorrect Guide to the Great Depression and the New Deal* (Washington, D.C.: Regnery Publishing, 2009), pp. 99–100. • **"did not return back to
1929 levels until 1941"** Robert P. Murphy, *The Politically Incorrect Guide to the Great
Depression and the New Deal* (Washington, D.C.: Regnery Publishing, 2009), pp. 110–
11. • **"Business was paralyzed as a result"** Robert Higgs, "Regime Uncertainty:
Why the Great Depression Lasted So Long and Why Prosperity Resumed After the
War," *The Independent Review* 1, no. 4, Spring 1997, https://www.independent.org/pdf
/tir/tir_01_4_higgs.pdf. • **PAGE 99: "An estimated four million workers lost
their jobs"** David B. Woolner, "Repeating Our Mistakes: The 'Roosevelt Recession' and the Danger of Austerity," The Roosevelt Institute, July 7, 2010, http://
rooseveltinstitute.org/repeating-our-mistakes-roosevelt-recession-and-danger-aus
terity/. • **" 'to make a Hell of earth' "** C. S. Lewis, *God in the Dock: Essays on Theology*, ed., Walter Hooper (Grand Rapids, MI: Wm. B. Eerdmans Publishing Company, 1970). • **" 'And an enormous debt to boot' "** Burton W. Folsom, *New Deal
Or Raw Deal?: How FDR's Economic Legacy Has Damaged America*, (New York:
Threshold Editions, 2009), p. 144. • **"the thing to get him there"** John T. Flynn,
The Roosevelt Myth, (Greenwich, CT: The Devin-Adair Publishing Company, 1948),
p. 281. • **" 'the downfall of New York in towers of flames' "** Eike Frenzel, "Operation Pastorius: Hitler's Unfulfilled Dream of a New York in Flames," *Der Spiegel*,
September 16, 2010, http://www.spiegel.de/international/zeitgeist/operation-pasto
rius-hitler-s-unfulfilled-dream-of-a-new-york-in-flames-a-716753-2.html.
• **PAGE 100: " 'including our own' "** Franklin D. Roosevelt, "Address at the
Annual Dinner of White House Correspondents' Association," (speech, Washing-

ton, D.C., March 15, 1941), The American Presidency Project at the University of California, Santa Barbara, http://www.presidency.ucsb.edu/ws/?pid=16089. • **"quantity of fabrics used in dresses"** Burton W. Folsom Jr. and Anita Folsom, *FDR Goes to War: How Expanded Executive Power, Spiraling National Debt, and Restricted Civil Liberties Shaped Wartime America* (New York: Threshold Editions, 2011), p. 119. • **"which procured raw materials"** John T. Flynn, *The Roosevelt Myth*, (Greenwich, CT: The Devin-Adair Publishing Company, 1948), p. 304. • **"spent $1.2 billion during the war"** John T. Flynn, *The Roosevelt Myth*, (Greenwich, CT: The Devin-Adair Publishing Company,1948), pp. 304–6. • **"the rubber from Haiti cost $546 per pound"** Burton W. Folsom Jr. and Anita Folsom, *FDR Goes to War: How Expanded Executive Power, Spiraling National Debt, and Restricted Civil Liberties Shaped Wartime America* (New York: Threshold Editions, 2011), p. 162. • **PAGE 101:** • **"'It all reminds me of my homeland'"** Anne Applebaum, "Gulag: Understanding the Magnitude of What Happened," The Heritage Foundation, October 16, 2003, http://www.heritage.org/research/lecture/gulag-under standing-the-magnitude-of-what-happened. • **"very understanding with people"** Henry A. Wallace, Soviet Asia Mission (New York: Reynal & Hitchcock, 1946), p. 82. • **"Wallace's welcoming committee"** Vadim J. Birstein, "Three Days in 'Auschwitz Without Gas Chambers': Henry A. Wallace's Visit to Magadan in 1944," The Wilson Center, April 30, 2012, https://www.wilsoncenter.org/publica tion/three-days-auschwitz-without-gas-chambers-henry-wallaces-visit-to -magadan-1944. • **PAGE 102:** **"'were razed in a single night'"** Elinor Lipper, *Eleven Years in Soviet Prison Camps* (Chicago: Henry Regnery Company, 1951). • **"'hundreds of thousands of the damned'"** Elinor Lipper, *Eleven Years in Soviet Prison Camps* (Chicago: Henry Regnery Company, 1951). • **"Thirty-five BEW Reds"** John T. Flynn, *The Roosevelt Myth*, (Greenwich, CT: The Devin-Adair Publishing Company, 1948), pp. 306–9 • **"take action to break up strikes"** Burton W. Folsom Jr. and Anita Folsom, *FDR Goes to War: How Expanded Executive Power, Spiraling National Debt, and Restricted Civil Liberties Shaped Wartime America* (New York: Threshold Editions, 2011), p. 121. • **PAGE 103: "mass shortages of basic goods"** Burton W. Folsom Jr. and Anita Folsom, *FDR Goes to War: How Expanded Executive Power, Spiraling National Debt, and Restricted Civil Liberties Shaped Wartime America* (New York: Threshold Editions, 2011), p. 140. • **"thirteen million man-days of labor lost"** Burton W. Folsom Jr. and Anita Folsom, *FDR Goes to War: How Expanded Executive Power, Spiraling National Debt, and Restricted Civil Liberties Shaped Wartime America* (New York: Threshold Editions, 2011), p. 159. • **"illegal black-market transactions"** Burton W. Folsom Jr. and Anita Folsom, *FDR Goes to War: How Expanded Executive Power, Spiraling National Debt, and Restricted Civil Liberties Shaped Wartime America* (New York: Threshold Editions, 2011), p. 166. • **"in the run-up to the 1944 election"** John T. Flynn, *The Roosevelt Myth*, (Greenwich, CT: The Devin-Adair Publishing Company, 1948), pp. 322–26. • **"Roosevelt was often suppressed"** John T. Flynn, *The Roosevelt Myth*, (Greenwich, CT: The Devin-Adair Publishing Company, 1948), p. 103. • **"'Taxes to beat the Axis'"** Burton W. Folsom Jr. and Anita Folsom, *FDR Goes to War: How Expanded Executive Power, Spiraling National Debt, and Restricted Civil Liberties Shaped Wartime America* (New York: Threshold Editions, 2011), pp. 189–90. • **PAGE 104: "even 'political friends'"** Burton W. Folsom Jr. and Anita Folsom, *FDR Goes to War: How Expanded Executive Power, Spiraling National Debt, and Restricted Civil Liberties Shaped Wartime America* (New York: Threshold Editions, 2011), p. 212. • **"and critical journalists"**

Burton W. Folsom Jr. and Anita Folsom, *FDR Goes to War: How Expanded Executive Power, Spiraling National Debt, and Restricted Civil Liberties Shaped Wartime America* (New York: Threshold Editions, 2011), pp. 211–13. • **"on behalf of actual opponents"** Burton W. Folsom Jr. and Anita Folsom, *FDR Goes to War: How Expanded Executive Power, Spiraling National Debt, and Restricted Civil Liberties Shaped Wartime America* (New York: Threshold Editions, 2011), p. 216. • **"consisted of six hundred thousand noncitizens"** Burton W. Folsom Jr. and Anita Folsom, *FDR Goes to War: How Expanded Executive Power, Spiraling National Debt, and Restricted Civil Liberties Shaped Wartime America* (New York: Threshold Editions, 2011), p. 226–29. • **"held disdain for 'inferior' peoples"** Greg Robinson, *By Order of the President: FDR and the Internment of Japanese Americans* (Cambridge, MA: Harvard University Press, 2003). • **"Japanese immigrants were inassimilable"** Rafael Medoff. "The Truth About FDR and the Jews," The Louis D. Brandeis Center For Human Rights Under Law, June 7, 2013, http://brandeiscenter.com/blog/the-truth-about-fdr-and-the -jews/. • **"praised the 'Teutonic race'"** John M. Cooper, Jr., *Reconsidering Woodrow Wilson: Progressivism, Internationalism, War, and Peace* (Washington, D.C.: Woodrow Wilson Center Press, 2008), p. 231. • **PAGE 105: "the spirit of Fascism here at home"** Franklin D. Roosevelt, "State of the Union Message to Congress," (speech, Washington, D.C., January 11, 1944), The Heritage Foundation, http:// www.heritage.org/initiatives/first-principles/primary-sources/fdrs-second-bill-of -rights. • **PAGE 106: "'a mere prelude to revolution'"** Raymond Moley, *How to Keep Our Liberty: A Program for Political Action* (New York: Knopf, 1952), pp. 82–83, https://mises.org/library/how-keep-our-liberty. • **PAGE 108: "'utterly broken, submissive, and repentant'"** Edmund Morris, *The Rise of Theodore Roosevelt* (New York: Random House Trade Paperbacks, 2001), p. 456. • **PAGE 109: "new city a federal priority"** "Teaching Eleanor Roosevelt Glossary: Arthurdale," The Eleanor Roosevelt Papers Project, George Washington University, accessed May 26, 2016, https://www.gwu.edu/~erpapers/teachinger/glossary/arthurdale.cfm. • **"managed by the Division of Subsistence Homesteads"** C. J. Maloney, *Back to the Land: Arthurdale, FDR's New Deal, and the Costs of Economic Planning* (Hoboken, NJ: Wiley & Sons, Inc., 2011). • **"designed to decentralize American industry"** C .J. Maloney, *Back to the Land: Arthurdale, FDR's New Deal, and the Costs of Economic Planning* (Hoboken, NJ: Wiley & Sons, Inc., 2011). • **"raising money for the program in Congress"** "Teaching Eleanor Roosevelt Glossary: Arthurdale," The Eleanor Roosevelt Papers Project, George Washington University, accessed May 26, 2016, https://www.gwu.edu/~erpapers/teachinger/glossary/arthurdale.cfm. • **PAGE 110: "talking about its future course"** "Teaching Eleanor Roosevelt Glossary: Arthurdale," The Eleanor Roosevelt Papers Project, George Washington University, accessed May 26, 2016, https://www.gwu.edu/~erpapers/teachinger/glossary/ar thurdale.cfm. • **"complete with indoor plumbing"** "Teaching Eleanor Roosevelt Glossary: Arthurdale," The Eleanor Roosevelt Papers Project, George Washington University, accessed May 26, 2016, https://www.gwu.edu/~erpapers/teachinger /glossary/arthurdale.cfm. • **"didn't fit the existing foundations"** Tom Stafford, "Looking Back: For Eleanor Roosevelt, Arthurdale Was a Chance to Help," *Springfield News-Sun*, August 23, 2010, http://www.springfieldnewssun.com/news/news /local/looking-back-for-eleanor-roosevelt-arthurdale-was-/nNxD9/. • **"made the homes three hundred percent more expensive"** Tom Stafford, "Looking Back: For Eleanor Roosevelt, Arthurdale Was a Chance to Help," *Springfield News-Sun*, August 23, 2010, http://www.springfieldnewssun.com/news/news/local/looking

-back-for-eleanor-roosevelt-arthurdale-was-/nNxD9/. • **"'the middle of no- where'"** C. J. Maloney, "The Peculiar History of Arthurdale," Mises Institute, August 8, 2007, https://mises.org/library/peculiar-history-arthurdale. • **"it too quickly shut down"** "Teaching Eleanor Roosevelt Glossary: Arthurdale," The Eleanor Roosevelt Papers Project, George Washington University, accessed May 26, 2016, https://www.gwu.edu/~erpapers/teachinger/glossary/arthurdale.cfm. • **PAGE 111: "sold off at steep discounts"** C. J. Maloney, "The Peculiar History of Ar- thurdale," Mises Institute, August 8, 2007, https://mises.org/library/peculiar-his tory-arthurdale.

CHAPTER 4: THIRD WAVE: LBJ AND THE POWER OF ENVY

PAGE 114: "'Uncle Cornpone and his little porkchop'" Robert Caro, *The Years of Lyndon Johnson: The Passage of Power* (New York: Knopf, 2012). • **"'if Lyndon was president'"** Rick Klein, "Jacqueline Kennedy Reveals that JFK Feared an LBJ Pres- idency," ABCNews.com, September 8, 2011, http://abcnews.go.com/Politics/Jac queline_Kennedy/jacqueline-kennedy-reveals-jfk-feared-lbj-presidency/story ?id=14477930. • **PAGE 115: "'a Baptist preacher'"** United Press International, "President Johnson Calls Himself Cross Between Cowboy, Preacher," *The Pittsburgh Press*, November 23, 1963, p. 11. • **PAGE 116: "to Congressman Richard Kle- berg"** "President Lyndon B. Johnson's Biography," LBJ Presidential Library, Uni- versity of Texas, accessed May 27, 2016, http://www.lbjlib.utexas.edu/john son/archives.hom/biographys.hom/lbj_bio.asp. • **"'in exchange for part-time jobs'"** "Lyndon B. Johnson to Allred: November 21, 1935," Texas State Library and Archives Commission, accessed May 27, 2016, https://www.tsl.texas.gov/governors /personality/allred-lbj.html. • **"'public buildings all over Texas'"** Lyndon B. Johnson to Allred: November 21, 1935," Texas State Library and Archives Commis- sion, accessed May 27, 2016, https://www.tsl.texas.gov/governors/personality/allred -lbj.html. • **PAGE 117: "'I support Franklin Roosevelt the full way'"** L. Pat- rick Hughes, "The Election of a Texas New Dealer: Lyndon Johnson's 1937 Race for Congress," Austin Community College, accessed May 27, 2016, http://www.austin cc.edu/lpatrick/his2341/election.html. • **"'Franklin D. and Lyndon B'"** Nero James Pruitt, *The Forty-Three Presidents: What They Said To and About Each Other* (self-published, and printed by iUniverse, 2015). • **"'horse radish for Roosevelt'"** William E. Leuchtenburg, *In the Shadow: From Harry Truman to Barack Obama* (Ithaca, NY: Cornell University Press, 2009). • **"met with the president no fewer than twenty-three times"** William J. vanden Heuvel, "Franklin Delano Roosevelt and Lyndon Baines Johnson: Architects of a Nation," (speech, Austin, Texas, March 14, 2000), Franklin D. Roosevelt Library and Museum, http://www.fdrlibrary.marist .edu/library/pdfs/vh_fdrlbj.pdf. • **"'soul needed support'"** William J. vanden Heuvel, "Franklin Delano Roosevelt and Lyndon Baines Johnson: Architects of a Nation," (speech, Austin, Texas, March 14, 2000), Franklin D. Roosevelt Library and Museum, http://www.fdrlibrary.marist.edu/library/pdfs/vh_fdrlbj.pdf. • **"'be- cause of him'"** William J. vanden Heuvel, "Franklin Delano Roosevelt and Lyn- don Baines Johnson: Architects of a Nation," (speech, Austin, Texas, March 14, 2000), Franklin D. Roosevelt Library and Museum, http://www.fdrlibrary.marist .edu/library/pdfs/vh_fdrlbj.pdf. • **PAGE 118: "'had more women by accident'"** Robert Dallek, "Three New Revelations About LBJ," *The Atlantic*, April 1998, http://www.theatlantic.com/magazine/archive/1998/04/three-new-revelations -about-lbj/377094/. • **"'groping' her"** Jan Jarboe Russell, "Alone Together," *Texas*

Monthly, August 1999, http://www.texasmonthly.com/politics/alone-together/.
• **"he was treating her as if she was invisible in public"** Jan Jarboe Russell,
"Alone Together," *Texas Monthly*, August 1999, http://www.texasmonthly.com/pol
itics/alone-together/. • **"'That's my prerogative'"** Stacy Conradt, "10 Unexpected Duties Performed by the Secret Service," *Mental Floss*, December 18, 2015,
http://mentalfloss.com/article/25170/10-unexpected-duties-performed-secret-ser
vice#comment-485137242. • **"'the only seat in the room'"** Matthew Pinsker,
"Richard Goodwin: Monday Morning Psychoanalyst," *The Harvard Crimson*, October 29, 1988, http://www.thecrimson.com/article/1988/10/29/richard-goodwin
-monday-morning-psychoanalyst-pbwbas/. • **PAGE 119: "their ticket barely
beat Nixon"** Peter Carlson, "Another Race to the Finish," *The Washington Post*,
November 17, 2000, https://www.washingtonpost.com/archive/politics/2000/11/17
/another-race-to-the-finish/c810a41c-7da9-461a-927b-9da6d36a65dc/. • **"'champion of everyday Americans'"** Kenneth T. Walsh, "The First 100 Days: Lyndon
Johnson Fulfilled Kennedy's Legacy," *U.S. News & World Report*, March 5, 2009,
http://www.usnews.com/news/history/articles/2009/03/05/the-first-100-days
-lyndon-johnson-fulfilled-kennedys-legacy. • **PAGE 121: "equality for all"** "John
Gardner: The Great Society," PBS, accessed May 27, 2016, http://www.pbs.org
/johngardner/chapters/4c.html. • **PAGE 122: "'Better than he did'"** Kenneth T.
Walsh, "The First 100 Days: Lyndon Johnson Fulfilled Kennedy's Legacy," *U.S.
News & World Report*, March 5, 2009, http://www.usnews.com/news/history/arti
cles/2009/03/05/the-first-100-days-lyndon-johnson-fulfilled-kennedys-legacy.
• **"'upward to the Great Society'"** Lyndon B. Johnson, "Commencement Address at the University of Michigan," (speech, Ann Arbor, MI, May 22, 1964), The
Heritage Foundation, http://www.heritage.org/initiatives/first-principles/primary
-sources/lbj-launches-the-great-society. • **PAGE 123: "'elevate our national
life'"** Lyndon B. Johnson, "Commencement Address at the University of Michigan," (speech, Ann Arbor, MI, May 22, 1964), The Heritage Foundation, http://
www.heritage.org/initiatives/first-principles/primary-sources/lbj-launches-the
-great-society. • **"'hunger for community'"** Lyndon B. Johnson, "Commenc
ement Address at the University of Michigan," (speech, Ann Arbor, MI, May 22,
1964), The Heritage Foundation, http://www.heritage.org/initiatives/first-princi
ples/primary-sources/lbj-launches-the-great-society. • **"'quantity of their
goods'"** Lyndon B. Johnson, "Commencement Address at the University of Michigan," (speech, Ann Arbor, MI, May 22, 1964), The Heritage Foundation, http://
www.heritage.org/initiatives/first-principles/primary-sources/lbj-launches-the
-great-society. • **"'marvelous products of our labor'"** Lyndon B. Johnson,
"Commencement Address at the University of Michigan," (speech, Ann Arbor, MI,
May 22, 1964), The Heritage Foundation, http://www.heritage.org/initiatives
/first-principles/primary-sources/lbj-launches-the-great-society. • **PAGE 124:
"big-government nonsense"** "Study Aid: Great Society Legislation," The Gilder
Lehrman Institute of American History, accessed May 27, 2016, https://www.gilder
lehrman.org/history-by-era/sixties/resources/study-aid-great-society-legisla
tion. • **PAGE 126: "'hidden social ties'"** "John Dewey and the Progressive Conception of Freedom: 1908," The Heritage Foundation, accessed May 27, 2016, http://
www.heritage.org/initiatives/first-principles/primary-sources/john-dewey-and
-the-progressive-conception-of-freedom. • **PAGE 127: "become 'a successful
businesswoman'"** Enid Nemy, "Lady Bird Johnson, 94, Dies; Eased a Path to
Power," *The New York Times*, July 12, 2007, http://www.nytimes.com/2007/07/12

/washington/12johnson.html?ex=1342065600&en=3085b9d85cb24e12&ei=5124 &partner=permalink&exprod=permalink&_r=0. • "'application was speedily approved'" Enid Nemy, "Lady Bird Johnson, 94, Dies; Eased a Path to Power," *The New York Times*, July 12, 2007, http://www.nytimes.com/2007/07/12/washington /12johnson.html?ex=1342065600&en=3085b9d85cb24e12&ei=5124&partner =permalink&exprod=permalink&_r=0. • **PAGE 128:** "'cable interests'" Enid Nemy, "Lady Bird Johnson, 94, Dies; Eased a Path to Power," *The New York Times*, July 12, 2007, http://www.nytimes.com/2007/07/12/washington/12johnson.html ?ex=1342065600&en=3085b9d85cb24e12&ei=5124&partner=permalink&exprod =permalink&_r=0. • **"ranches, real estate, and a bank"** Joe Holley, "Champion of Conservation, Loyal Force Behind LBJ," *The Washington Post*, July 12, 2007, http://www.washingtonpost.com/wp-dyn/content/article/2007/07/11/AR 2007071102146.html. • **"subsidiary of Halliburton"** "KBR History," KBR.com, accessed May 27, 2016, https://www.kbr.com/about/our-company/history. • **"sizable contributions to Johnson's political campaign"** John Burnett, "Halliburton Deals Recall Vietnam-Era Controversy," NPR, December 24, 2003, http:// www.npr.org/templates/story/story.php?storyId=1569483. • **PAGE 129:** "'thousands of dollars In campaign contributions'"** James M. Carter, "War Profiteering from Vietnam to Iraq," CounterPunch.org, December 11, 2003, http://www .counterpunch.org/2003/12/11/war-profiteering-from-vietnam-to-iraq/. • **"Lady Bird Johnson"** Ryan S. Walters, "From 'Lyin' Lyndon to 'Thieving Thad' The Eerie Similarities Between Texas'48 and Mississippi'14," Mississippi Conservative Daily, September 7, 2014, https://mississippiconservativedaily.com/2014/09/07 /from-lyin-lyndon-to-thieving-thad-the-eerie-similarities-between-texas-48-and -mississippi-14/. • **"'you'll get your war'"** Roger Stone and Phillip Nelson, "The Truth About LBJ and MLK," Breitbart, December 30, 2014, http://www.breitbart.com /big-government/2014/12/30/the-truth-about-lbj-and-mlk/. • **"'Dr. Johnny'"** Jay Martin, *The Education of John Dewey: A Biography* (New York: Columbia University Press, 2003), p. 492. • **PAGE 130:** "'economic stagnation followed'"** Brian M. Riedl, "Most New Spending Since 2001 Unrelated to the War on Terrorism," The Heritage Foundation, November 13, 2003, http://www.heritage.org/re search/reports/2003/11/most-new-spending-since-2001-unrelated-to-the-war-on -terrorism. • **"three times the amount of money'"** "Editorial: The Not-So -Great Society Turns a Rickety 50," *The Washington Post*, May 21, 2014, http://www .washingtontimes.com/news/2014/may/21/editorial-the-not-so-great-society/. • **PAGE 131:** "'negra' with others"** Adam Serwer, "Lyndon Johnson Was a Civil Rights Hero. But Also a Racist." MSNBC, April 12, 2014, http://www.msnbc.com /msnbc/lyndon-johnson-civil-rights-racism. • **"hordes of barbaric yellow dwarves'"** Adam Serwer, "Lyndon Johnson Was a Civil Rights Hero. But Also a Racist." MSNBC.com, April 12, 2014, http://www.msnbc.com/msnbc/lyndon -johnson-civil-rights-racism. • **"'pretend you're a goddamn piece of furniture'"** Adam Serwer, "Lyndon Johnson Was a Civil Rights Hero. But Also a Racist." MSNBC.com, April 12, 2014, http://www.msnbc.com/msnbc/lyndon-johnson -civil-rights-racism. • **"any civil rights legislation'"** Wynton Hall, "The Unknown History of Civil Rights," TownHall.com, February 4, 2008, http://townhall .com/columnists/wyntonhall/2008/02/04/the_unknown_history_of_civil_rights. • **"'the nigger bill'"** Adam Serwer, "Lyndon Johnson Was a Civil Rights Hero. But Also a Racist." MSNBC.com, April 12, 2014, http://www.msnbc.com/msnbc /lyndon-johnson-civil-rights-racism. • **"'everyone to know he's a nigger'"**

Adam Serwer, "Lyndon Johnson Was a Civil Rights Hero. But Also a Racist." MSNBC.com, April 12, 2014, http://www.msnbc.com/msnbc/lyndon-johnson -civil-rights-racism. • **PAGE 132: "'than Democrats'"** Alicia W. Stewart and Tricia Escobedo, "What You Might Not Know about the 1964 Civil Rights Act," CNN.com, April 10, 2014, http://www.cnn.com/2014/04/10/politics/civil-rights -act-interesting-facts/. • **"he became president himself"** Roger Stone and Phillip Nelson, "The Truth About LBJ and MLK," Breitbart, December 30, 2014, http:// www.breitbart.com/big-government/2014/12/30/the-truth-about-lbj-and-mlk/. • **"Democratic nomination in 1964"** Roger Stone and Phillip Nelson, "The Truth About LBJ and MLK," Breitbart, December 30, 2014, http://www.breitbart .com/big-government/2014/12/30/the-truth-about-lbj-and-mlk/. • **PAGE 133: "his marital infidelities"** Dia Kayyali, "FBI's 'Suicide Letter' to Dr. Martin Luther King, Jr., and the Dangers of Unchecked Surveillance," Electronic Frontier Foundation, November 12, 2014, https://www.eff.org/deeplinks/2014/11/fbis-sui cide-letter-dr-martin-luther-king-jr-and-dangers-unchecked-surveillance. • **"on the basis of 'national security'"** "June 16, 1967: LBJ Orders No Wiretapping," Today in Civil Liberties History, accessed May 27, 2016, http://todayinclh.com /?event=lbj-orders-no-wiretapping. • **"'is bared to the nation'"** Dia Kayyali, "FBI's 'Suicide Letter' to Dr. Martin Luther King, Jr., and the Dangers of Unchecked Surveillance," Electronic Frontier Foundation, November 12, 2014, https://www .eff.org/deeplinks/2014/11/fbis-suicide-letter-dr-martin-luther-king-jr-and-dan gers-unchecked-surveillance. • **PAGE 135: "as the population ages and people live longer"** John Stossel, "The Medicare Ponzi Scheme," TownHall.com, May 21, 2009, http://townhall.com/columnists/johnstossel/2009/05/20/the_medicare_ponzi _scheme. • **"'drug bills cut in half'"** "Bush Promotes Medicare Prescription Drug Plan," FoxNews.com, March 14, 2006, http://www.foxnews.com/story/2006 /03/14/bush-promotes-medicare-prescription-drug-plan.html. • **"$1.3 million for a family of four"** John Stossel, "The Medicare Ponzi Scheme," TownHall.com, May 21, 2009, http://townhall.com/columnists/johnstossel/2009/05/20/the_medi care_ponzi_scheme. • **"to spy on antiwar activists and other dissidents"** The Rockefeller Commission, *Report to the President by the Commission on CIA Activities Within the United States*, June 1975, Assassination Archives and Research Center, chap. 11, https://www.aarclibrary.org/publib/church/rockcomm/pdf/RockComm _Chap11_CHAOS.pdf. • **"files collected on them by the government"** David P. Hadley, "America's 'Big Brother': A Century of U.S. Domestic Surveillance," *Origins* 7, no. 3, December 2013, http://origins.osu.edu/article/americas-big-brother -century-us-domestic-surveillance. • **PAGE 136: "'Nothing more'"** Brendon O'Connor, *A Political History of the American Welfare System: When Ideas Have Conse- quences* (Lanham, MD: Rowan & Littlefield Publishers, Inc., 2004). • **"attended the Republican National Convention"** Brooks Jackson, "Hillary Worked for Gold- water?" FactCheck.org, March 27, 2008, http://www.factcheck.org/2008/03/hil lary-worked-for-goldwater/. • **"George McGovern's disastrous presidential campaign"** Martha T. Moore, "6 things to know about Hillary Clinton," *On Poli- tics* (blog), *USA Today*, April 12, 2015, http://www.usatoday.com/story/news/poli tics/onpolitics/2015/04/12/hillary-clinton-six-things-to-know/81596160/. • **PAGE 139: "'an inspiration'"** Lyndon B. Johnson, "Remarks Upon Accepting a Portrait of Franklin Delano Roosevelt," (Washington D.C., January 31, 1967), The Ameri- can Presidency at the University of California, Santa Barbara, http://www.presi dency.ucsb.edu/ws/?pid=28316. • **"'toward the broader horizons of human** hope'" Lyndon B. Johnson, "Remarks Upon Accepting a Portrait of Franklin Delano Roosevelt," (Washington D.C., January 31, 1967), The American Presidency at the University of California, Santa Barbara, http://www.presidency.ucsb.edu /ws/?pid=28316. • **PAGE 140: "'how many kids did you kill today'"** "Hey! Hey! LBJ!" *The Economist*, September 28, 2013, http://www.economist.com/news /united-states/21586830-what-current-fascination-lyndon-johnson-says-about -barack-obamas-america-hey-hey. • **"a decent political legacy"** "Lessons Learned: LBJ Announces He Will Not Seek Reelection," Council on Foreign Relations, March 27, 2012, http://www.cfr.org/world/lessons-learned-lbj-announces-he-not -seek-reelection/p27745. • **"'another term as your president'"** Lyndon B. Johnson, "Address to the Nation Announcing Steps to Limit the War in Vietnam and Reporting His Decision Not to Seek Reelection," (speech, Washington, D.C., March 31, 1968), LBJ Presidential Library, http://www.lbjlib.utexas.edu/johnson /archives.hom/speeches.hom/680331.asp. • **PAGE 142: "'tyrannical'"** Jacques Kelly and Carl Schoettler, "Philip Berrigan, Apostle of Peace, Dies at 79," *The Baltimore Sun*, December 7, 2002, http://articles.baltimoresun.com/2002-12-07/news /0212070391_1_philip-berrigan-vietnam-war-jonah. • **"by the age of five"** Shawn Francis Peters, *The Catonsville Nine: A Story of Faith and Resistance in the Vietnam Era* (New York: Oxford University Press, 2012). • **PAGE 143: "church's work in social justice"** Shawn Francis Peters, *The Catonsville Nine: A Story of Faith and Resistance in the Vietnam Era* (New York: Oxford University Press, 2012). • **PAGE 144: "ran over the cobblestone"** Terry Lenzner, *The Investigator: 50 Years of Uncovering the Truth* (New York: Penguin Group, 2013), p. 84. • **"cooked with whatever she had to spare"** Mary Pemberton, "1 [sic] Arrests Later, Phillip Berrigan Still Fighting for Peace," *The Seattle Times*, September 12, 1993, http://community.se attletimes.nwsource.com/archive/?date=19930912&slug=1720603. • **PAGE 146: "made to resemble napalm"** Mary Pemberton, "1 [sic] Arrests Later, Phillip Berrigan Still Fighting For Peace," *The Seattle Times*, September 12, 1993, http://com munity.seattletimes.nwsource.com/archive/?date=19930912&slug=1720603. • **"a 'grave' on the Rumsfelds' lawn"** Donald Rumsfeld, *Known and Unknown: A Memoir* (New York: Sentinel, 2011), p. 217. • **"six years in prison"** Mary Pemberton, "1 [sic] Arrests Later, Phillip Berrigan Still Fighting For Peace," *The Seattle Times*, September 12, 1993, http://community.seattletimes.nwsource.com/archive /?date=19930912&slug=1720603.

CHAPTER 5: FOURTH WAVE: THE HOPE AND CHANGE OF BARACK OBAMA

PAGE 149: "highly segregated city" Nate Silver, "The Most Diverse Cities Are Often the Most Segregated," FiveThirtyEight.com, May 1, 2015, http://fivethirty eight.com/features/the-most-diverse-cities-are-often-the-most-segregated/. • **"Hyde Park stands out as a vibrant, racially diverse"** Peter Slevin, "Uncommon Ground," *The Washington Post*, October 16, 2008, http://www.washingtonpost .com/wp-dyn/content/article/2008/10/15/AR2008101503728.html?sid=ST2008 101503923. • **"former domestic terrorists"** David Remnick, "Mr. Ayer's Neighborhood," *The New Yorker*, November 4, 2008, http://www.newyorker.com/the -new-yorker-blog/mr-ayerss-neighborhood. • **PAGE 150: "take any responsibility for it"** Joe Miller, "Obama a Constitutional Law Professor?" FactCheck.org, March 28, 2008, http://www.factcheck.org/2008/03/obama-a-constitutional-law -professor/. • **PAGE 150: "FBI's Ten Most Wanted list"** Ben Joravsky, "The

Long, Strange Trip of Bill Ayers," *The Chicago Reader*, November 8, 1990, http://www.chicagoreader.com/chicago/the-long-strange-trip-of-bill-ayers/Content?oid=876592. • **"killing those who got in the way"** "Bill Ayers," DiscoverThe Networks.org, accessed May 28, 2016, http://www.discoverthenetworks.org/individualProfile.asp?indid=2169. • **PAGE 151: "adhere to their beliefs"** Dinitia Smith, "No Regrets for a Love of Explosives; In a Memoir of Sorts, a War Protester Talks of Life with the Weathermen," *The New York Times*, September 11, 2001, http://www.nytimes.com/2001/09/11/books/no-regrets-for-love-explosives-memoir-sorts-war-protester-talks-life-with.html?pagewanted=all. • **"professor of law at Northwestern University"** "Bernardine Dohrn," DiscoverTheNetworks.org, accessed May 28, 2016, http://www.discoverthenetworks.org/individualProfile.asp?indid=2190. • **"murdered at least seven people"** Alfred S. Regnery, "They're All in This Together," *The American Spectator*, September 2, 2011, http://spectator.org/37001_theyre-all-together/. • **"didn't seem to have a whole lot of sympathy"** Guy Benson, "Confirmed: Bill Ayers Hosted Fundraiser for Obama," Townhall.com, November 30, 2011, http://townhall.com/tipsheet/guybenson/2011/11/30/confirmed_bill_ayers_hosted_a_fundraiser_for_obama. • **PAGE 152: "'some people have to die'"** Alfred S. Regnery, "They're All in This Together," *The American Spectator*, September 2, 2011, http://spectator.org/37001_theyre-all-together/. • **"calls himself a progressive"** Charles Kesler, *I Am the Change: Barack Obama and the Future of Liberalism* (New York: Broadside Books, 2012), p. x. • **PAGE 153: "he was destined for prominence"** Andrew Walden, "What Barack Obama Learned from the Communist Party," *American Thinker*, July 8, 2008, http://www.americanthinker.com/articles/2008/07/what_barack_obama_learned_from.html. • **"to be taken care of by her parents"** Thandeka, "Obama's Religious Roots," *UU World*, Fall 2012, October 8, 2012, http://www.uuworld.org/articles/obamas-religious-roots. • **"'after himself'"** Tim Jones, "Family Portraits: Strong Personalities Shaped a Future Senator, Barack Obama," *Chicago Tribune*, March 27, 2007, http://articles.chicagotribune.com/2007-03-27/features/0703270151_1_sen-barack-obama-stanley-ann-dunham-coffee-shops. • **"'What's wrong with Communism'"** Andrew Walden, "What Barack Obama Learned from the Communist Party," *American Thinker*, July 8, 2008, http://www.americanthinker.com/articles/2008/07/what_barack_obama_learned_from.html. • **PAGE 154: "'The Little Red Church on the Hill'"** Glenn Beck, "Barack Obama's Foundation," FoxNews.com, April 6, 2010, http://www.foxnews.com/story/2010/04/06/barack-obama-foundation.html. • **"'position-paper liberalism'"** Barack Obama, *Dreams from My Father: A Story of Race and Inheritance* (New York: Times Books, 1995), p. 75. • **"'how I go about the world of politics'"** Tim Jones, "Family Portraits: Strong Personalities Shaped a Future Senator, Barack Obama," *Chicago Tribune*, March 27, 2007, http://articles.chicagotribune.com/2007-03-27/features/0703270151_1_sen-barack-obama-stanley-ann-dunham-coffee-shops. • **"were chief aims of government"** Lisa Schiffren, "Confiscatory Tax Rate Dreams from my Father," *The Corner* (blog), *National Review*, August 19, 2008, http://www.nationalreview.com/corner/167359/confiscatory-tax-rate-dreams-my-father-lisa-schiffren. • **"with whom he spent his youth"** Paul Kengor, "Our First 'Red Diaper Baby' President?" *The American Spectator*, October 22, 2012, http://spectator.org/34558_our-first-red-diaper-baby-president/. • **"'resisting bourgeois society's stifling constraints'"** Gene Koprowski, "Obama Becomes Agitator in Chief," *The Detroit News*, February 11, 2010, http://www.realclearpolitics.com/2010

/02/11/obama_becomes_agitator-in-chief_229256.html. • **"'concerned with is-sues of social justice'"** Serge F. Kovaleski, "Old Friends Say Drugs Played Bit Part in Obama's Young Life," *The New York Times*, February 9, 2008, http://www.ny times.com/2008/02/09/us/politics/09obama.html?_r=1. • **"'a more practical road to socialism'"** John Drew, "Meeting Young Obama," *American Thinker*, February 24, 2011, http://www.americanthinker.com/articles/2011/02/meeting_young _obama.html. • **PAGE 155: "outright 'redistribution of income'"** Frances Fox Piven and Richard A. Cloward, "The Weight of the Poor: A Strategy to End Poverty," *The Nation*, March 8, 2010, http://www.thenation.com/article/weight-poor -strategy-end-poverty/. • **"necessitate radical change"** James Simpson, "Barack Obama and the Strategy of Manufactured Crisis," *American Thinker*, September 28, 2008, http://www.americanthinker.com/articles/2008/09/barack_obama_and_the _strategy.html. • **"over the next two decades"** James Simpson, "Barack Obama and the Strategy of Manufactured Crisis," *American Thinker*, September 28, 2008, http://www.americanthinker.com/articles/2008/09/barack_obama_and_the_strat egy.html. • **PAGE 156: "'socialist conferences'"** John McCormack, "Why Did Obama Attend Socialist Conferences?" *Weekly Standard*, July 18, 2008, http://www .weeklystandard.com/why-did-obama-attend-socialist-conferences/article/25175. • **"centenary of Karl Marx's death"** Stanley Kurtz, *Radical-in-Chief: Barack Obama and the Untold Story of American Socialism* (New York: Simon and Schuster, 2010). • **"Carol Mosely Braun to the U.S. Senate"** Aaron Klein, "Radicals Key to Career of Chicago Mayoral Candidate," WND.com, January 4, 2011, http:// www.wnd.com/2011/01/247365/. • **PAGE 157: "goal of a nuclear-free world"** Barack Obama, "Obama's 1983 College Magazine Article," *The New York Times*, accessed May 28, 2016, http://documents.nytimes.com/obama-s-1983-college-mag azine-article. • **"a world without nuclear weapons"** Barack Obama, "Remarks by President Barack Obama in Prague as Delivered," (remarks, Prague, Czech Republic, April 5, 2009), The White House, Office of the Press Secretary, https://www .whitehouse.gov/the-press-office/remarks-president-barack-obama-prague-deliv ered. • **"his progressive principles"** Byron York, "What Did Obama Do as a Community Organizer," *National Review*, September 8, 2008, http://www.national review.com/article/225564/what-did-obama-do-community-organizer-byron -york. • **"'problem-solving'"** "Obama's Socialist Roots and Worldview," DiscoverTheNetworks.org, accessed May 28, 2016, http://www.discoverthenetworks .org/viewSubCategory.asp?id=2374. • **"variety of leftist policies"** "Industrial Areas Foundation (IAF)," DiscoverTheNetworks.org, accessed May 28, 2016, http:// www.discoverthenetworks.org/groupProfile.asp?grpid=7493. • **"'a comparative handful'"** "Obama's Socialist Roots and Worldview," DiscoverTheNetworks.org, accessed May 28, 2016, http://www.discoverthenetworks.org/viewSubCategory.asp ?id=2374. • **"Obama's political rise"** Jim Geraghty, "The Alinsky Administration: Today, Reading 'Rules for Radicals' Is Illuminating and Worrisome," *National Review*, May 14, 2009, http://www.nationalreview.com/article/227500/alinsky-admin istration-jim-geraghty. • **"'Obama learned his lesson well'"** L. David Alinsky, "Son Sees Father's Handiwork in Convention," *The Boston Globe*, August 31, 2008, http://archive.boston.com/bostonglobe/editorial_opinion/letters/articles/2008/08 /31/son_sees_fathers_handiwork_in_convention/. • **"community organizers such as ACORN"** Mike Robinson, "Obama Got Start in Civil Rights Practice," *The Washington Post*, February 20, 2007, http://www.washingtonpost.com/wp-dyn /content/article/2007/02/20/AR2007022000045.html. • **PAGE 158: "Reverend**

Jeremiah Wright" Charles C. Johnson, "The Gospel According to Wright," *The American Spectator*, December 9, 2011, http://spectator.org/36529_gospel-according -wright/. • **"endemically racist"** Brian Ross and Rehab El-Buri, "Obama's Pastor: God Damn America, U.S. to Blame for 9/11," ABCNews.com, March 13, 2008, http://abcnews.go.com/Blotter/DemocraticDebate/story?id=4443788&page=1. • **"the progressivism Obama had imbibed"** Spengler, "The Peculiar Theology of Black Liberation," *Asia Times*, March 18, 2008, http://www.atimes.com/atimes/Front _Page/JC18Aa01.html. • **"make a progressive vision a reality"** Barack Obama, "Obama's 2006 Speech on Faith and Politics at the Call to Renewal's Building a Covenant for a New America Conference," (speech, Washington, D.C., June 28, 2006), *The New York Times*, http://www.nytimes.com/2006/06/28/us/politics/2006 obamaspeech.html?pagewanted=all. • **"whose famous book *Orientalism"*** Efraim Karsh and Rory Miller, "Did Edward Said Really Speak Truth to Power," *The Middle East Quarterly* 15, no. 1, Winter 2008, http://www.meforum.org/1811/did-ed ward-said-really-speak-truth-to-power. • **"colonialist oppressor of the Islamic world"** Joshua Muravchik, "Enough Said: The False Scholarship of Edward Said," *World Affairs*, March/April 2013, http://www.worldaffairsjournal.org/article/enough -said-false-scholarship-edward-said. • **"in the Left's historical reading"** Max Eden, "Book Review: 'Making David Into Goliath,'" review of *Making David Into Goliath: How the World Turned Against Israel*, by Joshua Muravchik, *The Washington Times*, July 21, 2014, http://www.washingtontimes.com/news/2014/jul/21/book -review-tracing-the-changed-perception-of-isra/. • **"Obama's unsuccessful 2000 congressional bid"** "Rashid Khalidi," DiscoverTheNetworks.org, accessed May 28, 2016, http://www.discoverthenetworks.org/individualProfile.asp?indid=1347. • **"during the 1990s"** Andrew C. McCarty, "The Obama/Ayers/Khalidi Connection," *National Review*, October 25, 2008, http://www.nationalreview.com/corner /172641/obamaayerskhalidi-connection-andrew-c-mccarthy. • **PAGE 159: "we must still be better"** Ron Radosh, "The Influence of Howard Zinn on the Loss of Patriotism, and the Antidote to Zinn, Dinesh D'Souza's America," PJ Media, July 4, 2014, https://pjmedia.com/ronradosh/2014/7/4/the-influence-of-howard-zinn-on -the-loss-of-patriotism-and-the-antidote-to-zinn-dinesh-dsouzas-movie-america/. • **"people have earned 'enough'"** Barack Obama, *The Audacity of Hope: Thoughts on Reclaiming the American Dream* (New York: Crown, 2006), Kindle edition, p. 193. • **"while protecting the environment"** Barack Obama, *The Audacity of Hope: Thoughts on Reclaiming the American Dream* (New York: Crown, 2006), Kindle edition, p. 119. • **"legitimate grievances"** Barack Obama, *The Audacity of Hope: Thoughts on Reclaiming the American Dream* (New York: Crown, 2006), Kindle edition, p. 233. • **PAGE 160: "we're all in it together"** Barack Obama, "Robert F. Kennedy Human Rights Award Ceremony & Commemoration of Robert F. Kennedy's 80th Birthday," (speech, Washington, D.C., November 16, 2005), Obama Speeches.com, http://obamaspeeches.com/039-Robert-F-Kennedy-Human-Rights -Award-Ceremony-Obama-Speech.htm. • **"'a progressive income tax'"** Barack Obama, "Remarks by the President on the Economy in Osawatomie, Kansas," (remarks, Osawatomie, KS, December 6, 2011, The White House, Office of the Press Secretary, https://www.whitehouse.gov/the-press-office/2011/12/06/remarks-pres ident-economy-osawatomie-kansas. • **PAGE 161: "'that makes this country work'"** Barack Obama, "Keynote Address at the Democratic National Convention," (speech, Boston, MA, July 27, 2004), *The Washington Post*, http://www.wash ingtonpost.com/wp-dyn/articles/A19751-2004Jul27.html. • **"'collective salva-**

tion'" Barack Obama, "Pritzker School of Medicine Commencement," (speech, Chicago, June 10, 2005), ObamaSpeeches.com, http://obamaspeeches.com/022 -Pritzker-School-of-Medicine-Commencement-Obama-Speech.htm. • **"by government intervention"** Rebecca Kaplan, "Obama: Income Inequality 'The Defining Challenge of Our Time,'" CBSNews.com, December 4, 2013, http:// www.cbsnews.com/news/obama-income-inequality-the-defining-challenge-of -our-time/. • **"'an ever-changing world'"** Barack Obama, *The Audacity of Hope: Thoughts on Reclaiming the American Dream* (New York: Crown, 2006), Kindle edition, p. 90. • **PAGE 162: "'social equality and social justice'"** Charles Kesler, *I Am the Change: Barack Obama and the Future of Liberalism* (New York: Broadside Books, 2012), pp. 190–91. • **"'openness to change'"** Charles Kesler, *I Am the Change: Barack Obama and the Future of Liberalism* (New York: Broadside Books, 2012), p. 192. • **PAGE 163: "Franklin Delano Roosevelt"** Charles Kesler, *I Am the Change: Barack Obama and the Future of Liberalism* (New York: Broadside Books, 2012), p. 11. • **"'run our factories'"** Barack Obama, "Inaugural Address," (speech, Washington, D.C., January 20, 2009), The White House, https://www.whitehouse.gov /blog/2009/01/21/president-barack-obamas-inaugural-address. • **"a retirement that is dignified'"** Barack Obama, "Inaugural Address," (speech, Washington, D.C., January 20, 2009), The White House, https://www.whitehouse.gov/blog /2009/01/21/president-barack-obamas-inaugural-address. • **PAGE 164 "'save the free market system'"** "'I've Abandoned Free Market Principles to Save the Free Market System'—George W. Bush," YouTube video, 1:05, from "Exit Interview with President Bush," by CNN, December 16, 2008, posted by "argusfest," January 14, 2013, https://www.youtube.com/watch?v=Tmi8cJG0BJo. • **"abrogating the property rights of creditors"** James Sherk and Todd Zywicki, "Auto Bailout or UAW Bailout? Taxpayer Losses Came from Subsidizing Union Compensation," The Heritage Foundation, June 13, 2012, http://www.heritage.org/research/reports /2012/06/auto-bailout-or-uaw-bailout-taxpayer-losses-came-from-subsidizing -union-compensation. • **"seize them"** Norbert J. Michael, "Repealing Dodd-Frank and Ending 'Too Big to Fail,'" The Heritage Foundation, November 3, 2014, http://www.heritage.org/research/reports/2014/11/repealing-doddfrank-and-end ing-too-big-to-fail. • **PAGE 165: "with the Department of Justice"** Sean Higgins, "Obama's Big Bank 'Slush Fund,'" *Washington Examiner*, January 18, 2016, http://www.washingtonexaminer.com/obamas-big-bank-slush-fund/article /2580431. • **"big banks have only grown even bigger**" Carrie Sheffield, "Dodd-Frank Is Killing Community Banks," *Forbes*, February 9, 2015, http://www.forbes .com/sites/carriesheffield/2015/02/09/dodd-frank-is-killing-community -banks/#23336d245ca4. • **"unless one was politically connected"** Tad De-Haven, "Obama's Stimulus: A Bit of Pork, a Lot of Opportunism," CATO Institute, January 10, 2013, http://www.cato.org/blog/obamas-stimulus-bit-pork-lot-oppor tunism. • **"an average of $260.6 million"** "Harvard Economist Says Stimulus Was Designed to Reward Democrat Constituencies," WinteryKnight.com, November 2, 2010, https://winteryknight.com/2010/11/02/harvard-economist-says-stimulus-was -designed-to-reward-democrat-constituencies/. • **"form of pork for Senate Democrats"** Ramesh Ponnuru, "The Stimulus Revisited," *The Corner* (blog), *National Review*, January 24, 2012, http://www.nationalreview.com/corner/289106 /stimulus-revisited-ramesh-ponnuru. • **"the 594,754 jobs allegedly 'created or saved,'"** "Harvard Economist Says Stimulus Was Designed to Reward Democrat Constituencies," WinteryKnight.com, November 2, 2010, https://winteryknight

.com/2010/11/02/harvard-economist-says-stimulus-was-designed-to-reward-democrat-constituencies/. • **"forestalled one million private-sector jobs"** John Hinderaker, "A Verdict on Obama's 'Stimulus' Plan," PowerlineBlog.com, May 15, 2011, http://www.powerlineblog.com/archives/2011/05/029042.php. • **"The IRS's 'slow-walking'"** Paul L. Caron, "The Media Ignores IRS Scandal: Column," *USA Today*, May 16, 2014, http://www.usatoday.com/story/opinion/2014/05/12/president-obama-irs-scandal-watergate-column/8968317/. • **PAGE 166: "including taking executive action"** Everett Rosenfeld, "Obama Announces Gun Control Plans: 'I believe in the Second Amendment,'" CNBC.com, January 5, 2016, http://www.cnbc.com/2016/01/05/obama-announces-gun-control-plans-i-believe-in-the-second-amendment.html. • **"'gun violence'"** Quinn Ford and Jeremy Gorner, "Chicago's Gun Violence Up from a Year Ago, Topping 1,000 Victims Earlier," *Chicago Tribune*, May 30, 2016, http://www.chicagotribune.com/news/ct-chicago-one-thousand-shootings-met-20150608-story.html. • **"'more guns equal less crime'"** John R. Lott Jr., *More Guns, Less Crime: Understanding Crime and Gun Control Laws* (Chicago: The University of Chicago Press, 1998). • **"authorized gun dealers to sell two thousand weapons"** Ian Tuttle, "El Chapo's Capture Puts 'Operation Fast and Furious' Back in the Headlines," *National Review*, January 21, 2016, http://www.nationalreview.com/article/430153/fast-furious-obama-first-scandal. • **PAGE 167: "'offensive' language"** "Stephen Coughlin on Fox and Friends 6.13.15," YouTube video, 2:42, from Fox and Friends, televised on Fox News, June 3, 2015, posted by "Javelin DC," June 3, 2015, https://www.youtube.com/watch?v=xuL3_fCqMfw. • **"al Qaeda's connection to the 1993 World Trade Center bombing"** "JW Report: 'U.S. Government Purges of Law Enforcement Training Material Deemed "Offensive" to Muslims'" *Press Room* (blog), Judicial Watch, December 9, 2013, http://www.judicialwatch.org/press-room/press-releases/judicial-watch-releases-new-special-report-u-s-government-purges-of-law-enforcement-training-material-deemed-offensive-to-muslims/. • **"'nihilistic'"** Barack Obama, "Remarks on the Execution of Journalist James Foley by Islamic State," (remarks, Martha's Vineyard, MA, August 20, 2014), *The Washington Post*, https://www.washingtonpost.com/politics/transcript-president-obamas-remarks-on-the-execution-of-journalist-james-foley-by-islamic-state/2014/08/20/f5a63802-2884-11e4-8593-da634b334390_story.html. • **"'counter violent extremism'"** Benjamin Weingarten, "10 Troubling Aspects of President Obama's 'Countering Violent Extremism' Summit," TheBlaze, February 28, 2015, http://www.theblaze.com/contributions/10-troubling-aspects-of-president-obamas-countering-violent-extremism-summit/. • **"hostile speech toward Muslims by Americans"** John Stanton, "Loretta Lynch: 'Actions Predicated on Violent Talk' Toward Muslims Will Be Prosecuted," Buzzfeed, December 3, 2015, https://www.buzzfeed.com/johnstanton/loretta-lynch-actions-predicated-on-violent-talk-toward-musl?utm_term=.xl4Aa6zNG#.poXEQG8Wb. • **"global warming is the greatest threat to the planet"** Jerome Hudson, "22 Times Obama Admin Declared Climate Change a Greater Threat Than Terrorism," Breitbart, November 14, 2015, http://www.breitbart.com/big-government/2015/11/14/22-times-obama-admin-declared-climate-change-greater-threat-terrorism/. • **"billions of public dollars"** Larry Bell, "In Their Own Words: Climate Alarmists Debunk Their 'Science,'" *Forbes*, February 15, 2013, http://www.forbes.com/sites/larrybell/2013/02/05/in-their-own-words-climate-alarmists-debunk-their-science/#4fa6022476fb. • **"citing environmental concerns"** Juliet Eilperin and Katie Zezima, "Obama Vetoes Keystone XL Bill," *The Washington Post*, February 24, 2015, https://www.washington-post.com/news/post-politics/wp/2015/02/24/keystone-xl-bill-a-k-a-veto-bait-heads-to-presidents-desk/. • **"funding to back 'green jobs'"** Hans Bader, "More Failed Stimulus Spending: Green Jobs Boondoggles Promoted by Obama Fail, Go Bankrupt, but Obama Wants More," Competitive Enterprise Institute, September 2, 2011, https://cei.org/blog/more-failed-stimulus-spending-green-jobs-boondoggles-promoted-obama-fail-go-bankrupt-obama. • **PAGE 168: "would reduce its emissions by between twenty-six percent and twenty-eight percent"** William Mauldin and Colleen McCain Nelson, "U.S., China Build on Plan to Cut Emissions," *The Wall Street Journal*, September 15, 2015, http://www.wsj.com/articles/u-s-china-build-on-climate-accord-1442342194. • **"create a GDP loss of $650 billion"** Matt Vespa, "Obama's War on Coal Is Projected to Cost Us 125,800 Jobs and $650 Billion," HotAir.com, November 25, 2015, http://hotair.com/archives/2015/11/25/obamas-war-on-coal-is-projected-to-cost-us-125800-jobs-and-650-billion/. • **"in the service of their ideological agenda"** Erica Martinson, "Uttered in 2008, Still Haunting Obama," *Politico*, April 5, 2012, http://www.politico.com/story/2012/04/uttered-in-2008-still-haunting-obama-in-2012-074892. • **"entitlement, now cast as a civil rights issue"** Nia-Malika Henderson, "Obama Links Civil Rights, Health Care," *Politico*, September 26, 2009, http://www.politico.com/story/2009/09/obama-links-civil-rights-health-care-027613. • **"big f*cking deal'"** "Joe Biden to Obama: 'This is a Big Fucking Deal,'" YouTube video, :49, from when President Obama signed the Patient Protection and Affordable Care Act into law, March 23, 2010, posted by "FaceBook Day," March 23, 2010, https://www.youtube.com/watch?v=HHKq9tt50O8. • **"socialized medicine down the road"** Charles Kesler, *I Am the Change: Barack Obama and the Future of Liberalism* (New York: Broadside Books, 2012), p. 13. • **PAGE 169: "partnerships between industry and government"** Charles Kesler, *I Am the Change: Barack Obama and the Future of Liberalism* (New York: Broadside Books, 2012), p. 233. • **"enlightened technocrats'"** Charles Kesler, *I Am the Change: Barack Obama and the Future of Liberalism* (New York: Broadside Books, 2012), pp. 206–7. • **"a living constitution"** Charles Kesler, *I Am the Change: Barack Obama and the Future of Liberalism* (New York: Broadside Books, 2012), p. 207. • **"without any Republican votes"** Guy Benson, "Three Years Ago, Today: Democrats Ram Through Obamacare," TownHall.com, March 21, 2013, http://townhall.com/tipsheet/guybenson/2013/03/21/three-years-ago-today-democrats-ram-through-obamacare-n1544594. • **"shun the checks and balances"** "Obama's Deal: Chronology," Frontline, PBS.org, accessed May 29, 2016, http://www.pbs.org/wgbh/pages/frontline/obamasdeal/etc/cron.html. • **"Jonathan Gruber, an architect of the legislation"** Marc Thiessen, "Thanks to Jonathan Gruber for Revealing Obamacare Deception," *The Washington Post*, November 17, 2014, https://www.washingtonpost.com/opinions/marc-thiessen-thanks-to-jonathan-gruber-for-revealing-obamacare-deception/2014/11/17/356514b2-6e72-11e4-893f-86bd390a3340_story.html. • **PAGE 170: "'we're going to get health care reform passed'"** David M. Herszenhorn and Robert Pear, "While Confident Health Care Will Pass This Year, Democrats Still Search for a Plan," *The New York Times*, January 28, 2010, http://www.nytimes.com/2010/01/29/health/policy/29health.html • **"Are you serious?'"** Geoffrey Dickens, "Flashback: Pelosi Responds with 'Are You Serious?' to Question about ObamaCare's Constitutionality," NewsBusters.org, March 26, 2012, http://newsbusters.org/blogs/geoffrey-dickens/2012/03/26/flashback-pelosi-responds-are-you

-serious-question-about-obamacare. • **"Using recess appointment power"** Adam Liptak, "Supreme Court Rebukes Obama on Right of Appointment," *The New York Times*, June 26, 2014, http://www.nytimes.com/2014/06/27/us/supreme -court-president-recess-appointments.html?_r=0. • **"'fairness' and 'justice'"** "Education Experts Blast DOJ's Apparent Call for Race-Based System of Punishment of Schoolkids," FoxNews.com, January 10, 2014, http://www.foxnews.com /2014/01/10/education-experts-blast-obama-administration-call-for-race-based -punishment.html. • **"strip protections from college students"** Caroline Kitchens, "Overreaching on Campus Rape," *National Review*, May 13, 2014, http://www .nationalreview.com/article/377878/overreaching-campus-rape-caroline-kitchens. • **"give thirty days' notice to Congress"** Josh Hicks, "Guantanamo Prisoner Transfer for Bowe Bergdahl Violated Laws, Review Finds," *The Washington Post*, August 21, 2014, https://www.washingtonpost.com/news/federal-eye/wp/2014/08 /21/gao-pentagon-broke-law-with-guantanamo-transfer-for-bowe-bergdahl/. • **"unconstitutional nationwide speech code"** David Bernstein, "Two Cheers for President Obama's Support for Free Speech on Campus," *The Washington Post*, November 18, 2015, https://www.washingtonpost.com/news/volokh-conspiracy /wp/2015/11/18/two-cheers-for-president-obamas-support-for-free-speech-on -campus/. • **PAGE 171:** • **"risen to 45.8 million***"* United States Department of Agriculture, Food and Nutrition Service, "Supplemental Nutrition Assistance Program Participation and Costs," fns.usda.gov, May 6, 2016, http://www.fns.usda.gov /sites/default/files/pd/SNAPsummary.pdf. • **"now fallen to five percent"** Benjamin Weingarten, "Everything You Though You Knew About the Unemployment Rate Is Wrong," GenFKD.com, December 26, 2015, http://www.genfkd.com/ev erything-you-knew-about-unemployment-rate-wrong. • **"Obama's 'recovery'"** Stephen Moore, "The Obama Recovery That Wasn't," *The Washington Times*, January 3, 2016, http://www.washingtontimes.com/news/2016/jan/3/stephen-moore -the-obama-economic-recovery-that-was/. • **"have been hit particularly hard"** United States Department of Labor "Labor Force Statistic from the Current Population Survey," bls.gov, May 31, 2016, http://data.bls.gov/timeseries/LNS14000000. • **"forty-nine states seeing premium hikes in 2016"** Ali Meyer, "Forty-Nine of 50 States Will See Premium Hikes in 2016," The Washington Free Beacon, January 11, 2016, http://freebeacon.com/issues/49-of-50-states-will-see-premium-hikes -2016/. • **"at least a thousand ongoing investigations"** Adam Kredo, "Rise in U.S. Terror Plots Tied to 'Unprecedented' Spike in Immigration," *The Washington Free Beacon*, January 14, 2016, http://freebeacon.com/national-security/rise-in-u-s -terror-plots-tied-to-unprecedented-spike-in-immigration/. • **"debt rose from $10.6 trillion"** Phillip Bump, "The Story Behind Obama and the National Debt, in 7 Charts," *The Washington Post*, January 7, 2015, https://www.washingtonpost.com /news/the-fix/wp/2015/01/07/the-story-behind-obama-and-the-national-debt-in -7-charts/. • **"more than $19 trillion as of February 2016"** Romina Boccia, "The US Debt Just Exceeded $19 Trillion. Here's How We Got Here," *The Daily Signal*, February 2, 2016, http://dailysignal.com/2016/02/02/the-us-debt-just-ex ceeded-19-trillion-heres-how-we-got-here/. • **"$20 trillion by the end of his presidency"** Dave Boyer, "$20 Trillion Man: National Debt Nearly Doubles During Obama Presidency," *The Washington Times*, November 1, 2015, http://www .washingtontimes.com/news/2015/nov/1/obama-presidency-to-end-with-20-tril lion-national-/?page=all. • **"rejected unanimously by the Supreme Court***"* David Bernstein, *Lawless: The Obama Administration's Unprecedented Assault on the Con-*

stitution and the Rule of Law (New York: Encounter Books, 2015), pp. 58–64. • **PAGE 172: "international coalitions and norms"** Tamas Magyarics, "Wilsonianism—A Blueprint for 20th Century American Foreign Policy?" (paper, Cold War History Research Center, Corvinus University of Budapest), accessed May 29, 2016, http://www.coldwar.hu/html/en/publications/wilsonianism.html. • **PAGE 173: "'unclench your fist'"** Barack Obama, "Inaugural Address," (speech, Washington, D.C., January 20, 2009), The White House, https://www.whitehouse.gov/blog/2009/01/21/president-barack-obamas-inaugural-address. • **"nefarious jihadist designs"** Benjamin Weingarten, "Obama Makes the Worst Trade in US History: Israel for Iran," TheBlaze, March 3, 2015, http://www.theblaze.com/contributions/obama-makes-the-worst-trade-in-u-s-history-israel-for-iran/. • **"violating the deal's terms"** Jon Gambrell, "Iran Fires 2 Missiles Marked with 'Israel Must Be Wiped Out,'" Yahoo! News, March 9, 2016, https://*www*.yahoo.com/news/iran-fires-2-missiles-marked-israel-must-wiped-071612751.html?ref=gs. • **PAGE 174: "self-determination for oppressed peoples**" Vladimir Lenin, "The Socialist Revolution and the Right of Nations to Self-Determination," Marxists.org, accessed May 29, 2016, https://www.marxists.org/archive/lenin/works/1916/jan/x01.htm. • **"above the advice of his national security team"** Kate Scanlon, "Former Defense Secretary Says Obama Went Against the 'Entire National Security Team' on Egypt Coup," TheBlaze, March 17, 2016, http://www.theblaze.com/stories/2016/03/17/former-defense-secretary-says-obama-went-against-the-entire-national-security-team-on-egypt-coup/. • **"'fully representative democracy'"** CNN Wire Staff, "Obama Says Egypt's Transition 'Must Begin Now,'" CNN.com, February 2, 2011, http://www.cnn.com/2011/POLITICS/02/01/us.egypt.obama/. • **"monetary aid and heavy weaponry"** Spencer Case, "How Obama Sided with the Muslim Brotherhood," *National Review*, July 3, 2014, http://www.nationalreview.com/article/381947/how-obama-sided-muslim-brotherhood-spencer-case. • **"had repressed jihadist forces"** Nic Robertson and Paul Cruickshank, "Islamic Militants Among Prisoners Free from Libyan Jail," CNN.com, August 26, 2011, http://www.cnn.com/2011/WORLD/africa/08/26/libya.militants.analysis/. • **"disarming in response to America's invasion of Iraq"** Ron Suskind, "The Tyrant Who Came in from the Cold," *Washington Monthly*, October 2006, http://www.washingtonmonthly.com/features/2006/0610.suskind.html. • **"aiding the 'rebels'"** Washington Post Editorial Board, "What Obama Botched in Libya," *The Washington Post*, May 5, 2014, https://www.washingtonpost.com/opinions/what-obama-botched-in-libya/2014/05/05/3aef7176-d47a-11e3-95d3-3bcd77cd4e11_story.html. • **PAGE 175: "jihadists diving into the swimming pool"** Tom Rogan, "Jihadists in the Swimming Pool," *National Review*, September 2, 2014, http://www.nationalreview.com/article/386832/jihadists-swimming-pool-tom-rogan. • **"approximately sixty-five hundred ISIS fighters"** Jim Sciutto, Barbara Starr, and Kevin Liptak, "ISIS fighters in Libya Surge as Group Suffers Setbacks in Syria, Iraq," CNN.com, February 4, 2016, http://www.cnn.com/2016/02/04/politics/isis-fighters-libya-syria-iraq/. • **"'hostilities' under the law"** David Bernstein, *Lawless: The Obama Administration's Unprecedented Assault on the Constitution and the Rule of Law* (New York: Encounter Books, 2015), p. xxi. • **"keeping Ambassador Stevens in the country"** Robert Young Pelton, "Low Profile in Benghazi: When Political Correctness Kills," DangerousMagazine.com, May 8, 2013, http://dangerousmagazine.com/project/low-profile-in-benghazi-when-political-correctness-kills/. • **"only liberal democracy in the Middle East"** Ben Shapiro, "A Complete

Timeline of Obama's Anti-Israel Hatred," Breitbart, March 20, 2015, http://www.breit
bart.com/national-security/2015/03/20/a-complete-timeline-of-obamas-anti-israel
-hatred/. • **"strengthening the Palestinian Arabs**" Charles Krauthammer, "What
Obama Did to Israel," *The Washington Post*, May 26, 2011, https://www.washington
post.com/opinions/what-obama-did-to-israel/2011/05/26/AGJfYJCH_story.html.
• **"boycott, divestment and sanctions (BDS) movement"** "Kerry Adds Fuel to
BDS Fire," *The New York Jewish Week*, February 4, 2014, http://www.thejewish
week.com/editorial-opinion/editorial/kerry-adds-fuel-bds-fire. • **PAGE 176: " 'Israel and the West Bank' "** Jennifer Rubin, "Obama Winks at BDS," *Right Turn*
(blog), *The Washington Post*, July 2, 2015, https://www.washingtonpost.com/blogs
right-turn/wp/2015/07/02/obama-winks-at-bds/. • **" 'greatest geopolitical catastrophe' "** "Putin: Soviet Collapse a 'Genuine Tragedy,' " NBCNews.com,
April 25, 2005, http://www.nbcnews.com/id/7632057/ns/world_news/t/putin-so
viet-collapse-genuine-tragedy/#.V03bs-crIy5. • **"cyber-attacks on U.S. businesses"** "Pentagon: China's Man-Made Islands Growing, Now Thousands of
Acres," FoxNews.com, August 22, 2015, http://www.foxnews.com/politics/2015
/08/21/defense-official-china-grabs-50-percent-more-land-through-man-made-is
lands.html. • **" 'open hand' policy"** "Chinese Cyberattacks on U.S. Companies
Continue, Report Says," NBCNews.com, October 19, 2015, http://www.nbcnews
.com/tech/tech-news/chinese-cyberattacks-u-s-companies-continue-report
-says-n447016. • **PAGE 177: " 'counterfeit' progressive"** Thomas Frank, "Cor-
nel West: 'He Posed as a Progressive and Turned Out to Be Counterfeit. We Ended
Up with a Wall Street Presidency, a Drone Presidency,' " *Salon*, August 24, 2014,
http://www.salon.com/2014/08/24/cornel_west_he_posed_as_a_progressive
_and_turned_out_to_be_counterfeit_we_ended_up_with_a_wall_street_presi
dency_a_drone_presidency/. • **PAGE 178: " 'Git your black ass in the car with
us' "** Paul Kengor, *The Communist* (New York: Threshold Editions/Mercury Ink,
2012), p. 23. • **PAGE 179: " 'whole hour piss in their faces' "** Paul Kengor, *The
Communist* (New York: Threshold Editions/Mercury Ink, 2012), p. 24. • **" 'horses,
cattle, and furniture' "** Paul Kengor, *The Communist* (New York: Threshold Edi-
tions/Mercury Ink, 2012), p. 25. • **" 'lukewarm liberals' "** Paul Kengor, *The Communist* (New York: Threshold Editions/Mercury Ink, 2012), p. 239. • **"home for his
interracial marriage"** Toby Harnden, "Frank Marshall Davis, Alleged Communist, Was Early Influence on Barack Obama," *The Telegraph*, August 22, 2008, http://
www.telegraph.co.uk/news/worldnews/barackobama/2601914/Frank-Marshall
-Davis-alleged-Communist-was-early-influence-on-Barack-Obama.html. • **PAGE
180: "ran to six hundred pages"** Paul Kengor, "The Washington Post Sugarcoats
Obama's Communist Mentor," *American Thinker*, March 26, 2015, http://www
.americanthinker.com/articles/2015/03/the_washington_empostem_sugarcoats
_obamas_communist_mentor.html#ixzz3VanoJC9E. • **"testimony in front of
the U.S. Senate"** Paul Kengor, "Dreams from Frank Marshall Davis," *The American
Spectator*, October 12, 2012, http://spectator.org/34799_dreams-frank-marshall-da
vis/. • **"photographs of nude women"** Jim Hoft, "Your Right to Know: More
Racy Photos of Obama's Mother Discovered (Video)," TheGatewayPundit.com,
June 19, 2012, http://www.thegatewaypundit.com/2012/06/your-right-to-know
-more-racy-photos-of-obamas-mother-discovered-video/. • **"should Hawaii ever
need to be targeted"** Michelle Ye Hee Lee, "Frank Marshall Davis: Obama's
'Communist mentor'?" *The Washington Post*, March 23, 2015, https://www.washing
tonpost.com/news/fact-checker/wp/2015/03/23/frank-marshall-davis-obamas

-communist-mentor/. • **"drink together"** Paul Kengor, "Dreams from Frank Marshall Davis," *The American Spectator,* October 12, 2012, http://spectator.org/34799 _dreams-frank-marshall-davis/. • **PAGE 181: "'African, and an American'"** "From the Vault—Barack Obama—Sep 1995," YouTube video, 56:42, from "Barack Obama Speaking at the Cambridge Public Library," on 22-City View, September 20, 1995, posted by "22-City View—Cambridge, MA," March 12, 2015, https://www .youtube.com/watch?v=w5JlqDnoqlo. • **"'get used to these frustrations'"** "From the Vault—Barack Obama—Sep 1995," YouTube video, 56:42, from "Barack Obama Speaking at the Cambridge Public Library," on 22-City View, September 20, 1995, posted by "22-City View—Cambridge, MA," March 12, 2015, https://www .youtube.com/watch?v=w5JlqDnoqlo. • **"'black people have a reason to hate'"** Bob Unruh, "See Obama Admit Seeking Advice from Communist," WND.com, April 15, 2015, http://www.wnd.com/2015/04/see-obama-admit-seeking-counsel -from-communist/. • **PAGE 182: "'picturing him there'"** Paul Kengor, "Obama's Purge: Why Has Frank Marshall Davis Been Quietly Removed from 'Dreams from My Father,'" TheBlaze, October 3, 2012, http://www.theblaze.com/contributions /obama%E2%80%99s-purge-why-has-frank-marshall-davis-been-quietly-removed -from-dreams-from-my-father/. • **"'planet on which we reside'"** Gerald Horne, "Rethinking the History and Future of the Communist Party," *Political Affairs,* March 29, 2007, http://www.politicalaffairs.net/rethinking-the-history-and-future -of-the-communist-party-41925/. • **"purged Davis's name"** Tiffany Gabbay, "Why Was Obama's Audio Book Version of 'Dreams from My Father' Purged of All References to Communist Mentor?" TheBlaze, October 3, 2012, http://www.the blaze.com/stories/2012/10/03/why-would-obamas-audio-book-version-of-dreams -from-my-father-have-been-purged-of-all-references-to-communist-mentor/. • **"'satisfaction of radical ends'"** Glenn Beck, "Van Jones, In His Own Words," FoxNews.com, September 1, 2009, http://www.foxnews.com/story/2009/09/01 /van-jones-in-his-own-words.html.

PART II: THE LIES

INTRODUCTION: THE GREAT LIE
PAGE 191: "a 'moderate' and a sellout" Clare Foran, "What Does It Mean to Be a 'Real Progressive'?," *The Atlantic,* February 4, 2015, http://www.theatlantic.com /politics/archive/2016/02/progressive-sanders-clinton/459978/. • **PAGE 192: "'find a more accomplished and passionate progressive'"** Dan Merica, "Clinton 'a little disappointed' Sanders' Comments," CNN.com, February 3, 2016, http:// www.cnn.com/2016/02/03/politics/hillary-clinton-bernie-sander-disappointed/. • **"'the root of that word . . . is progress'"** Gregory Krieg, "What 'Progressive' Means to Hilary Clinton vs. What 'Progressive' Means to Bernie Sanders," CNN.com, February 5, 2016, http://www.cnn.com/2016/02/04/politics/hillary -clinton-bernie-sanders-progressive-fight/. • **"'I make no bones about it'"** Maya Rhodan, "President Obama: 'I Still Believe in a Politics of Hope'" *Time,* February 11, 2016, http://time.com/4215851/barack-obama-springfield/. • **PAGE 196: "'that we can change the gun culture'"** Liz Kreutz, "Clinton Holds Emotional Town Hall with Family Members of Sandy Hook Victims," ABC News, April 21, 2016, http://abcnews.go.com/Politics/emotional-town-hall-hillary-clinton-concerted -effort-undermine/story?id=38580530. • **PAGE 196: "This is how we will be judged"** Barack Obama and Joe Biden, "Remarks by the President and the Vice

President on Gun Violence" (remarks, Washington, D.C., January 16, 2013), The White House, Office of the Press Secretary, https://www.whitehouse.gov/the-press -office/2013/01/16/remarks-president-and-vice-president-gun-violence. • **PAGE 198: "'Wheeler controlled the Prohibition Bureau'"** John Kobler, *Ardent Spirits: The Rise and Fall of Prohibition* (Boston: Da Capo, 1993), p. 274. • **"'costs many lives and long years of effort'"** Lily Rothman, "The History of Poisoned Alcohol Includes an Unlikely Culprit: The US Government," *Time*, January 14, 2015, http:// time.com/3665643/deadly-drinking/. • **"poisoned some ten thousand Americans"** Deborah Blum, "The Chemist's War: The Little-Told Story of How the US Government Poisoned Alcohol During Prohibition with Deadly Consequences," *Slate*, February 19, 2010, http://www.slate.com/articles/health_and_science/medi cal_examiner/2010/02/the_chemists_war.html. • **"'in order to further the investigation'"** Lauren Keane, "The Justice Department Cartel Strategy, October 2009," *The Washington Post* online, July 26, 2011, http://www.washingtonpost.com /wp-srv/nation/documents/atf-fast-and-furious-2.html. • **"found its way to the kingpin through Fast and Furious"** Ian Tuttle, "El Chapo's Capture Puts 'Operation Fast and Furious' Back in the Headlines," *National Review*, January 21, 2016, http://www.nationalreview.com/article/430153/fast-furious-obama-first-scandal. • **PAGE 199: "'regardless of the politics'"** Tom Cohen, "Wiping Away Tears, Obama Mourns Children Killed in School Shooting," CNN.com, December 15, 2012, http://www.cnn.com/2012/12/14/us/obama-school-shooting/. • **"'This is how we will be judged'"** Barack Obama and Joe Biden, "Remarks by the President and the Vice President on Gun Violence," (remarks, Washington, D.C., January 16, 2013), The White House, Office of the Press Secretary, https://www .whitehouse.gov/the-press-office/2013/01/16/remarks-president-and-vice-presi dent-gun-violence. • **"'over the profits of the gun lobby'"** Hillary Clinton Presidential Campaign, "Gun Violence Prevention: It Is Past Time We Act on Gun Violence," HillaryClinton.com, accessed May 30, 2016, https://www.hillaryclinton.com /issues/gun-violence-prevention/. • **"'that we can change the gun culture'"** Liz Kreutz, "Clinton Holds Emotional Town Hall with Family Members of Sandy Hook Victims," ABC News, April 21, 2016, http://abcnews.go.com/Politics/emotional -town-hall-hillary-clinton-concerted-effort-undermine/story?id=38580530. • **PAGE 200: "'fact that the AR-15 has been in the news'"** Justin Peters, "The New Assault Weapons Ban Deserved to Die," *Crime* (blog), *Slate*, March 20, 2016, http://www.slate.com/blogs/crime/2013/03/20/dianne_feinstein_gun_control _the_new_assault_weapons_ban_deserved_to_die.html. • **"'to protect its citizens' safety'"** Richard Simon, "Senate Votes Down Feinstein's Assault Weapons Ban," *Los Angeles Times*, April 17, 2013, http://articles.latimes.com/2013/apr/17 /news/la-pn-dianne-feinstein-assault-weapons-vote-20130417. • **"compiled data on causes of death"** Jason Howerton, "Infographic: Fears Versus Reality When It Comes to Death—Including 5 Things More Likely to Kill You Than a Firearm," TheBlaze.com, April 5, 2016, http://www.theblaze.com/stories/2016/04/05/info graphic-fears-vs-reality-when-it-comes-to-death-including-5-things-more-likely -to-kill-you-than-a-firearm/. • **PAGE 201: "'just making my kids and I less safe?'"** Justin Wm. Moyer, "Meet the Pro-Gun Rape Survivor Who Challenged Obama on CNN," *The Washington Post*, January 8, 2016, https://www.washington post.com/news/morning-mix/wp/2016/01/08/meet-kimberly-corban-the-pro -gun-rape-survivor-who-challenged-obama-on-cnn/. • **"'firearm in a home leads to a tragic accident'"** Justin Wm. Moyer, "Meet the Pro-Gun Rape Survivor Who Challenged Obama on CNN," *The Washington Post*, January 8, 2016, https://www.washingtonpost.com/news/morning-mix/wp/2016/01/08/meet -kimberly-corban-the-pro-gun-rape-survivor-who-challenged-obama-on-cnn/. • **"'He kind of dodged the question'"** Justin Wm. Moyer, "Meet the Pro-Gun Rape Survivor Who Challenged Obama on CNN," *The Washington Post*, January 8, 2016, https://www.washingtonpost.com/news/morning-mix/wp/2016/01/08/meet -kimberly-corban-the-pro-gun-rape-survivor-who-challenged-obama-on-cnn/. • **PAGE 202: "after her husband was shot and killed on a commuter train"** Rick Hampson, "'Gun Lady' Carolyn McCarthy Finally Going Home," *USA Today*, January 2, 2016, http://www.usatoday.com/story/news/nation/2015/01/02/carolyn -mccarthy-retiring/20599293/. • **PAGE 203: "'time to rise again to secure our future'"** Al Gore and Davis Guggenheim, *An Inconvenient Truth* (Hollywood, CA: Paramount, 2006). • **"'and our planet began to heal'"** Barack Obama, "Full Speech: Obama Declares Victory," ABC News, June 3, 2008, http://abcnews.go .com/Politics/Vote2008/story?id=4988344&page=1. • **"that was the scientific Left's theory in the 1970s"** Popular Technology, "1970s Global Cooling Alarmism," PopularTechnology.net, February 28, 2013, http://www.populartechnology.net /2013/02/the-1970s-global-cooling-alarmism.html. • **PAGE 204: "'result from unchecked climate change'"** Hillary Clinton Presidential Campaign, "Climate Change and Clean Energy: Making America the World's Clean Energy Superpower and Meeting the Climate Change Challenge," HillaryClinton.com, accessed May 30, 2016, https://www.hillaryclinton.com/issues/climate/. • **"'ravages our planet and our people'"** Bernie Sanders Presidential Campaign, "Combating Climate Change to Save the Planet: #Peoplebeforepolluters," BernieSanders.com, accessed May 30, 2016, https://berniesanders.com/people-before-polluters/. • **"and our planet began to heal"** Barack Obama, "Full Speech: Obama Declares Victory," ABC News, June 3, 2008, http://abcnews.go.com/Politics/Vote2008/story?id=498 8344&page=1. • **"'the proliferation of weapons of mass destruction'"** "Caitlin Werrell and Francesco Femia, "Secretary Kerry on the Security Threat of Climate Change," ClimateandSecurity.org, February 17, 2014, https://climateandse curity.org/2014/02/17/secretary-kerry-on-the-security-threat-of-climate-change/. • **PAGE 205: "made his hedge-fund money in fossil fuels"** Richard Valdmanis, "Exclusive: Billionaire Green Activist Steyer Not Ready to Back Clinton, Open to Sanders," Reuters, January 20, 2016, http://www.reuters.com/article/us -usa-election-steyer-idUSMTZSAPEC1K9038AB. • **"top super-PAC donors in the 2016 elections"** Matea Gold and Anu Narayanswamy, "The New Gilded Age: Close to Half of All Super-PAC Money Comes from 50 Donors," *The Washington Post*, April 15, 2016, https://www.washingtonpost.com/politics/the-new-gilded-age -close-to-half-of-all-super-pac-money-comes-from-50-donors/2016/04/15/63dc 363c-01b4-11e6-9d36-33d198ea26c5_story.html. • **"'Why didn't they wake up when they had a chance?'"** Al Gore and Davis Guggenheim, *An Inconvenient Truth* (Hollywood, CA: Paramount, 2006). • **PAGE 206: "'what Howard Zinn and Noam Chomsky were thirty years ago'"** Larissa Macfarquhar, "Outside Agitator: Naomi Klein and the New Left," *The New Yorker*, December 8, 2008, http:// www.newyorker.com/magazine/2008/12/08/outside-agitator. • **"'and build something radically better'"** Naomi Klein, *This Changes Everything* (New York: Simon & Schuster, 2014). • **"'the best chance we're ever gonna get to build a better world'"** "This Changes Everything: Int'l Trailer," YouTube video, 2:22, posted by ThisChangesEverything, August 27, 2016, https://www.youtube.com/watch

?v=IpuSt_ST4_U. • **PAGE 207:** " **'problems such as deforestation or the ozone hole'** " Anthony Watts, "IPCC Official: 'Climate Policy Is Redistributing the World's Wealth," Watt's Up with That?, November 18, 2010, https://wattsupwith that.com/2010/11/18/ipcc-official-%E2%80%9Cclimate-policy-is-redistributing -the-worlds-wealth%E2%80%9D/. • " **'distribution of the world's resources will be negotiated'** " Anthony Watts, "IPCC Official: 'Climate Policy Is Redistributing the World's Wealth," Watt's Up with That?, November 18, 2010, https://wattsup withthat.com/2010/11/18/ipcc-official-%E2%80%9Cclimate-policy-is-redistribut ing-the-worlds-wealth%E2%80%9D/. • " **'at least 150 years, since the industrial revolution'** " United Nations Regional Information Centre for Western Europe, "Figueres: First Time the World Economy Is Transformed Intentionally," Unric.org, February 3, 2015, http://www.unric.org/en/latest-un-buzz/29623-figueres-first -time-the-world-economy-is-transformed-intentionally. • **PAGE 209:** " **'wisdom of our founders and the Constitution'** " Elizabeth Titus, "Hillary and Jeb, Friends for a Night," *Politico*, September 10, 2013, http://www.politico.com/story /2013/09/hillary-clinton-jeb-bush-philadelphia-096587. • " **'and true to our founding documents'** " Barack Obama, "The President's Inaugural address," (speech, Washington, D.C., January 21, 2009), The White House, https://www .whitehouse.gov/blog/2009/01/21/president-barack-obamas-inaugural-address. • **PAGE 210:** " **'according to the Darwinian principle'** " First Principles editors, "Woodrow Wilson Asks 'What Is Progress,' " First Principles, Heritage.org, accessed May 31, 2016, http://www.heritage.org/initiatives/first-principles/primary-sources /woodrow-wilson-asks-what-is-progress. • " **'most marvelously elastic compi- lation of rules'** " Franklin D. Roosevelt, "Address as Governor of New York," (speech, New York, NY, March 2, 1930), Lexrex.com, accessed May 31, 2016, http:// www.lexrex.com/enlightened/writings/fdr_address.htm. • **PAGE 211: "reelected with fewer votes than his first election"** Ed Krayewski, "Barack Obama First President Re-Elected with Less Popular, Electoral Support Second Time Around," *Hit and Run* (blog), Reason.com, November 19, 2012, http://reason.com/blog /2012/11/19/barack-obama-first-president-re-elected. • **PAGE 213:** " **'placed by the Founding Fathers in the Constitution'** " Mark Tapscott, "Bombshell: Obama Endorsed 'Redistribution of Wealth' in 2001 WBEZ Interview," *Washington Examiner*, October 26, 2008, http://www.washingtonexaminer.com/bombshell -obama-endorsed-redistribution-of-wealth-in-2001-wbez-interview/article /136302/section/elizabeth-warren. • " **'must do on your behalf'** " Mark Tapscott, "Bombshell: Obama Endorsed 'Redistribution of Wealth' in 2001 WBEZ Inter- view," *Washington Examiner*, October 26, 2008, http://www.washingtonexaminer.com /bombshell-obama-endorsed-redistribution-of-wealth-in-2001-wbez-interview /article/136302/section/elizabeth-warren. • " **'the Colonial culture nascent at that time'** " David A. Patten, "Obama: Constitution Is 'Deeply Flawed,' " News- max, October 27, 2008, http://www.newsmax.com/InsideCover/obama-constitu tion/2008/10/27/id/326165/. • **PAGE 214:** " **'flaw of this country that contin- ues to this day'** " David A. Patten, "Obama: Constitution Is 'Deeply Flawed,' " Newsmax, October 27, 2008, http://www.newsmax.com/InsideCover/obama-con stitution/2008/10/27/id/326165/. • **PAGE 215:** " **'distrust of the democratic principle'** " Herbert Croly, *The Promise of American Life*, quoted in David Levy, *Herbert Croly of the New Republic: The Life and Thought of an American Progressive* (Princeton, NJ: Princeton University Press, 1984), p. 103. • " **'feeling of its pecu- liarly sacred character'** " Herbert Croly, "Introduction to *Progressive Democracy*," in

American Progressivism: A Reader, ed. Ronald J. Pestritto and William J. Atto (Lanham, MD: Lexington Books, 2008), p. 295. • **"earlier Articles of Confederation government"** Charles Beard, "An Economic Interpretation of the Constitution of the United States," TeachingAmericanHistory.org, accessed May 31, 2016, http://teachingamericanhistory.org/library/document/an-economic-interpretation-of-the-constitution-of-the-united-states/. • **" 'democracy rallied to an undemocratic Constitution' "** Herbert Croly, *Progressive Democracy* (New Brunswick, NJ: Transaction Publishers, 2006), p. 49–51. • **PAGE 216: " 'serve the purposes for which it was intended' "** Charles R. Kesler, *I Am the Change: Barack Obama and the Future of Liberalism* (New York: Broadside Books, 2012), p 45–46. • **PAGE 217: " 'throwback to the Gilded Age of the robber barons' "** Benjy Sarlin, "Hillary Clinton Slams Inequality in Populist Speech," MSNBC.com, May 16, 2014, http://www.msnbc.com/msnbc/hillary-clinton-goes-populist. • **" 'if we're going to have a vibrant middle class' "** Greg Sargent, "Bernie Sanders Calls for Downward 'Transfer' of Wealth of Top One Percent," *The Washington Post,* May 26, 2015, https://www.washingtonpost.com/blogs/plum-line/wp/2015/05/26/bernie-sanders-calls-for-downward-transfer-of-wealth-of-top-one-percent/. • **"one of the 'biggest issues we face' "** Correct the Record editors, "Hillary Clinton: A Lifetime Champion of Income Opportunity," CorrectRecord.org, accessed May 31, 2016, http://correctrecord.org/the-points/hillary-clinton-a-lifetime-champion-of-income-opportunity/. • **" 'reshuffle the deck' to address the issue"** James Pethokoukis, "Hillary Clinton's Inequality Plan Has Big Problems," *The Week,* January 7, 2016, http://theweek.com/articles/597696/hillary-clintons-inequality-plan-big-problems. • **"both 'income inequality' and 'wealth inequality' during his campaign"** Bernie Sanders Presidential Campaign, "Issues: Income and Wealth Inequality," BernieSanders.com, accessed May 31, 2016, https://berniesanders.com/issues/income-and-wealth-inequality/. • **"Liberal outlets like the *New York Times* routinely publish columns"** Peter Georgescu, "Capitalists, Arise: We Need to Deal with Income Inequality," *The New York Times,* August 7, 2015, http://www.nytimes.com/2015/08/09/opinion/sunday/capitalists-arise-we-need-to-deal-with-income-inequality.html?_r=2. • **PAGE 218: "Moore's worth at around $50 million"** Noel Sheppard, "OWS Supporter Michael Moore Lies on National Television About His Wealth: No, I'm Not Worth Millions," NewsBusters.org, October 26, 2011, http://newsbusters.org/blogs/noel-sheppard/2011/10/26/ows-supporter-michael-moore-lies-national-television-about-his-wealth. • **"was a net worth of $20 million"** Peter Coy, "The Richest Are in a Class by Themselves: For a Lucky Few, It's a Return to the Roaring Twenties," Bloomberg, April 3, 2014, http://www.bloomberg.com/news/articles/2014-04-03/top-tenth-of-1-percenters-reaps-all-the-riches. • **"Neil Young, with a net worth of $65 million"** "Neil Young Net Worth," CelebrityNetWorth.com, accessed May 31, 2016, http://www.celebritynetworth.com/richest-celebrities/rock-stars/neil-young-net-worth/. • **"and let him use his music at rallies"** Tessa Berenson, "Here's What Neil Young Thinks About Donald Trump Using His Music," *Time,* September 27, 2015, http://time.com/4051260/neil-young-donald-trump-music/. • **"Tim Robbins and Susan Sarandon . . . threw their weight separately"** Christie D'Zurilla, Kyle Kim, Armand Emadjomeh, "Celebrity Endorsement Tracker," *Campaign 2016* (blog), *Los Angeles Times,* accessed May 31, 2016, http://graphics.latimes.com/celebrity-presidential-endorsements/. • **"a combined net worth of more than $100 million"** "Tim Robbins Net Worth," CelebrityNetWorth.com, accessed May 31, 2016, http://

www.celebritynetworth.com/richest-celebrities/actors/tim-robbins-net-worth/.
"Susan Sarandon Net Worth," CelebrityNetWorth.com, accessed May 31, 2016,
http://www.celebritynetworth.com/richest-celebrities/actors/susan-sarandon-net
-worth/. • **"amassed a net worth of $30 million**" "Dick Van Dyke Net Worth,"
CelebrityNetWorth.com, accessed May 31, 2016, http://www.celebritynetworth.com
/richest-celebrities/richest-comedians/dick-van-dyke-net-worth/. • **PAGE 219:
"a 'New Deal Democrat' from the Franklin Roosevelt era"** Christie D'Zu-
rilla, Kyle Kim, Armand Emadjomeh, "Celebrity Endorsement Tracker," *Campaign
2016* (blog), *Los Angeles Times*, accessed May 31, 2016, http://graphics.latimes.com/ce
lebrity-presidential-endorsements/. • **"made $3 million for giving three
speeches in 2013"** Zaid Jilani, "Hillary Clinton Made More in Twelve Speeches to
Big Banks Than Most of Us Earn in a Lifetime," TheIntercept.com, January 8, 2016,
https://theintercept.com/2016/01/08/hillary-clinton-earned-more-from-12
-speeches-to-big-banks-than-most-americans-earn-in-their-lifetime/. • **"an astounding $19 trillion in new taxes"** Philip Klein, "Here's a List of Bernie Sand-
ers's $19.6 Trillion in Tax Hikes," *Washington Examiner*, January 19, 2016, http://
www.washingtonexaminer.com/heres-a-list-of-bernie-sanders-19.6-trillion-in
-tax-hikes/article/2580846. • **PAGE 220: "minimum wage has been increased
nine times**" US Department of Labor, "Wage and Hour Division: History of Federal Minimum Wage Rates Under the Fair Labor Standards Act 1938–2009," dol
.gov, accessed May 31, 2016, https://www.dol.gov/whd/minwage/chart.htm.
• **"poverty level is now sixteen percent—a three percent *increase*"** United
States Census Bureau, "Income, Poverty, and Health Insurance Coverage in the
United States: 2013," press release, Census.gov, September 16, 2014, http://www
.census.gov/newsroom/press-releases/2014/cb14-169.html. • **"cost the economy
as many as two hundred thousand jobs"** David Neumark, "The Effects of Minimum Wages on Employment," Federal Reserve Bank of San Francisco, frbsf.org,
December 21, 2015, http://www.frbsf.org/economic-research/publications/eco
nomic-letter/2015/december/effects-of-minimum-wage-on-employment/. • **PAGE
221: "in Switzerland, they've proposed $2,700 a month"** Kathleen Caulder-
wood, "$2,700 a Month No Matter What? Some Swiss Ask Government to Assure
Income," *International Business Times*, November 12, 2013, http://www.ibtimes
.com/2700-month-no-matter-what-some-swiss-ask-government-assure-income
-1466508. • **"even some conservatives have gotten on board"** Noah Gordon,
"The Conservative Case for a Guaranteed Basic Income," *The Atlantic*, August 6,
2014, http://www.theatlantic.com/politics/archive/2014/08/why-arent-reformicons
-pushing-a-guaranteed-basic-income/375600/. • **"an astounding thirty percent
of Switzerland's GDP"** "Basically Unaffordable" *The Economist*, May 23, 2015,
http://www.economist.com/news/finance-and-economics/21651897-replacing
-welfare-payments-basic-income-all-alluring. • **"'bringing their own toilet
paper'"** Dave Shiflett, "Laughing in the Face of Despair," *The Wall Street Journal*,
November 20, 2015, http://www.wsj.com/articles/laughing-in-the-face-of-despair
-1448044955. • **PAGE 222: "'the more they did for themselves, and became
richer'"** The Federalist Papers Project, "Benjamin Franklin on the Price of Corn
and Management of the Poor, November 1766," TheFederalistPapers.org, accessed
May 31, 2016, http://www.thefederalistpapers.org/founders/franklin/benjamin
-franklin-on-the-price-of-corn-and-management-of-the-poor-november-1766.
• **"and work is an important part of one's happiness"** Arthur C. Brooks, "A
Formula for Happiness," *The New York Times*, December 14, 2013, http://www.ny

times.com/2013/12/15/opinion/sunday/a-formula-for-happiness.html?_r=0.
• **PAGE 224: "'to achieve the universal aspirations of mankind'"** George
H. W. Bush, "Address Before a Joint Session of the Congress on the State of the
Union" (speech, Washington, DC, January 29, 1991), The American Presidency
Project at University of California, Santa Barbara, http://www.presidency.ucsb.edu
/ws/?pid=19253. • **"'I'm a George W. Bush conservative'"** "Transcript: Bret
Baier Interviews President Bush," FoxNews.com, December 17, 2008, http://www
.foxnews.com/politics/2008/12/17/transcript-bret-baier-interviews-president-bush
.html. • **PAGE 226: "as a senile fool or a dangerous loose cannon"** Matt Lat-
imer, "Nancy Reagan's Passing Marks the Death of the GOP Establishment," *Politico
Magazine*, March 6, 2016, http://www.politico.com/magazine/story/2016/03/nancy
-reagan-death-gop-establishment-213703. • **"'limits one or more of the major
life activities'"** Americans with Disabilities Act of 1990, Public Law 101-336.
108th Congress, 2nd Session (July 26, 1990). • **PAGE 227: "'communicating and
interacting with others'"** James Bovard, "The Failure of the Americans with
Disabilities Act," The Future of Freedom Foundation, fff.org, October 1, 2015,
http://fff.org/explore-freedom/article/failure-americans-disabilities-act/. • **"lawsuits
against private industries"** James Bovard, "How Disability Law Went Nuts: Column," *USA Today*, July 29, 2015, http://www.usatoday.com/wlna/opinion/2015
/07/27/ada-americans—disabilities-act-lawsuits/30702519/. • **"toilet stall was at
an improper height"** James Bovard, "How Disability Law Went Nuts: Column,"
USA Today, July 29, 2015, http://www.usatoday.com/wlna/opinion/2015/07/27
/ada-americans—disabilities-act-lawsuits/30702519/. • **"'if an individual without
a disability performed the job'"** Kenneth Ofgang, "Ninth Circuit Rejects One-
Eyed Drivers' Bias Claims Against UPS," *Metropolitan News-Enterprise*, September 16,
2005, http://www.metnews.com/articles/2005/eeoc091605.htm. • **"lawsuits
against businesses under the ADA"** Joseph Perkins, "Abuse of ADA a Plague on
California Small Businesses," *The Orange County Register*, April 24, 2015, http://
www.ocregister.com/articles/ada-659192-mccarthy-lawsuits.html. • **PAGE 229:
"deal McConnell had made to keep the Export–Import Bank open"** Jordain
Carney, "Cruz Accuses McConnell of Lying," *Floor Action* (blog), *The Hill*, http://
thehill.com/blogs/floor-action/senate/249076-cruz-accuses-mcconnell-of-lying
-to-him-on-ex-im-bank. • **"'Capitol Hill humming along as it was designed
to"** Politico Staff, "Senate Sends Transportation Infrastructure Bill to Obama," *Politico*, December 3, 2015, http://www.politico.com/story/2015/12/senate-transpor
tation-package-ex-im-renewal-216420. • **PAGE 231: "'fighting for equality for
all Americans'"** Priorities USA, "What's at Stake: Fighting for Equal Rights,"
PrioritiesUSAAction.org, accessed May 31, 2016, http://prioritiesusaaction.org/whats
-at-stake/. • **"'and to reform our broken criminal justice system'"** Bernie
Sanders Presidential Campaign, "Sanders in North Charleston Caps South Carolina
Tour," press release, BernieSanders.com, August 22, 2015, https://berniesanders.com
/press-release/sanders-in-charleston-caps-south-carolina-tour/?source=twitter
08222015&utm_source=twitter&utm_medium=post&utm_campaign=twitter
08222015. • **"'struggle with racism remains far from finished'"** Hillary Clinton Presidential Campaign, "Racial Justice: America's Struggle with Race Is Far
From Finished," HillaryClinton.com, accessed May 31, 2016, https://www.hillary
clinton.com/issues/racial-justice/. • **PAGE 232: "'own them, and then change
them'"** Hillary Clinton Presidential Campaign, "Racial Justice: America's Struggle
with Race Is Far From Finished," HillaryClinton.com, accessed May 31, 2016,

https://www.hillaryclinton.com/issues/racial-justice/. • " 'fight harder to end in-stitutional racism' " Elizabeth Landers and Eugene Scott, "New Sanders Video Features Martin Luther King Jr. and Jesse Jackson," CNN.com, February 13, 2016, http://www.cnn.com/2016/02/13/politics/bernie-sanders-martin-luther-king-jr-hillary-clinton-south-carolina/. • " 'they like me. I like them' " Janell Ross, "Donald Trump's Intriguing Comments About Sandra Bland. Yes, Really," *The Fix* (blog), *The Washington Post*, July 23, 2016, https://www.washingtonpost.com/news/the-fix/wp/2015/07/23/donald-trumps-intriguing-comments-about-sandra-bland-yes-really/. • **"declared in the photo's caption: 'I love Hispanics!' "** Donald J. Trump, Twitter post, May 5, 2016, 11:57 a.m., https://twitter.com/realDonald Trump/status/728297587418247168?ref_src=twsrc%5Etfw. • " 'the rights of Americans with disabilities' "** Hillary Clinton Presidential Campaign, "Disabil-ity Rights: We Must Continue to Expand Opportunities for All Americans," Hillary Clinton.com, accessed May 31, 2016, https://www.hillaryclinton.com/issues/dis ability-rights/. • " 'and achieve a high quality of life' " Bernie Sanders Presiden tial Campaign, "Issues: Fighting for Disability Rights," Bernie Sanders.com, ac-cessed May 31, 2016, https://berniesanders.com/issues/fighting-for-disability -rights/. • **PAGE 233: " 'birth control could be a valuable tool of eugenics' "** Thomas C. Leonard, *Illiberal Reformers: Race, Eugenics, and American Economics in the Progressive Era* (Princeton, NJ: Princeton University Press, 2016), p. 116. • **PAGE 234: " 'certain criminals and other mental defectives' "** Talya Nevins, "Eu-genics at Princeton," *Nassau Weekly*, April 12, 2015, http://www.nassauweekly.com /eugenics-at-princeton/. • " 'broad enough to cover cutting the Fallopian tubes"** *Buck v. Bell*, 274 U.S. 200, 47 S. Ct. 584 (1927). • " 'Three generations of imbeciles are enough"** *Buck v. Bell*, 274 U.S. 200, 47 S. Ct. 584 (1927). • **"the Nazis quoted Justice Holmes's opinion in *Buck v. Bell*"** Edwin Black, "Eugen-ics and the Nazis: The California Connection," *SF Gate*, November 9, 2003, http:// www.sfgate.com/opinion/article/Eugenics-and-the-Nazis-the-California-2549771 .php. • **PAGE 235: "more than three hundred thousand abortions every year***" Jamie Bryan Hall and Roger Severino, *Disentangling the Data on Planned Parent-hood Affiliates' Abortion Services and Receipt of Taxpayer Funding*, Issue Brief, (Washing-ton, D.C.: The Heritage Foundation, September 30, 2015), http://www.heritage.org /research/reports/2015/09/disentangling-the-data-on-planned-parenthood-affili ates-abortion-services-and-receipt-of-taxpayer-funding. • **"accounted for 35.7% of all abortions in 2010"** Jerome Hudson, "Proof Ben Carson Is Right About Planned Parenthood Targeting Black Neighborhoods," Breitbart.com, August 13, 2015, http://www.breitbart.com/big-government/2015/08/13/proof-ben-carson-is -right-about-planned-parenthood-targeting-black-neighborhoods/. • **PAGE 238: " 'winning over the masses on his way to power' "** William L. Shirer, *The Rise and Fall of the Third Reich*, (New York: Simon & Schuster, 1990), p. 205. • " 'Now we've got a new bunch of Hitlers' "** Doug Heye, "The Left's Limited Outrage at Hitler Comparisons," *US News & World Report*, October 6, 2011, http://www.us news.com/opinion/blogs/doug-heye/2011/10/06/celebs-should-avoid-the-hitler -president-comparison-be-it-bush-or-obama. • **PAGE 239: "war crimes in 1945 is foreign policy in 2003"** "MoveOn Stays on Bush-Hitler Theme," WND.com, 1/14/2004, http://www.wnd.com/2004/01/22750/. • **"images of Senator John McCain alongside Hitler***" Jocelyn Vena, "Madonna Compares Hitler to John Mc-Cain at Tour Opener; Campaign Calls Slam 'Outrageous,' "** MTV.com, August 25, 2008, http://www.mtv.com/news/1593432/madonna-compares-john-mccain-to

-hitler-at-tour-opener-campaign-calls-slam-outrageous/. • **"because they both used Swiss bank accounts"** Tony Lee, Slate Blogger Matthew Yglesias Compares Mitt Romney to Hitler," *Breitbart*, July 9, 2012, http://www.breitbart.com/big-jour nalism/2012/07/09/slate-blogger-matthew-yglesias-compares-mitt-romney-to-hit ler/. • **"campaign efforts in Illinois as a 'Mittzkrieg'"** Tim Cavanaugh, "Axel-rod Stay Class with Romney/Hitler Comparison," *Hit and Run* (blog), Reason.com, March 19, 2012, http://reason.com/blog/2012/03/19/axelrod-stays-classy-with -romneyhitler-c. • **"akin to 'Jews for Hitler'"** Meera Jagannathan, "Joy Behar Rips Caitlyn Jenner's Ted Cruz Support: 'Transgenders for Cruz Is Like Jews for Hitler,'" *New York Daily News*, March 15, 2016, http://www.nydailynews.com/en tertainment/tv/joy-behar-caitlyn-cruz-support-jews-hitler-article-1.2565331. • **"supporters of Stalin, for example, as 'conservatives'"** Gregory Bovt, "Back to Stalin's Soviet Union," *The Moscow Times*, February 15, 2013, http://www.the moscowtimes.com/opinion/article/back-to-stalins-soviet-union/475589.html. • **"'Why U.S. Conservatives Love Russia's Vladimir Putin'"** Ishaan Tharoor, "Why U.S. Conservatives Love Russia's Vladimir Putin," *The Washington Post*, Au-gust 25, 2014, https://www.washingtonpost.com/news/worldviews/wp/2014/08/25 /why-u-s-conservatives-love-russias-vladimir-putin/. • **PAGE 240: "'shut on the fingers of millions of citizens'"** Norman Vieira and Leonard Gross, *Supreme Court Appointments: Judge Bork and the Politicization of Court Appointments*, (Carbon-dale, IL: Southern Illinois University Press, 1998), p. 26. • **"'to escape altogether from its relentless logic'"** Jonah Goldberg, *Liberal Fascism: The Secret History of the American Left, from Mussolini to the Politics of Meaning* (New York: Crown, 2009), p. 21. • **"'absolutely necessary to get the state in order'"** Jonah Goldberg, *Liberal Fascism: The Secret History of the American Left, from Mussolini to the Politics of Meaning* (New York: Crown, 2009), p. 21. • **PAGE 241: "negotiated by British prime minister Neville Chamberlain"** Clive Irving, "Joe Kennedy's Answer to the 'Jewish Question': Ship Them to Africa," *The Daily Beast*, February 1, 2015, http:// www.thedailybeast.com/articles/2015/02/01/joe-kennedy-s-answer-to-the-jewish -question-ship-them-to-africa.html. • **"led him to argue that they should be shipped to Africa"** Clive Irving, "Joe Kennedy's Answer to the 'Jewish Question': Ship Them to Africa," *The Daily Beast*, February 1, 2015, http://www.thedailybeast .com/articles/2015/02/01/joe-kennedy-s-answer-to-the-jewish-question-ship -them-to-africa.html. • **"told the *Boston Globe*. 'It may be here'"** Thomas Mal-lon, review of *Hostage to Fortune: The Letters of Joseph P. Kennedy*, ed. Amanda Smith, *New York Times*, December 31, 2000, https://www.nytimes.com/books/00/12/31 /reviews/001231.31mallont.html. • **"'The right thing for Germany'"** Allan Hall, "How JFK Secretly ADMIRED Hitler: Explosive Book Reveals Former Pres-ident's Praise for the Nazis as He Traveled Through Germany Before the Second World War," *Daily Mail*, May 23, 2013, http://www.dailymail.co.uk/news/article -2329556/How-JFK-secretly-ADMIRED-Hitler-Explosive-book-reveals-Presi dents-praise-Nazis-travelled-Germany-Second-World-War.html#ixzz46rv0Eouu. • **"have pointed out, a 'man of the left'"** Jonah Goldberg, *Liberal Fascism: The Secret History of the American Left, from Mussolini to the Politics of Meaning* (New York: Crown, 2009), p. 53. • **"'others, including democratic socialists, thought so too'"** George Watson, "Hitler and the Socialist Dream," *The Independent*, Novem-ber 21, 1998, http://www.independent.co.uk/arts-entertainment/hitler-and-the-so cialist-dream-1186455.html. • **"'as I do not hesitate to admit'"** George Watson, "Hitler and the Socialist Dream," *The Independent*, November 21, 1998, http://www

.independent.co.uk/arts-entertainment/hitler-and-the-socialist-dream-1186455. html. • **"first with providing the opportunity for a livelihood'"** Bill Flax, "Obama, Hitler, and Exploding the Biggest Lie in History," *Forbes*, September 1, 2011, http://www.forbes.com/sites/billflax/2011/09/01/obama-hitler-and-explod ing-the-biggest-lie-in-history/#325ff0292b98. • **PAGE 242: "'experiment in reconciling individualism and socialism'"** George Dunlap Burns Jr., *Our Dying Republic: The Cause and the Cure*, (self-published, and printed by Xulon Press, 2011), p. 27. • **"hailed the Soviet Union as 'the future'"** Jonah Goldberg, *Liberal Fascism: The Secret History of the American Left, from Mussolini to the Politics of Meaning* (New York: Crown, 2009), p. 28. • **"run by 'petty persons with petty purposes'"** Jonah Goldberg, *Liberal Fascism: The Secret History of the American Left, from Mussolini to the Politics of Meaning* (New York: Crown, 2009), p. 103. • **"'formed' by God 'out of the rib of Italy'"** Jonah Goldberg, *Liberal Fascism: The Secret History of the American Left, from Mussolini to the Politics of Meaning* (New York: Crown, 2009), p. 28. • **"'the able and courageous Mussolini'"** Billie James Jensen, *"Philip Dru*, the Blueprint of a Presidential Adviser," *American Studies Journal* 12, no. 1 (Spring 1971): 55, https://journals.ku.edu/index.php/amerstud/article/view/2434/2393. • **"'piece of social machinery I've ever seen'"** Jonah Goldberg, *Liberal Fascism: The Secret History of the American Left, from Mussolini to the Politics of Meaning* (New York: Crown, 2009), p. 11. • **"'action against a Hitler-backed fifth column'"** Ron Capshaw, "Henry Wallace: Unsung Hero of the Left," *National Review*, April 4, 2015, http:// www.nationalreview.com/article/416450/henry-wallace-unsung-hero-left-ron-cap shaw. • **PAGE 243: "he wrote in the *Times* on November 15, 1931"** Arnold Beichman, "Pulitzer-Winning Lies," *The Weekly Standard*, June 12, 2003, http:// www.weeklystandard.com/pulitzer-winning-lies/article/4040. • **"'entire matter is exaggerated'"** Arnold Beichman, "Pulitzer-Winning Lies," *The Weekly Standard*, June 12, 2003, http://www.weeklystandard.com/pulitzer-winning-lies/article /4040. • **"'dying at a rate of 25,000 a day'"** Arnold Beichman, "Pulitzer-Winning Lies," *The Weekly Standard*, June 12, 2003, http://www.weeklystan dard.com/pulitzer-winning-lies/article/4040. • **"'I have met in fifty years of journalism'"** Arnold Beichman, "Pulitzer-Winning Lies," *The Weekly Standard*, June 12, 2003, http://www.weeklystandard.com/pulitzer-winning-lies/article /4040. • **"'to which they had dedicated their lives'"** Arnold Beichman, "Pulitzer-Winning Lies," *The Weekly Standard*, June 12, 2003, http://www.weekly standard.com/pulitzer-winning-lies/article/4040. • **"let the lies stand"** "*New York Times* Statement About 1932 Pulitzer Prize Awarded to Walter Duranty," press release, *The New York Times*, accessed June 1, 2016, http://www.nytco.com/new-york -times-statement-about-1932-pulitzer-prize-awarded-to-walter-duranty/.

PART III: FEAR THE FUTURE
PAGE 248: "Planned Parenthood" Betsy Woodruff, "Donald Trump Is Planned Parenthood's Favorite Republican," *The Daily Beast*, August 11, 2015, http://www .thedailybeast.com/articles/2015/08/11/donald-trump-is-planned-parenthood-s-fa vorite-republican.html. • **"contributor to the Clintons"** Nick Gass, "Trump has Spent Years Courting Hillary and Other Dems," *Politico*, June 16, 2015, http://www .politico.com/story/2015/06/donald-trump-donations-democrats-hillary-clinton -119071. • **"even Walter Mondale"** James V. Grimaldi, "Records Show Scant Reagan-Trump Ties," *The Wall Street Journal*, September 15, 2015, http://www.wsj .com/articles/records-show-scant-reagan-trump-ties-1442359829. • **PAGE 249:**

"**including MIT**" Richard Vangermeersch, "The Marking of Stuart Chase as a 'Red Accountant'—An Epic (1917–1921)" Special Collections Publications, Paper 8, p. 4, http://digitalcommons.uri.edu/cgi/viewcontent.cgi?article=1007&context=sc _pubs. • "**Intercollegiate Socialist Society (ISS)**" Zygmund Dobbs, *Keynes at Harvard: Economic Deception as a Political Credo* (New York: Probe Research, Inc., 1969), chap. 3, http://www.keynesatharvard.org/book/KeynesatHarvard-ch03.html. • "'**influence and guidance' of Fabian socialists**" Zygmund Dobbs, Keynes at Harvard: Economic Deception as a Political Credo (New York: Probe Research, Inc., 1969), chap. 3, http://www.keynesatharvard.org/book/KeynesatHarvard-ch03 .html. • "**to do something about it**" William Alan Hodson and John M. Carfora, "Stuart Chase: Brief life of a public thinker: 1888–1985," *Harvard Magazine*, September–October 2004, http://harvardmagazine.com/2004/09/stuart-chase-html. • **PAGE 250: "'knows where they are going'"** William Alan Hodson and John M. Carfora, "Stuart Chase: Brief life of a public thinker: 1888–1985," *Harvard Magazine*, September–October 2004, http://harvardmagazine.com/2004/09/stuart -chase-html. • **PAGE 251: "a thin veneer for eugenics"** Albert Sonnichsen, James Peter Warbasse et al., *Consumer's Cooperation: Organ of the Consumers' Cooperative Movement in the U.S.A.*, (Charleston, SC: Nabu Press, 2011), vol. 3. • "**with the Federal Trade Commission**" Richard Vangermeersch, "The Marking of Stuart Chase as a 'Red Accountant'—An Epic (1917–1921)" Special Collections Publications, Paper 8, p. 79, http://digitalcommons.uri.edu/cgi/viewcontent.cgi?article=10 07&context=sc_pubs. • "'**Red accountant'**" William Alan Hodson and John M. Carfora, "Stuart Chase: Brief life of a public thinker: 1888–1985," *Harvard Magazine*, September–October 2004, http://harvardmagazine.com/2004/09/stuart-chase -html. • **PAGE 252: "'inflated' government data"** Richard Vangermeersch, "The Marking of Stuart Chase as a 'Red Accountant'—An Epic (1917–1921)" Special Collections Publications, Paper 8, p. 79, http://digitalcommons.uri.edu/cgi/view content.cgi?article=1007&context=sc_pubs. • "**wrote books on economics**" Gary McCulloch and David Cook, eds., *The Routledge International Encyclopedia of Education* (New York: Routledge, 2008), p. 594. • "'**First American Trade Union Delegation'**" Stuart Chase, Robert Dunn, and Rex Tugwell, eds. *Soviet Russia in the second decade: a joint survey by the technical staff of the first American Trade Union Delegation* (New York: John Day, 1928) • "'**bowled over'**" Nick Gillespe, "Remembering 'The Forgotten Man,'" Reason.com, December 18, 2007, http://reason.com /archives/2007/12/18/remembering-the-forgotten-man/print. • "'**the world of Stalin'**" Nick Gillespe, "Remembering 'The Forgotten Man,'" Reason.com, December 18, 2007, http://reason.com/archives/2007/12/18/remembering-the-for gotten-man/print. • "'**influenced by Moscow'**" Nick Gillespe, "Remembering 'The Forgotten Man,'" Reason.com, December 18, 2007, http://reason.com/ar chives/2007/12/18/remembering-the-forgotten-man/print. • "**increased federal spending**" William Alan Hodson and John M. Carfora, "Stuart Chase: Brief life of a public thinker: 1888–1985," *Harvard Magazine*, September–October 2004, http:// harvardmagazine.com/2004/09/stuart-chase-html. • "'**remaking a world'**" Nick Gillespe, "Remembering 'The Forgotten Man,'" Reason.com, December 18, 2007, http://reason.com/archives/2007/12/18/remembering-the-forgotten-man/print. • **PAGE 253: "'first-class temperament'"** Charles Krauthammer, "Hail Mary vs. Cool Barry," *The Washington Post*, October 3, 2008, http://www.washingtonpost .com/wp-dyn/content/article/2008/10/02/AR2008100203043.html. • "'**a new deal for the American people'**" Franklin D. Roosevelt, "Address Accepting the

Presidential Nomination at the Democratic National Convention in Chicago," (speech, Chicago, July 2, 1932), The American Presidency Project at the University of California, Santa Barbara, http://www.presidency.ucsb.edu/ws/?pid=75174. • "'foremost public analysts and interpreters'" Nancy Capace, *Encyclopedia of New Hampshire* (Santa Barbara: Somerset Publishers, Inc., 2000), p. 183. • "'the inevitability of a planned economy'" Ronald Sullivan, "Stuart Chase, 97; Coined Phrase 'A New DEA,'" *The New York Times*, November 17, 1985, http://www.ny times.com/1985/11/17/nyregion/stuart-chase-97-coined-phrase-a-new-dea.html. • "'teaching the American people more about economics'" William Alan Hodson and John M. Carfora, "Stuart Chase: Brief life of a public thinker: 1888–1985," *Harvard Magazine*, September–October 2004, http://harvardmagazine.com /2004/09/stuart-chase-html. • **PAGE 254: "'exploratory reports on postwar problems'"** Stuart Chase, *The Road We Are Traveling 1914–1942: Guide Lines to America as Reported to The Twentieth Century Fund* (New York: The Twentieth Century Fund, Inc.,1942), https://ia802600.us.archive.org/29/items/TheRoadWeAre Traveling/TheRoadWeAreTraveling.pdf. • **PAGE 255: "'must be to win'"** Stuart Chase, *The Road We Are Traveling 1914–1942: Guide Lines to America as Reported to The Twentieth Century Fund* (New York: The Twentieth Century Fund, Inc.,1942), p. 1, https://ia802600.us.archive.org/29/items/TheRoadWeAreTraveling/TheRoad WeAreTraveling.pdf. • "'centralized, collective controls has continued'" Stuart Chase, *The Road We Are Traveling 1914–1942: Guide Lines to America as Reported to The Twentieth Century Fund* (New York: The Twentieth Century Fund, Inc.,1942), p. 95, https://ia802600.us.archive.org/29/items/TheRoadWeAreTraveling/The RoadWeAreTraveling.pdf. • "'lease-lending around the globe'" Stuart Chase, *The Road We Are Traveling 1914–1942: Guide Lines to America as Reported to The Twentieth Century Fund* (New York: The Twentieth Century Fund, Inc., 1942), p. 99, https://ia802600.us.archive.org/29/items/TheRoadWeAreTraveling/TheRoad WeAreTraveling.pdf. • **PAGE 256: "didn't seem to fit the bill"** Stuart Chase, *The Road We Are Traveling 1914–1942: Guide Lines to America as Reported to The Twentieth Century Fund* (New York: The Twentieth Century Fund, Inc.,1942), p. 97, https:// ia802600.us.archive.org/29/items/TheRoadWeAreTraveling/TheRoadWeAre Traveling.pdf. • "'all over the world'" Stuart Chase, *The Road We Are Traveling 1914–1942: Guide Lines to America as Reported to The Twentieth Century Fund* (New York: The Twentieth Century Fund, Inc.,1942), p. 95, https://ia802600.us.archive .org/29/items/TheRoadWeAreTraveling/TheRoadWeAreTraveling.pdf. • **PAGE 257: "'state control of communications and propaganda'"** Stuart Chase, *The Road We Are Traveling 1914–1942: Guide Lines to America as Reported to The Twentieth Century Fund* (New York: The Twentieth Century Fund, Inc., 1942), pp. 95–96, https://ia802600.us.archive.org/29/items/TheRoadWeAreTraveling/TheRoadWe AreTraveling.pdf. • "'doctrines of Adam Smith'" Stuart Chase, *The Road We Are Traveling 1914–1942: Guide Lines to America as Reported to The Twentieth Century Fund* (New York: The Twentieth Century Fund, Inc.,1942), p. 97, https://ia802600.us.ar chive.org/29/items/TheRoadWeAreTraveling/TheRoadWeAreTraveling.pdf. • **PAGE 258: "'applicable in some degree to the United States'"** Stuart Chase, *The Road We Are Traveling 1914–1942: Guide Lines to America as Reported to The Twentieth Century Fund* (New York: The Twentieth Century Fund, Inc.,1942), p. 97, https://ia802600.us.archive.org/29/items/TheRoadWeAreTraveling/TheRoad WeAreTraveling.pdf. • "'underwriting of social security'" Ronald Sullivan, "Stuart Chase, 97; Coined Phrase 'A New DEA,'" *The New York Times*, Novem-

ber 17, 1985, http://www.nytimes.com/1985/11/17/nyregion/stuart-chase-97
-coined-phrase-a-new-dea.html. • **"a federal deficit of more than $500 billion"**
"Current U.S. Federal Budget Deficit," About.com, February 23, 2016, http://
useconomy.about.com/od/fiscalpolicy/p/deficit.htm. • **PAGE 259: "'U.S. Freedom of Information Act'"** Ted Bridis, "The Obama Administration Keeps Getting Less Transparent," *Business Insider*, March 18, 2015, http://www.businessinsider
.com/government-transparency-is-the-worst-its-been-since-obama-took-office
-2015-3. • **PAGE 260: "'since the Nixon administration'"** Rebecca Kaplan,
"Report: Obama Administration Most Aggressive Toward Press Since Nixon,"
CBSNews.com, October 10, 2013, http://www.cbsnews.com/news/report-obama
-administration-most-aggressive-toward-press-since-nixon/. • **"dump 30 million
pounds of the fruit onto the ground"** Ron French, "Cherry Wars: The Crazy
Economics of Michigan's Favorite Pitted Fruit," MLive.com, May 22, 2015, http://
www.mlive.com/business/index.ssf/2014/07/cherry_wars_the_crazy_economic
.html. • **"visited the White House 104 times"** Michelle Ye Hee Lee, "Giuliani's
Claim the White House Invited Al Sharpton up to 85 Times," *The Washington Post*,
December 30, 2014, https://www.washingtonpost.com/news/fact-checker/wp/2014
/12/30/giulianis-claim-the-white-house-invited-al-sharpton-up-to-85-times/.
• **"'response, and recovery'"** Corporation for National Community Service,
"FEMA Corps: About FEMA Corps," NationalService.gov, accessed May 30, 2016,
http://www.nationalservice.gov/programs/americorps/fema-corps. • **PAGE 261:**
"conjured up some unpleasant associations*" U.S. Department of Homeland
Security, "Welcome to the FEMA Corps Inaugural Class," dhs.gov, September 12,
2012, https://www.dhs.gov/blog/2012/09/14/welcome-fema-corps-inaugural-class.
• **"'seek better understanding'"** Ronald Sullivan, "Stuart Chase, 97; Coined
Phrase 'A New DEA,'" *The New York Times*, November 17, 1985, http://www.ny
times.com/1985/11/17/nyregion/stuart-chase-97-coined-phrase-a-new-dea.html.
• **"'intervention in the economy'"** Ronald Sullivan, "Stuart Chase, 97; Coined
Phrase 'A New DEA,'" *The New York Times*, November 17, 1985, http://www.ny
times.com/1985/11/17/nyregion/stuart-chase-97-coined-phrase-a-new-dea.html.
• **PAGE 263: "'haphazard reactions to modern liberalism's excesses'"**
Charles Kesler, *I Am the Change: Barack Obama and the Future of Liberalism* (New York:
Broadside Books, 2012), p. xxiii.

EPILOGUE: DEFEATING THE FEAR FACTORY
PAGE 277: "highest per-capita income" CQ Researcher editors, *Urban Issues*
(Washington, D.C.: CQ Press, 2013), p. 109. • **"'so long as it is black'"** Henry
Ford and Samuel Crowther, *My Life and Work* (Garden City, NY: Garden City Pub-
lishing Company, 1922), p. 72. • **"bureaucrats who operated by fiat"** Arthur
Herman, *Freedom's Forge: How American Business Produced Victory in WWII* (New
York: Random House, 2012), p. 163. • **PAGE 278: "Britain, and the Soviet
Union combined"** Arthur Herman, "Bill Knudsen's Business Skills Saved the U.S.
at the Dawn of World War II," *The Daily Beast*, June 16, 2012, http://www.thedaily
beast.com/articles/2012/06/16/bill-knudsen-s-business-skills-saved-the-u-s-at-the
-dawn-of-world-war-ii.html. • **"unemployment was one percent"** Arthur Herman, "Bill Knudsen's Business Skills Saved the U.S. at the Dawn of World War II,"
The Daily Beast, June 16, 2012, http://www.thedailybeast.com/articles/2012/06/16/
bill-knudsen-s-business-skills-saved-the-u-s-at-the-dawn-of-world-war-ii.html.
• **"called *Once in a Great City: A Detroit Story*"** David Maraniss, *Once in a Great*

City: A Detroit Story (New York: Simon & Schuster, 2015). • **"Chicago, St. Louis, Baltimore, and New Orleans"** Mark Reutter, "Baltimore Surges Past Detroit in Number of Homicides in 2015," *Baltimore Brew*, August 7, 2015, https://www.balti morebrew.com/2015/08/07/baltimore-surges-past-detroit-in-number-of-homi cides-in-2015/. • **"remained twice the national average"** Keith A. Owens, "Detroit Unemployment Remains More Than Twice Level of State, Nation," *Michigan Chronicle*, July 28, 2015, http://michronicleonline.com/2015/07/28/detroit-unem ployment-remains-more-than-twice-level-of-state-nation/. • **PAGE 279: "'em- ployees who are ready to work and skilled'"** Keith A. Owens, "Detroit Unemployment Remains More Than Twice Level of State, Nation," *Michigan Chron- icle*, July 28, 2015, http://michronicleonline.com/2015/07/28/detroit-unemploy ment-remains-more-than-twice-level-of-state-nation/. • **"who are illiterate hold high school degrees"** "Detroit's 'Shocking' 47 Percent Illiteracy Rate," *The Week*, May 6, 2011, http://theweek.com/articles/484910/detroits-shocking-47-percent-il literacy-rate."Nearly Half of Detroit's Adults Are Functionally Illiterate, Report Finds," *Huffington Post*, May 7, 2011, http://www.huffingtonpost.com/2011/05/07 /detroit-illiteracy-nearly-half-education_n_858307.html. • **PAGE 280: "and built public housing"** Sanford Ikeda, "FDR's Friend in New York," review of *City of Ambition*, by Mason B. Williams, Reason.com, June 11, 2013, http://reason.com/ar chives/2013/06/11/fdrs-friend-in-new-york. • **PAGE 281: "'tax and tax, and elect and elect'"** Michael Hiltzik, *The New Deal: A Modern History* (New York: Free Press, 2011) p. 438. • **PAGE 282: "'center of the radical universe in those days'"** Coleman Young and Lonnie Wheeler, *Hard Stuff: The Autobiography of Mayor Coleman Young* (New York: Viking, 1994), p. 128. • **"too bad they didn't kill that [expletive]"** David M. Lewis Colman, *Race Against Liberalism: Black Workers and the UAW in Detroit* (Champaign, IL: University of Illinois Press, 2008), p. 37. • **"Communist-dominated Progressive Party"** Wilbur C. Rich, *Colman Young and Detroit Politics: From Social Activist to Power Broker* (Detroit: Wayne State Univer- sity Press, 1989), p. 67. • **"ran for state senator as a progressive"** Coleman Young and Lonnie Wheeler, *Hard Stuff: The Autobiography of Mayor Coleman Young* (New York: Viking, 1994), 37. • **"officially labeled a Communist front"** Martin Hal- pern, *Unions, Radicals, and Democratic Presidents: Seeking Social Change in the Twentieth Century* (Santa Barbara, CA: Praeger, 2003), p. 70. Wilbur C. Rich, *Colman Young and Detroit Politics: From Social Activist to Power Broker* (Detroit: Wayne State Univer- sity Press, 1989), p. 71. • **"he took the Fifth Amendment"** Coleman Young and Lonnie Wheeler, *Hard Stuff: The Autobiography of Mayor Coleman Young* (New York: Viking, 1994), pp. 120–21. *See also:* Martin Halpern, *Unions, Radicals, and Democratic Presidents: Seeking Social Change in the Twentieth Century* (Santa Barbara, CA: Praeger, 2003), p. 70. • **"elected as a state senator"** Wilbur C. Rich, *Colman Young and Detroit Politics: From Social Activist to Power Broker* (Detroit: Wayne State University Press, 1989), p. 85. • **PAGE 283: "'have sprung up in their place'"** *Encyclopedia of Detroit Online*, "Cavanagh, Jerome," Detroit Historical Society, Accessed May 30, 2016, http://detroithistorical.org/learn/encyclopedia-of-detroit/cavanagh-jerome. • **"ignited by a police raid on an African-American nightclub"** "July 23 1967: The 12th Street Riot," *This Day in History* (blog), History.com, July 23, 2010, http:// www.history.com/this-day-in-history/the-12th-street-riot. • **"left the city a fis- cal and social wreck'"** James Q. Wilson, "The Closing of the American City," review of *Official Negligence: How Rodney King and the Riots Changed Los Angeles and the LAPD*, by Lou Cannon, and *Someone Else's House: America's Unfinished Struggle for*

Integration, by Tamar Jacoby, *New Republic,* May 11, 1998, https://newrepublic.com /article/101313/la-riots-1992-racism-rodney-king-trial. • **" 'the sort of polarization that other politicians dread' "** Isabel Wilkerson, "The Nation: After Four Terms, Us Versus Them Still Plays in Detroit," *The New York Times,* September 17, 1989, http://www.nytimes.com/1989/09/17/weekinreview/the-nation-after-four -terms-us-versus-them-still-plays-in-detroit.html. • **" 'Renaissance Center' in Detroit's fading downtown"** Robin Meredith, "GM Buys a Landmark of Detroit for Its Home," *The New York Times,* May 17, 1996, http://www.nytimes.com /1996/05/17/us/gm-buys-a-landmark-of-detroit-for-its-home.html. • **PAGE 284: "ten thousand of the city's ninety thousand abandoned homes"** "Nearly Half of Detroit's Adults Are Functionally Illiterate, Report Finds," *Huffington Post,* May 7, 2011, http://www.huffingtonpost.com/2011/05/07/detroit-illiteracy-nearly-half-ed ucation_n_858307.html. • **" 'We had to make a culture change' "** Alex P. Kellogg, "Detroit Shrinks Itself, Historic Homes and All," *Wall Street Journal,* May 14, 2010, http://www.wsj.com/articles/SB100014240527487039508045752424334353 38728. • **PAGE 285: "on a house so it will be worth $400,000' "** Alex P. Kellogg, "Detroit Shrinks Itself, Historic Homes and All," *Wall Street Journal,* May 14, 2010, http://www.wsj.com/articles/SB10001424052748703950804575242433435338728. • **"Few citizens ever used the 'People Mover' "** Derek Hunter, "Detroit: My City Was Gone," TownHall.com, July 28, 2016, http://townhall.com/colum nists/derekhunter/2013/07/28/detroit-my-city-was-gone-n1650664. • **"later sold it to General Motors for $80 Million***"* Isabel Wilkerson, "The Nation: After Four Terms, Us Versus Them Still Plays in Detroit," *The New York Times,* September 17, 1989, http://www.nytimes.com/1989/09/17/weekinreview/the-nation-after-four -terms-us-versus-them-still-plays-in-detroit.html. • **"federal investigators probed his efforts"** "Colman A. Young, 79, Mayor of Detroit and Political Symbol for Blacks, Is Dead," *The New York Times,* December 1, 1997, http://www.nytimes .com/1997/12/01/us/coleman-a-young-79-mayor-of-detroit-and-political-symbol -for-blacks-is-dead.html?pagewanted=all. • **"His Honor is scheduled to be released in 2041"** Elisha Anderson, "Kwame Kilpatrick's Conviction and Sentence Upheld," *Detroit Free Press,* August 14, 2016, http://www.freep.com/story/news /local/michigan/detroit/2015/08/14/kwame-kilpatrick-appeal-conviction-upheld /31724407/. • **PAGE 286: "once upon a time, a 'Poletown' "** "Poletown" should not be confused with next-door, once-overwhelmingly Polish-American Ham-tramck, a community now with a Muslim-American majority on its city council: Sarah Pulliam Bailey, "In the First Majority-Muslim US City, Residents Tense About Its Future," *The Washington Post,* November 21, 2015, https://www.washing tonpost.com/national/for-the-first-majority-muslim-us-city-residents-tense-about -its-future/2015/11/21/45d0ea96-8a24-11e5-be39-0034bb576eee_story.html. • **PAGE 286: "No, thank you. We don't want to move."** James Risen, "Poletown Becomes Just a Memory: GM Plant Opens, Replacing Old Detroit Neighborhood," *Los Angeles Times,* September 18, 1985, http://articles.latimes.com/1985-09-18/busi ness/fi-6228_1_gm-plant. • **PAGE 287: " 'like we were a bunch of criminals' "** Jeanine Wylie, *Poletown: Community Betrayed* (Champaign, IL: University of Illinois Press, 1990), p. 111. • **"costing twenty-five hundred workers their jobs"** Jeanine Wylie, *Poletown: Community Betrayed* (Champaign, IL: University of Illinois Press, 1990), p. 255.

Answer Key to Quiz on Page 184

Scoring Per Question

a = 5 points
b = 4 points
c = 3 points
d = 2 points
e = 1 point

0–20 = Ron Paul (Libertarian)
21–35 = Ted Cruz (Conservative)
36–60 = Jeb Bush (Moderate)
61–80 = Donald Trump (Moderate Progressive)
81–100 = Hillary/Obama (Liberal Progressive)
100+ = Bernie Sanders (Socialist Progressive)